CASE ANALYSES FOR ABNORMAL PSYCHOLOGY

Case Analyses for Abnormal Psychology, second edition uses case studies to explore the etiology, biology, and dynamics of psychiatric disorders in the DSM-5. Readers will learn about the new classifications and treatments for disorders while simultaneously reading the personal history of each consumer both before and during the development of each case. Every case ends with a section on the particular disorder presented, as viewed from a biological perspective. This updated edition bridges advances in abnormal psychology and neuroscience in understanding mental illness.

Randall E. Osborne, PhD, is Professor of Psychology at Texas State University.

Joan Esterline Lafuze, PhD, is Professor of Biology at Indiana University East, Richmond and Research Associate at Indiana University School of Medicine, Indianapolis.

David V. Perkins, PhD, is Professor of Psychological Science at Ball State University.

CASE ANALYSES FOR ABNORMAL PSYCHOLOGY

Learning to Look Beyond the Symptoms

Second edition

Randall E. Osborne, Joan Esterline Lafuze, and David V. Perkins

Routledge
Taylor & Francis Group

NEW YORK AND LONDON

Second edition published 2016
by Routledge
711 Third Avenue, New York, NY 10017

and by Routledge
2 Park Square, Milton Park, Abingdon, Oxon, OX14 4RN

Routledge is an imprint of the Taylor & Francis Group, an informa business

First edition published by Routledge 2000

Library of Congress Cataloging-in-Publication Data
Names: Osborne, Randall E., author. | Lafuze, Joan, author. | Perkins, David V., author.
Title: Case analyses for abnormal psychology : learning to look beyond the symptoms / Randall E. Osborne, Joan Esterline Lafuze, and David Perkins.
Description: 2nd edition. | Milton Park, Abingdon, Oxon ; New York, NY : Routledge, 2016. | Includes bibliographical references and index.
Identifiers: LCCN 2015042813 | ISBN 9781138904521 (hbk : alk. paper) | ISBN 9781138904538 (pbk : alk. paper) | ISBN 9781315696287 (ebk)
Subjects: LCSH: Psychology, Pathological—Case studies.
Classification: LCC RC465 .O83 2016 | DDC 616.89—dc23
LC record available at http://lccn.loc.gov/2015042813

ISBN: 978-1-138-90452-1 (hbk)
ISBN: 978-1-138-90453-8 (pbk)
ISBN: 978-1-315-69628-7 (ebk)

Typeset in Bembo
by Apex CoVantage, LLC

Printed and bound in the United States of America by Publishers Graphics, LLC on sustainably sourced paper.

This book is dedicated to:

Diane Osborne, simply because she is wonderful, and Joseph Osborne, for being the true joy of his father's life, the entire Esterline Lafuze family, especially to Robert for teaching us all so well, and Kristin and Jason, with love and admiration.

CONTENTS

ABOUT THE AUTHORS

Randall E. Osborne received his PhD in social psychology from the University of Texas at Austin. Since that time, he has taught at the university level, and remained active in research on biased first impressions and the development and maintenance of self-concept and self-esteem. Dr. Osborne also has team-taught a course on the biology of mental illness with coauthor Dr. Joan Esterline Lafuze.

Joan Esterline Lafuze, PhD, is a systems medical physiologist who has spent the last 18 years educating many—including college students, professional providers, families, and persons who are mentally ill—about the strong biological component of the neurobiological disorders we call "mental illnesses." Dr. Esterline Lafuze is also actively engaged in mental health services research through the Indiana Consortium for Mental Health Services Research (ICMHSR).

David V. Perkins is a professor of Psychological Science at Ball State University. His research concerns community-based supports and services for persons with serious mental illness and their families. He is coauthor of *Principles of Community Psychology: Perspectives and Applications*, 2nd Edition, and author or coauthor of more than 30 articles in professional journals. Dr. Perkins received a BA with honors in psychology from Oberlin College, and a PhD in psychology from Indiana University.

PREFACE

You may immediately wonder why a casebook for abnormal psychology is needed. That is a good question and one that has guided us as we prepared this text. Casebooks for such courses are only as useful as the student's ability to learn from them. So, first and foremost, we wanted to create a casebook that would support and enhance your learning of course content. In addition, we were interested in providing a model that would demonstrate the relationship between the disorder from which the individual may suffer and the behaviors in which that individual may engage. Although it is tempting to assume that abnormal behaviors are, in and of themselves, the problem, you will soon discover that the behaviors may only be a pale manifestation of the larger problem.

In order to help you develop a fuller understanding of the complex nature of abnormal behavior, we will provide detailed cases that illustrate the major disorders you may discuss in your abnormal psychology course. Each case will begin with information about the history of the client discussed and progress through the diagnostic process, follow the individual into and through treatment, and end with a discussion of the long-term prognosis for the person based on his or her response to the treatment regimen. Within the cases we will illustrate a spectrum of treatment techniques that could be employed.

Many methods of treatment for mental illness can be categorized as either psychotherapeutic or "somatic." The root word *somatic* means "body," so somatic treatments focus on the brain as a biological entity. Such treatments include drugs, Electroconvulsive Therapy (ECT), and other brain stimulation procedures (such as vagus nerve stimulation). Treatments that fall under the heading of "psychotherapeutic" are all designed, in some way, to change the way someone thinks and/or behaves. Such approaches predominantly include psychotherapy and behavior therapies. Psychotherapies are often categorized as individual, group or family and behavior therapies often include relaxation, exposure training, or cognitive-behavioral combinations.

It was our intention to create a casebook that provided readers with a more expansive view of the challenges of abnormal psychology. Rather than focusing our attention on specialized aspects of the therapeutic process, such as primarily addressing diagnosis or treatment, we chose to take you through the complete process. As you will learn when you read the case of Ricky G, an intervention may often begin because someone has reached "rock bottom." Other times, the intervention may begin more swiftly because an early assessment has been made. Given that not each person ends up in treatment for the same reasons or at the same point in the progression of the illness or disorder, a question to bear in mind as you read through the cases is, "Does the timing of the intervention relate in any way to the success of the treatment outcome?"

Students often are curious to learn more about the authors of the books they are assigned. In order to provide you with more background on the perspective of this text, let us tell you a little bit about what we bring to this project. These brief introductions will also help you to understand the nature of this book and the intended outcomes we have for you as a reader of this text.

Dr. Osborne teaches psychology and stresses the relationships between psychological, biological, and behavioral processes. As such, he brings to this text an interest in the interconnections between biological changes and the resulting impact such changes may have on psychological states, behavioral choices, or both. He firmly believes students should be taught to see beyond behaviors and ask more critical questions about cause and effect. More often than not the unusual behaviors that usually get someone labeled as "abnormal" are only behavioral manifestations of a bigger problem: "If all we do is treat the behavior, we have done little more than put a bandage on a broken finger."

Dr. Esterline Lafuze is a medical physiologist who has an intense interest in severe mental illnesses. Her medical training provides her with a detailed understanding of the structures and functions of the human brain. In addition, her understanding of the biochemistry of the brain is especially important for understanding how and why certain psychoactive medications have the effects on mental illnesses they do. Dr. Esterline Lafuze's well-known advocacy for persons and families suffering with mental illness provides a humane touch to a subject that is often far removed from the experience of most people.

Dr. Perkins has taught abnormal psychology to undergraduate students for 30 years and a course in psychotherapy to graduate students for 20 years. He also brings diagnostic and therapeutic experience to this project. As a result of his expertise we have developed and included an assessment model in this text. This model provides a framework for thinking about the clinical process. In addition, the model provides questions for critical analysis that become the focal points for making progress with each of the cases. Rather than simply accepting behaviors at face value, for example, Dr. Perkins encourages readers to ask questions such as, "What behavioral symptoms am I witnessing?" "What are the possible causal explanations for such behaviors?" "What less-obvious symptoms (such as cognitive and affective symptoms) may also be occurring?" and "What do I need to know about the onset and progression of those symptoms?"

As you can see from these brief descriptions, we bring a unique combination of expertise and interests to this project. It is our belief that this association will give you a more complete picture of the nature of mental illness and disorders. In addition, we provide you with a look at possible alternative explanations for each disorder. We then critically analyze the available evidence, make a diagnosis, explain how and why that particular diagnosis was made, describe a potential treatment regimen, and discuss the evaluative mechanisms that will be used to assess the relative success of the decided upon treatment program.

We include questions for critical thinking in many cases and encourage you to answer these. They are intended to help you develop a more analytical approach to thinking about and understanding abnormal behaviors and the discipline of abnormal psychology. We wish you the best of luck in using this text and welcome any and all feedback you have about it. Please let us know what you think!

ACKNOWLEDGMENTS

Randall Osborne thanks Texas State University for its support during the writing of this book. In addition, he thanks a myriad of persons who shared their stories to make the cases in this book realistic and accurate. Though these persons wish to remain anonymous, we are indebted to them and acknowledge their dedication and their courage. He would also like to thank Diane Osborne for her guidance and feedback in the development of this book and his coauthors David and Joan for their professionalism and the sheer joy writing this book has been.

Joan Esterline Lafuze sends her thanks to Mary Moller, Mary Comer, and Soroya Allen who served as consultants for specific portions of this casebook. She also acknowledges the Indiana Consortium for Mental Health Services Research for funding a portion of this project and for providing a multidisciplinary forum for understanding effective approaches for the provision of services. Thank you to the Indiana Department of Mental Health and Indiana University Collaborative Project, especially to coleaders Janet Corson, director of the Division of Mental Health, and Ted Petti, psychiatric consultant to the division, for emphasizing the importance of interdisciplinary treatment teams including stakeholders. She is grateful to her many National Alliance for the Mentally Ill (NAMI) and Key Consumer friends for their support and encouragement, and to Margaret Trauner and Bruce Van Dusen for leading her to appreciate the meaning of recovery.

David V. Perkins thanks the Indiana Consortium for Mental Health Services Research for financial support and for helping him understand better the social context of mental disorders, and members of the National Alliance for the Mentally Ill–Indiana for providing him with many personal stories about family experiences with mental illness. He would like to thank Deborah W. Balogh, Diana M. Gray, and Curtis J. Jones for their help with some of the cases described in this book.

INTRODUCTION

A Guiding Theme

If there is one statement that guides the nature and structure of this casebook, it is "What you see isn't necessarily what you get." It is easy and perhaps efficient to assume that what we see is reality. If we see a man on the street kick a dog, for example, it is quite easy (and possibly even "safe" assuming you might have to walk by this man) to conclude that this is an aggressive person. But what type of information have we used to draw this rapid conclusion? We have based our entire decision about the kind of person he is on one piece of behavioral evidence. Although, certainly, what people do (how they act) can indicate the type of person they are, there are other pieces of evidence available to us that we can use to verify or nullify the accuracy of the impressions we have formed.

Forming Impressions—The Road to Bias and Back Again

Daniel Gilbert and his colleagues (e.g., Gilbert, Pelham, & Krull, 1988) have suggested that the cognitive resources necessary for forming impressions of others is limited. We cannot expend more of those resources (such as the amount of time we have to consider what someone else is like) than we have available. At the same time that we are expending mental resources to form impressions, we are also utilizing mental resources to complete other cognitive tasks, such as trying to remember what we were supposed to pick up at the grocery store. Thus, we may not always have the mental resources available to truly consider the kind of person we are observing or with whom we are interacting.

In addition, Gilbert and colleagues (1988) suggest that forming an accurate impression requires a two-step process. To the extent that an individual does *not* complete both steps, the resulting impression that is formed will be biased in some fashion. The two steps required for forming an accurate impression are: making a dispositional inference, and engaging in situational correction.

When making a dispositional inference, the person perceiving the behavior of another will assume that the behavior indicates the type of person that is being observed. With our example of the man kicking the dog, the perceiver (the person witnessing the event and attempting to form an impression) will judge the behavior at face value. In other words, if a man kicks a dog, he is an aggressive person.

The second step in the impression formation process requires more effort (therefore it will require the expenditure of more of our cognitive resources) than the first. It is quite easy to assume that the behavior defines the person. It is quite another thing, however, to assess the situation in which that behavior is occurring and judge whether the situation could have had any impact on that behavior. According to Gilbert and colleagues (1988), many impressions are formed solely on the basis of the dispositional inference because perceivers are often too busy or not highly enough motivated to engage in the more effortful process of situational correction. In our dog example, situational correction will require the perceiver to assess the situation and make appropriate adjustments to his or her impression of the man.

Perhaps we could ask a few people who witnessed the same event what they think the behavior indicates. Maybe some of these people will have more information about what happened than we do. It is possible that one of the other "witnesses" observed what led up to the kicking episode. Would you change your opinion of the man, for example, if you discovered that his son is cowering behind his leg and the dog had tried to bite the 5-year-old? Probably. In this case, the situational-correction process would cause us to change our impression of the man. What would happen to your impression if the other people present tell you that the man was yelled at by his girlfriend and he just "stormed up to the dog and kicked it in the ribs" after that? Maybe you would become even more certain that this is an aggressive person. The point we are making is this: When someone engages in a behavior, we have to know more than just what the behavior was in order to understand why that behavior occurred.

Once biased impressions have formed, they are extremely resistant to change. A teacher who has heard from another teacher that an incoming student is a "behavior problem" will have a difficult time resisting the use of that biased impression in interactions with that student. But recovery from bias is possible. Gilbert and Osborne (1989) suggested individuals can correct biased impressions, but only under a specific set of circumstances. Specifically, the person who has formed the impression must have both: (a) the cognitive resources available to reconsider that impression and, (b) must be motivated to expend the mental energy that changing that impression will require (Osborne & Gilbert, 1992).

A clinician wanting to form an accurate impression of a client must focus effort on doing so. This may require her or him to talk with the individual prior to reading case history information. In this manner the clinician may begin to form an impression without allowing prior information to introduce bias into that process. If the clinician reads the case history first and a previous doctor has suggested that the client might suffer from schizophrenia, could that prior conclusion interfere with the current clinician's ability to objectively observe and interview that client? Yes. The beliefs that people have, whether those persons are clinicians or laypersons, directly affect the assumptions those persons will make. Sometimes those assumptions—and the conclusions that will be drawn based on those assumptions—will be valid and accurate. Many times, however, they will not be.

Treating the Symptoms Versus Seeking the Cause

Thousands of people a day will go to a medical doctor with some illness. Let us say that you have some bacterial infection that is causing a severe cut on your finger to hurt. The doctor may prescribe an over-the-counter painkiller to ease the pain. Although this medication may provide temporary relief from the pain caused by the infection, will it "cure" the problem? No. If the doctor is going to provide you with a cure, it will have to be in the form of an antibiotic that can "kill" the infectious agent.

This same analogy applies in understanding the relationship between the symptoms of a disorder and the nature of the underlying cause. It would behoove us to provide you with an example to clarify the point. If you saw someone sitting on a bench waiting for the city bus and constantly waving his hands by his ears, you might think that this is odd behavior. If you fall victim to this pattern of thinking, however, you will have made the first mistake that will make it difficult to truly understand abnormal psychology. As a general rule in abnormal psychology, the symptoms we can observe (in this case the waving of the hands) are only a reflection of the underlying problem.

If we did not seek the causal explanation for why this man is waving his hands by his ears, we may not truly provide him with the assistance he needs. Maybe we decide to use a behavioral modification technique to get him to stop engaging in the waving behavior. Would this "cure" the man? Certainly not. What if we discover that the man is suffering from paranoid schizophrenia and he is hearing voices telling him to do bad things. Suddenly, waving his hands by his ears does not seem so odd anymore. In fact, given that he is hearing voices, the behavior might make perfect sense. Since he is unaware of the source of the voices, he may be attempting to shoo the sounds away.

The Components of Disorders

In order to aid you in connecting the affective, behavioral, and cognitive symptoms of each disorder, we will provide case information that focuses on all three. After presenting this case information, then, each chapter will progress into critical questions that will influence the diagnosis that is selected, cover potential treatment options and the strengths and disadvantages of each, provide information on case progress or setbacks, and conclude with information about the typical prognosis (long-term probability of success) for such a case.

Major issues that confront clinical psychologists will be woven into the cases. Clinical psychologists often confront difficulties in diagnosing various disorders that are strikingly similar. How psychologists go about resolving those issues will be incorporated into the text so that you can learn to engage in the critical reflection process that accurate diagnosis requires. Part of this difficulty comes from the intricate underlying biology of the brain. A number of the disorders discussed will involve many of the same brain structures or neurotransmitters or both. Only subtle differences, then, may determine which disorder is at play.

We also incorporate into the text the relationship between diagnosis and treatment. After exploring the potential diagnoses a clinician may consider based on the prevalent symptoms in each case, potential treatment plans will be discussed. These discussions of diagnosis and treatment are important, as they illustrate the critical analysis process that clinicians must use. Treatment decisions are complex and many crucial concepts must be considered in developing, maintaining, assessing, and altering a treatment program.

You will become actively involved in the development of each case. Most chapters will include "Critical Thinking and Questioning" pauses that engage you in the analysis process. These reflection questions will also serve as springboards into the next section of the chapter, as you are encouraged to reflect on unresolved questions and issues that will then become focal points for discussion in that next section of the chapter. You will be given the opportunity to utilize diagnostic information and suggest a diagnosis before it is actually revealed in the chapter. The same will occur when treatment strategies are discussed. The section following the diagnosis will discuss the choices the clinician made and why those choices were made. The emphasis is more on the critical analysis process and much less on the specifics of actual treatment.

It is extremely important that you understand our use of terminology throughout this text. Several times it might seem as if we do not make definitive statements. You will notice that we often use terms such as "may be caused by," "might be indicative of," or "normally is associated with." Such cautious wording is not an attempt to avoid making absolute statements. The nature of mental illness and the relatively rapid increase in knowledge about these illnesses, however, requires us to be cautious with our word choices. We have attempted to provide you with the most accurate and most complete, yet most expansive, coverage of the illnesses as we can. For this reason, many of the cases will include a discussion of multiple potential causes as well as the multiple treatment paths that may be considered.

A Word About the "Medical Student Syndrome"

We are very aware that some students complete abnormal psychology courses assuming they can now diagnose. It is also possible for students to complete such courses believing they see major disorders in each person they know. We wish to avoid fostering such assumptions by developing the critical thinking and reflection model previously described. The clinician will model the difficult task of accurate assessment, the challenge of developing feasible treatment strategies, and the difficulties with evaluating the relative success of the treatment or treatments being used. We believe this will aid you in gaining an appreciation for the complexity of the clinical process and how each answer leads to more questions.

A Note About Clinicians

We would like you to understand that we believe that clinicians are extremely adept at utilizing the critical analysis process to which we have alluded. These professionals have been trained to look beyond symptoms and to seek underlying causes. The reason we will emphasize the importance of this process is not to insinuate that clinicians do not do this. Instead, we emphasize this process as a learning tool. The more often this difference between symptom and underlying cause is illustrated, the more this relationship will be reinforced. With practice, then, we hope you will also become more successful with separating behaviors and other symptoms and the complex underlying illness that may be causing them.

Mental Illness From a Biological Perspective

Biology is the study of life. Therefore, a biologist looks at subjects of interest from that perspective. A poet might look at a field of flowers in terms of an emotion the scene might evoke. A biologist might look at the same field of flowers and think of pollination patterns.

In the scientific arena we turn to another example: The chemist might look at bone as a depository of calcium and phosphate salts. A biologist would probably see that same bone in terms of a living tissue with a blood and nerve supply. A medical professional would be very much interested in the most modern techniques to image the broken portion for diagnosis and appropriate treatment.

When a biologist looks at behaviors, he or she begins by considering how the body works from its most basic components—its cells. Cells work together as tissues. Nervous tissue has properties that allow it to send an electrical signal to stimulate muscles that are attached to bone. Thus, a nerve tells a muscle to contract and move a bone appropriately for a behavior to result. This behavior may be a rapid, predictable, automatic response to a stimulation. That kind of response is called a *reflex*. It could also be a voluntary, well-planned movement. Both are behaviors that biologists in specialized disciplines study.

Understanding behaviors is very complicated and requires us to consider other information in addition to the biology involved. Other disciplines become involved and move beyond the biological bases of the behaviors. How one learns to behave or misbehave, how one motivates desired behaviors in oneself and others, and how one discourages others moves into the realms of education and psychology.

When behaviors become symptoms of disorders that society categorizes as illness, health-care professionals such as clinical psychologists, nurses, physicians, and clinical social workers diagnose, intervene, treat, support, and rehabilitate. Behaviors that become symptoms of illnesses include reactions to feeling and responding to pain, developing fevers, paralysis, or losing consciousness. Treatments may include interventions such as medication, surgery, changes in lifestyle, and specific exercises. Frequently, the medications used act on neurotransmitter function. To better understand these mechanisms, we will review briefly what a neurotransmitter is and how it functions.

Excitable membranes (nerve and muscle) are able to support a nerve impulse or action potential. This impulse is like a wave of electricity that moves along the plasma membrane. The impulse is generated when a sodium ion that is generally outside the cell is let in through sodium channels. The membrane at rest (prior to the impulse) is negative inside relative to the outside. When the sodium ion enters, the polarity is reversed. This process is called *depolarization*. The impulse is generated and propagated down the nerve plasma membrane (neurolemma) until it comes to the end. There, at the end, the impulse meets the gap or synapse between itself and the waiting muscle or second nerve. The problem is how to get the impulse across the gap or synapse. The solution is that a chemical message is sent in the form of a neurotransmitter that goes across the synapse and joins with a receptor on the postsynaptic membrane. The receptor determines how the message of the neurotransmitter is "translated" by the recipient cell.

Although the behaviors have become symptoms of disease or disorders, they are still within the realm of interest of a biologist. There is a special area of biology called *pathobiology* or *pathophysiology*—and biologists or "life scientists" teach not only the basic biology that underlies behavior, but also what happens when symptoms of illness (or pathology) occur.

Many mental illnesses have been studied by biologists who have determined that the basic biological structures and functions of the body have been altered in such a way that symptoms of disorders or disease result. The behaviors exhibited by persons who have illnesses such as schizophrenia, bipolar illness, clinical depression, obsessive-compulsive disorder, panic and anxiety disorders, and personality disorders have been linked to evidence that indicates the strong possibility of biological changes. Frequently these changes are found in the neuroendocrine systems of those who are ill.

Because study of the brain was limited by lack of technology until modern imaging techniques such as positive emission tomography (PET) and magnetic resonance imaging (MRI) were developed, biologists lagged behind other disciplines in analyzing the brain bases of behaviors—especially those behaviors that mark mental illness. Psychological testing for diagnoses and psychoanalytic interventions were well developed before biology had a chance to contribute very effectively toward understanding mental illness.

Some exciting studies have correlated biological understandings with perspectives of those from other disciplines that have studied the behaviors of persons who have the neurobiological disorders that are called "mental illness." For example, an early study reported in 1992 in the *New England Journal of Medicine* indicated that in a small group of men with schizophrenia there was a significant correlation between their scores on a test called the Thought Disorder Index and a reduced blood-flow volume of a portion of the brain called the posterior, superior temporal gyrus (Shenton et al., 1992). More recent studies have shown that brain temperature may be more involved than actual blood flow. Brain temperature has been shown to be related to symptoms of schizophrenia but not to individuals with Bipolar Disorder. Hence, dysfunctional thermoregulation in the brain may be an important component of schizophrenia (Ota et al., 2014). Thus, biologists and psychologists have found a possible link in perspectives.

1

MAJOR PERSPECTIVES AND THE ASSUMPTIONS EACH MAKES ABOUT HUMAN BEHAVIOR

One important aspect to understanding any science (and psychology is a science) is an awareness of what "data" the scientist is using. Psychologists seek to understand human behavior and mental processes in sometimes complex circumstances. To the extent that not all of those circumstances can be taken into account at any one time, the scientist tends to focus his or her awareness on a subset of those circumstances.

This focusing of awareness and concentration, then, determines the kinds of data that scientist will use to try and understand and explain human behavior and mental processes. If we decide, for example, that the *behavior* of someone else is more important to understanding a situation than the person's *thought processes* prior to engaging in that behavior, then we will use behavior as our data in trying to figure out the person we are observing.

Most therapeutic approaches are linked fairly closely with the psychological perspective. You no doubt will note the tentative manner in which that sentence was written. It is not all cut-and-dried. Perspectives are often presented as if they come in nice tidy packages with clearly established boundaries separating them. For a long time in the history of psychopathology, that was predominantly the case. If one adopted a psychodynamic perspective, then one would employ a psychodynamic approach to treatment. Likewise, if one believed that abnormal behaviors were learned, then one adopted a behavioral approach to treatment. But this linear approach has been tried and, for the most part, has failed (e.g., Barlow & Durand, 1999).

In the history of treating mental illness, perspectives on treatment have been limited by the technology of the time. Clearly, Freud was constrained by technology. Many students do not realize that Freud was trained as a medical doctor and truly believed that a medical explanation could be found for the mental disorders of the day. But technology limited his ability to locate such causes. Rather than being diverted by this lack of technology, however, Freud sought out a different path of explanation.

Needless to say, times have changed. Brain scanning technology, neural tissue staining methods, and the development of microscopic electrodes with which the electrical activity of single neurons can be measured have changed the face of psychopathology. Few clinicians adopt a single perspective for assessing and treating mental illness. Most, in fact, follow Barlow and Durand's (1999) advice and utilize an "integrative approach." Ultimately, the best approach would appear to be one that assumes that abnormal behavior is the result of multiple factors and successful treatment will require that each of these factors be confronted and dealt with.

With serious illnesses, such as schizophrenia, multiple strategies from more than one of the perspectives may need to be employed. As an example, schizophrenia involves disturbances in thought processes, emotions, sensory and perceptual processes, and even motor movements. Clearly no single approach could effectively treat all symptoms. Before beginning our in-depth look at the cases, then, we will briefly introduce these perspectives and their link to therapeutic strategies in enough detail that you can recognize these when they are being employed by the care providers in the cases that come next in this book.

The Scenario. As an example, we will examine an event that might not be very unusual (and therefore, not likely to labeled as "abnormal") in American culture. Consider the following situation:

> You have just entered the arena to watch a hockey game because you have heard that one of the players is a woman. The players skate out onto the ice, and the action begins. Within a few moments, two players collide, and one slams the other hard into the wall. Immediately following this, a large portion of the audience begins to shout, "Kill, kill, kill!" Subsequently, the player who was slammed into the wall skates after the other player, and beats that player upside the head several times into unconsciousness. The crowd immediately starts to cheer, and the avenging hockey player raises her arms and hockey stick in triumph.

The Question. How would a psychologist interpret this complex situation? There are so many different details and nuances to focus on that it is difficult to know where to start. The scenario can be interpreted from a variety of perspectives and these tend to be where the psychologist will start.

The perspective that a psychologist takes tends to direct his or her focus in trying to determine why the events that occurred unfolded the way they did. To understand both the assumptions a psychologist will make about a situation, and the direction in which he or she will seek answers, it is useful to understand the multiple perspectives.

Perspectives That Provide Possible Answers

There are seven basic perspectives that a psychologist might take to explain behavior and mental processes: biological, psychodynamic, humanistic, behavioral, cognitive, sociocultural, and evolutionary.

Let's take a quick look at each of these perspectives and figure out what aspects of the scenario just described would be of the most interest to a psychologist working from that perspective.

Biological

The biological perspective focuses on what biological factors might be playing a role in the situation. This perspective might focus on the emotions of the players or the audience members. How might the emotions being experienced influence such physiological measures as heart rate, blood pressure, and respiration? If we change the biological aspects of the person (e.g., lower his or her heart rate), will this result in a change in the way the person thinks?

Psychodynamic

The psychodynamic perspective is primarily associated with the psychoanalytic method and theories originally developed by Sigmund Freud and expanded upon by his followers. The focus with this perspective would be on the personality and motives (primarily unconscious) of the key persons involved. Freud theorized that human beings are driven by two categories of instincts. Instincts toward life (which he called "Eros") motivate persons to procreate and to care for others. Instincts toward death (which he called "Thanatos") motivate people to want to hurt and even kill. This approach also assumes that people can "vent" some of this aggressive instinctual energy by engaging in or witnessing aggressive and violent activity. How do individual characteristics and motives influence the level of aggressive behavior displayed? What personality characteristics and motives influenced these players to choose hockey as a profession or an audience member to pay money to see the event?

Humanistic

The humanistic perspective developed as a reaction against the perceived pessimism of Freud's version of psychodynamic theory. Unlike Freud, who felt that human beings are driven primarily by aggressive and sexual urges, those operating from the humanistic perspective assume that all human beings have a unique capacity for self-actualization and will develop to that potential unless too many obstacles intervene. Psychologists operating from this perspective might want to know what unique capacities each person is attempting to fulfill or what makes each person feel "special." Living among such enormous numbers and varieties of other people, we all have a need to believe that, somehow, "I am special" within that context. In addition, this perspective might want to know what needs are being met by the persons involved. One need, for example, is to be physiologically fulfilled. Perhaps the players engage in the game to earn a paycheck so they can eat and survive. A second need could be mastery. According to this perspective, human beings have a strong need to master their environment. As such, humans will generally strive to be as good as they can be at what they do.

Behavioral

The behavioral perspective assumes that we do not need to assess unconscious motives or even biological drives to understand why people do the things they do. According to this perspective, people engage in the behaviors they do because they have learned to behave and think that way. Positive reinforcement and punishment are used to shape and mold the way people behave. A person operating from this perspective would emphasize the events that are occurring and attempt to predict how people have been influenced to behave in specific ways. This approach is interested in defining the consequences of behavior (e.g., Was the person positively reinforced or punished for doing it?). As a result of knowing the consequences of a behavior, then, we can predict whether the person will engage in that action in the future.

Cognitive

The cognitive perspective would focus on the thoughts of the individuals involved. What was the player thinking that caused him to "slam" the other player into the wall? What did his opponent think about that action that may have caused her to retaliate? What was the audience thinking would happen when they chanted "kill, kill, kill"? This perspective clearly emphasizes the linkage between what and how people think and the resulting behaviors.

Sociocultural

A person operating from the sociocultural perspective would focus on social and cultural factors that might be influencing the observed events and how people are interpreting those events. Why would more aggressive sports such as hockey be more popular in some cultures than others? If hockey is a male-dominated sport, how did the woman involved gain entry into this sport?

Evolutionary

The focus of the evolutionary perspective is on inherited human tendencies. In other words, to what extent were the actions of those involved (e.g., the initial slamming, the chanting to kill, the revenge-type action, and the crowd cheering) influenced by tendencies of the human species? Does aggressiveness in sports represent some more basic level of human aggressiveness passed on from our past? Do the types of stimulating activities people choose represent a human need for excitement? The focus here is not on the individual and his or her heredity (that would be more in line with the biological perspective). The focus is on characteristics of the species that might explain current behavior patterns.

A Brief Connection to Historical Thoughts About Abnormal Behaviors

These same perspectives may play a role in determining the assumptions that a psychologist might make about abnormal behavior. Not all of these perspectives are as popular as the others and some have been more popular in the past than they are in the present. The psychodynamic perspective is a good example. This was one of the first and most influential perspectives in all of psychology. Yet, contrary to the thoughts of some, this was not the first perspective to make assumptions about the origins of abnormal behaviors. One of the earliest perspectives was postulated by Hippocrates (yes, the one known as the "father" of modern medicine), and then later refined by Galen. Hippocrates proposed a biologically based system for mental disorders. In addition, this system was developed by Galen into the first diagnostic system for classifying abnormal behaviors.

Hippocrates believed that human beings had four kinds of fluids in their bodies that he called "humors." In order to understand this theory, it is important to remember that Hippocrates was a physician. As such, he saw a lot of persons suffering from all types of ailments. Hippocrates noticed that virtually all major illnesses involved excesses or disruptions of bodily fluids. A bad infection, for example, might cause the sore to seep a yellowish pus. This led Hippocrates to believe that one of the major humors (bodily fluids) was yellow bile. His hypothesis was that if the fluids were brought back in balance, the illness would go away. Hippocrates proposed four humors that would affect the physical state of the body. These humors were: black bile, blood, phlegm, and yellow bile. Hippocrates believed that the balance of these fluids was vital to the health of the body. In addition, he believed that excesses of these humors would affect the physical status of the individual.

Galen built upon this work and extended the concept to characteristics of persons. His assumption was that the presence of an excess of one of these fluids would be associated with a different negative personality type and associated characteristics. Excess yellow bile, for example, was associated with a personality type referred to as "choleric." Choleric individuals were believed to have irritability as their most dominant personality characteristic, according to Galen's typology. This concept—that bodily status and personality characteristics are linked—is still found in contemporary theories. It is also a part of our popular culture. We might assume, for example, that a large, round man will be gentle

TABLE 1.1 Galen's Diagnostic Categories

Type	Humor (or fluid)	Characteristics
Sanguine	Blood	Happy, optimistic
Melancholic	Black bile	Introverted, sentimental, sad
Choleric	Yellow bile	Short-tempered, ambitious
Phlegmatic	Phlegm	Sluggish, cowardly

and jolly, while a muscle-bound man will be harsh and aggressive. Although many of these assumptions may not be true, we tend to draw such conclusions nonetheless.

Galen completed his theory by connecting personality types to the four humors and the four physical elements of air, earth, fire, and water, as illustrated in Table 1.1.

You will note from this table that this system also served as an early diagnostic method. If an individual had an excess of black bile, for example, the personality type would be "melancholic." Just like the term *melancholia* suggests, these individuals were observed to have a depressed temperament.

From this classification, then, early methods of treatment were derived. "Sanguine" individuals (those believed to have an excess of blood) were optimistic. Now, there does not appear to be anything inherently wrong with being optimistic. But what if that optimism is so extreme as to become mania? What kind of a treatment might this system recommend for a person with an excess of blood? One of the early treatments used was bloodletting. With this method, some of the patient's blood was drained. Another technique used to ease the mania presumed to be brought about by an excess of blood was to use leeches.

Although bloodletting and the use of leeches would strike most persons as barbaric, think about the rationale employed in making such decisions. Considering that this theory was proposed in medieval times (even earlier if you look at the foundation work for this theory done by Hippocrates), it was really quite ahead of its time. There are several important reasons to consider this theory groundbreaking, including: (a) the classification of individuals into types, which was an early precursor to trait approaches to personality, (b) the assumption that the underlying cause of abnormal behavior involved imbalances in the biology of the body, (c) the belief that such imbalances could be corrected, and (d) the incorporation of those corrections into a treatment methodology.

Conclusions

This chapter lays the foundation upon which the rest of this text is based. Perspectives drive the assumptions we make about why people do the things they do. In addition, perspectives provide a framework around which ideas about treatment can be built. Although this chapter has presented the perspectives as if they are isolated and mutually exclusive, we have done so only to illustrate the differences between them. In reality, most clinicians, psychologists, therapists, case workers, and counselors will use a combination of approaches. Many individuals needing an intervention will show a variety of symptoms, have available different coping resources, and pursue specific goals for recovery. Thus, even people with the same diagnosis are not always treated the same way or viewed from the same perspective. Each perspective is incomplete and oversimplified when considered alone.

A man who is seeking counseling for alcohol use disorder, for example, will need more than just help to get over his physical addiction to alcohol. It is also very likely that his personal relationships have suffered, his self-esteem may be low, and he may have difficulty imagining that he has the willpower to overcome the allure of the alcohol. Surely, the professional engaging in treatment with this person will want to consider what to do from multiple fronts. The person is likely to suffer biological challenges during withdrawal from the alcohol. But there will be psychological concerns to deal with as well. In the end, the treatment regimen that is utilized will depend upon the particulars of the case being considered.

When appropriate in the cases that come later in this text, we will illustrate how multiple treatment methods may be employed when multiple problems are present. As you read the following chapters, we will provide you with opportunities to reflect on these perspectives, the assumptions each makes about the underlying causes of abnormal behavior, and the treatment techniques each perspective would suggest we employ in order to bring those abnormal behaviors "back in line."

2

CASE FORMULATION INTERVIEWS

The Importance of Critical Thinking in the Clinical Process

Before discussing the process of diagnostic interviewing, we want to say a few words about the concept of assessment. *Assessment* is a word with which most people are familiar, yet it is difficult to define. Nietzel, Bernstein, and Milich (1994) define assessment as "the process of collecting information to be used as the basis for informed decisions by the assessor or by those to whom results are communicated." An important part of the clinical process involves the assessment. Clinical assessment "is the evaluation and measurement of psychological, biological and social factors in an individual with a possible psychological disorder" (Durand & Barlow, 2013).

In order for a diagnosis to be made, the clinician must gather the appropriate information. Every one of us utilizes the process of assessment on a daily basis. Whether we work in customer service for a retail store, are teachers attempting to grade a student paper, or are trying to make judgments about which interviewees to hire for a new position in our company, many of our daily tasks involve gathering information and trying to make informed judgments about that data. Clinical assessment is not fundamentally different from this. We must, however, remind ourselves of the importance of this assessment process. Many dramatic decisions can be made on the basis of this assessment. As such, the quality of the assessment is crucial to the well-being of the individual with whom we are working. If the assessment data that we are gathering is to be used to make diagnostic decisions about a person, it is easy to understand how much care we should take in making that assessment. We will cover assessment in detail in the next chapter. It is important, however, to understand the important connection between the Case Formulation Interview and the broader concept of assessment.

What Is a Case Formulation Interview?

An interview is the most widely used assessment tool in clinical psychology. Regardless of what other information might exist about a particular client and a particular case, nothing currently seems likely to replace the importance of the interview. Both the manner in which the person is interviewed and the content of that interview are crucial. Working with a client requires the development of a trusting relationship. This sense of trust will begin to develop during the interview process.

An interview is a directed conversation between two persons in which there is a defined goal. In fact, interviews can include multiple goals for each of the members of the interview relationship. If it is a job interview, the goal for the applicant is to do well during the interview and get the offer while the goal for the interviewer is to find the best possible person to fill the job opening. Both participants will engage in behaviors designed to maximize the likelihood for fulfilling the desired goals. The interviewee will attempt to answer all questions with clarity and obvious knowledge. The interviewer will attempt to ask quality questions to elicit pertinent details and behaviors from the applicant so that the person's appropriateness for the position can be assessed.

Rather than approaching assessment like a traditional interview (such as for a job), many clinicians now emphasize Case Formulation skills as fundamental to providing effective treatment. In an early review of the literature on Case Formulation skills, Eells, Kendjelic, and Lucas (1998) found "strikingly little research on such skills." According to these authors, Case Formulations share three features regardless of whether they are designed to follow psychodynamic, cognitive-behavioral, interpersonal, behavioral, or blended orientations. These features are: "(1) They emphasize levels of inference that can readily be supported by a patient's statements in therapy, (2) The information they contain is based largely on clinical judgment rather than patient self-report, and (3) The Case Formulation is compartmentalized into preset components that are addressed individually in the formulation process and then assembled into a comprehensive formulation" (Eells et al., 1998, p. 145).

How to Structure the Interview

Structure is an important issue to consider in the interview process. On one hand, the clinician needs to ensure that there is enough structure to the interview to provide guidance and ensure progress. Yet, on the other hand, there needs to be enough flexibility in the interview to allow for it to move in directions consistent with the client's responses.

If you have ever interviewed for a job, you will know that interviews are structured in such a way as to gather as much relevant information as possible, yet, at the same time, place the interviewee at ease. If the individual who is being interviewed feels comfortable, he or she is significantly more likely to open up and respond honestly than if he or she feels that the interview is hostile or confrontational. One of the challenges to constructing and conducting a successful Case Formulation interview is to maintain a sense of relevancy. The person being interviewed needs to sense that the questions being asked are relevant to the help that he or she may need. There is a balance to strike here and a good clinician will adjust the degree of structure within the interview to maximize what is learned.

The goals of the interview will also aid the clinician in determining the amount of structure that would be appropriate. If the interview is taking place in response to a crisis—a person rushed to a facility after a suicide attempt, for example—the interview will be much more highly structured. If, however, there is not an emergency—as in the case of a person voluntarily seeking treatment for anxiety—the clinician will probably use a less structured, more nondirected technique. With a nondirective interview technique, the clinician will allow and actively encourage the client to do the majority of the talking. While the client is talking, the clinician will listen, perhaps take notes, and will encourage the client to take the interview in directions that the client chooses.

Interviews, like a book or course paper, need to tell a story. There needs to be enough information available so that the "reader" knows where the story starts, understands what occurred to mark the transition (perhaps such as what prompted the individual to seek out or be referred for services), and has some sense of where this particular person might be going in the very near future.

To understand where the story starts, the interviewer will need to gather honest feedback from the person being interviewed. Again, this is only likely to the extent that the interviewer can establish a sense of comfort about the interview process. One effective method for establishing this comfort is to be honest about the interview process itself. Regardless of how the individual came to the interview setting, he or she is bound to be nervous and apprehensive about that process. Explaining the process can put the individual more at ease.

Another successful technique involves establishing the boundaries of the early part of the interview. The interviewer might want to let the client know, for example, that he or she does not have to answer questions that feel too uncomfortable to discuss. It should be made clear, however, that these questions will be asked again and that, to maximize the process, the questions will eventually need to be answered. This takes some of the pressure off of the client when the interview process is new and unknown. Such an approach also establishes the fact that all questions are important even if they are not all answered during the initial part of the interview process.

Once a sense of comfort or rapport has been established, most interviews will progress into the fact-finding stage. During this stage of the interview, the goal is to discover information relevant to understanding the particular case. Eells and colleagues (1998) recommend four broad categories of information that are contained in most Case Formulation methods:

1. symptoms and problems
2. precipitating stressors or events
3. predisposing life events or stressors
4. a mechanism that links the preceding categories together and offers an explanation of the precipitants and maintaining influences of the individual's problems.

In "The Art of Case Formulation," Dr. Adam Blatner points out that Case Formulation is "not a case summary." According to Dr. Blatner, "formulating a case involves making appropriate inferences about a person's problem in light of an understanding of the nature of normal and pathological development. Drawing inferences and constructing a story goes beyond a mere summary of the relevant facts of a case and addresses a higher level of abstraction" (Blatner, 2006).

In addition, Blatner suggests a summary "should include the distilled elements of the history, physical and mental status examination, relevant tests, etc. These should be distilled down into the key positives and negatives sufficient to make a descriptive diagnosis. A formulation then draws those facts into a meaningful pattern. Admittedly, there's a knack to this skill, and it develops with practice and clinical experience" (Blatner, 2006).

Table 2.1 illustrates Blatner's recommended system for a Case Formulation interview. As one can see from this listing, it is more a system of questions to be answered than an exact framework for going about answering those questions. The framework often comes from one's clinical perspective and experience.

More recent efforts at Case Formulation (often referred to as Case Conceptualization), come from Sperry (2010; Sperry & Sperry, 2012). In Sperry's view, an effective Case Conceptualization (after having gathered the necessary background information on the client) accomplishes four things. First, a successful Case Conceptualization develops a diagnostic formulation that emphasizes

TABLE 2.1 Systems of Organizing a Formulation

Blatner's recommended system for addressing the various aspects of a case:

1. What are the relevant factors at the different levels of psychological organization—somatic, intrapsychic, family, social network, culture, etc.?
2. What are the current roles and role strains, conflicts, imbalances, or deficiencies?
3. What are the stressors and precipitants in the case?
4. What are the psychodynamic issues?
5. What is the status of the relevant prognostic variables?
6. How can the Case Formulation be further summarized, considering the different types of causation?

TABLE 2.2 Siassi's Mental Status Exam

1. General appearance and behavior
2. Speech and thought
3. Consciousness
4. Mood and affect
5. Perception
6. Obsessions and compulsions
7. Orientation
8. Memory
9. Attention and concentration
10. Fund of general information
11. Intelligence
12. Insight and judgment
13. Higher intellectual functioning

symptoms, but not those noted from the background information. Instead, it focuses on symptoms as presented within the context of the therapy. Second, the Case Conceptualization requires the therapist to develop a clinical formulation in which she or he attempts to understand how the symptoms developed and what might be occurring in the client's situation that is keeping the symptoms going. Third, a successful Case Conceptualization requires understanding the individual from a cultural standpoint. The bottom line here is quite simple: Culture impacts how symptoms are expressed. There are, for example, cultural differences in the words people use to express physical pain (e.g., Campbell & Edwards, 2012). It would not be a surprise, then, to find out culture likely would also influence how psychological symptoms are expressed. Fourth, a successful Case Conceptualization is the treatment formulation. Based on the first three steps, the therapist develops a picture of what the primary symptoms are, how they developed and are being expressed, and the role that culture plays in the expression and, therefore, the treatment of those symptoms.

Interview Tactics

The determination as to what interviewing tactics to use is just as important as the choice the clinician makes about how to structure the interview. Again, the tactics can be more or less directive. Nondirective interview tactics may: (a) encourage the client to expand on what was said, (b) rephrase what the client said, or (c) ask open-ended questions that allow the client to respond in ways with which he or she is comfortable.

Questions that encourage the client to say more about a topic should remain as nondirective as possible. This means that questions should encourage more information but not guide the direction toward which that information will proceed. If a client suggests, for example, that his job might be causing his anxiety, a follow-up response might be to ask a question seeking more details. Two examples are:

1.   Could you tell me more about that?
2.   How often do you feel that way?

In both cases, the clinician responds to the comment by encouraging more information, but in such a way that the assumption the client is making has neither been confirmed nor challenged.

The primary goal with nondirective questions is to keep the client talking. In addition, the nature of the questions encourages the client to focus on whatever topics he or she is interested in discussing. The drawback to such techniques, however, is the fact that the conversation may continue down a path that eventually proves to be fruitless.

Interview questions, however, can also be direct. With direct questions, the clinician will make more specific requests based on prior case history information or as a result of questions answered earlier during the same interview. Examples of such questions include:

1.   When was the first time you noticed this?
2.   Have there been other times when this has been a problem for you?
3.   Do you think this is related to your job in any way?
4.   What have you done to deal with this in the past?

The most common interview would begin with the clinician offering some information to let the client know the purpose and nature of the interview, proceed to a discussion designed to help build rapport between the interviewer and the client, progress to nondirected questions to begin accessing information about the person and the nature of the problem or problems prompting the diagnostic interview, and then transition into direct questions based on the progression of the interview. When the interview is over, the process is not complete. The clinician may make some preliminary summary statements to the client—focusing on positives as much as possible. Again, this helps build rapport and establishes a sense that the person has already made good progress. Last, the clinician will probably schedule a follow-up session to begin planning a treatment program or to gather additional information if making a diagnosis is not currently possible.

3

CLASSIFICATION AND DIAGNOSIS

The *Diagnostic and Statistical Manual of Mental Disorders*

Classification and diagnosis generally follow successful interviewing with a client. As mentioned in an earlier chapter, attempts to create a classification system for abnormal behavior date back to Galen and his use of the four bodily fluids (humors) to make predictions about personality and temperament. But modern classification and diagnosis is much more sophisticated. The American Psychiatric Association brought classification and diagnosis into the modern era with the development of the *Diagnostic and Statistical Manual of Mental Disorders* (DSM) in 1952. Since that date, the DSM has been revised four times, the most recent prior edition being the DSM-IV-TR, released in 1994.

There were two versions of the DSM published during the 1980s. The DSM-III was published in 1980 and the DSM-III-R (a revised version of DSM-III) was published in 1987. The versions of the DSM-III departed significantly from both DSM and DSM-II. These earlier editions of the DSM mainly included abstract diagnostic terms and theoretical concepts. As such, their usefulness as diagnostic tools was somewhat limited. The newer versions of the DSM, however, include significantly more information about symptomology, timing of onset, and descriptions of behaviors indicative of the disorders included.

The DSM-III-R was also the first version of the DSM to include specific categories for childhood and adolescent disorders. Prior to this revision, children were primarily diagnosed using the adult symptom criteria. With the DSM-IV publication in 1994, the American Psychiatric Association modernized the classification system to reflect recent changes in psychiatry. These changes include the use of the term *Dissociative Identity Disorder* to replace the often misused and misunderstood term *Multiple Personality* and the use of the term *Bipolar Disorder* to replace the misleading term *Manic-Depression* (American Psychiatric Association, 1994). DSM-IV was revised (somewhat) in 2000 and retitled DSM-IV-TR. The changes were mainly in diagnostic codes and some text sections of disorders were updated.

The most recent version, DSM-5, was published in 2013. This version of the DSM includes 20 chapters that restructure disorders from DSM-IV-TR based on how "related" disorders appear to be with each other. The changes were also designed to align the DSM with the World Health Organization's (WHO) *Internal Classification of Diseases*, 11th Edition (ICD-11). This was done in an effort to facilitate improved communication and create more common use of diagnoses across disorders (APA, 2013a).

Knowing the rationale behind developing a classification system like the DSM is more important for your understanding in an abnormal psychology course than knowing how to use the system. The DSM is a tool that a clinician can use to focus his or her assessment efforts. As such, it is useful. But the DSM is not the only tool a clinician should use. Instead, using it should be considered an important step in the overall assessment, classification, diagnosis, and treatment process.

Prior to the development of the DSM, there were few standard methods by which a clinician could arrive at a diagnosis. It would not be unusual in these early years for two clinicians to assess the same client and arrive at fundamentally different diagnoses. Although this can still happen, the detailed symptom listings for each disorder included in the DSM guide the clinician on what to look for within any given diagnostic category. As such, we can expect a greater degree of consistency within the major classifications.

The Major Diagnostic Categories

Although your primary textbook will most likely include an extensive description of each of the major diagnostic categories of the DSM-5, a brief description of each category here will aid your understanding of the major cases that we will be describing in detail in subsequent chapters. Most of these major disorders will have a case devoted to them in the case chapters. The major disorders categorized by DSM-5 are outlined in Table 3.1. Following is a brief description of each category (APA, 2013b).

Neurodevelopmental Disorders

This category is one of the revised categories added to DSM-5. Disorders in this category primarily begin in infancy, childhood, or adolescence. Although you are probably familiar with several of these disorders such as autism or mental retardation (now referred to as "intellectual disability" or "intellectual development disorder"), there are many others with which you may be less familiar, such as

TABLE 3.1 Specific Disorders of DSM-5

Neurodevelopmental Disorders
Schizophrenia Spectrum and Other Psychotic Disorders
Bipolar and Related Disorders
Depressive Disorders
Anxiety Disorders
Obsessive-Compulsive and Related Disorders
Trauma-and-Stressor-Related Disorders
Dissociative Disorders
Somatic Symptom Disorders
Feeding and Eating Disorders
Elimination Disorders
Sleep-Wake Disorders
Sexual Dysfunctions
Gender Dysphoria
Disruptive, Impulse Control, and Conduct Disorders
Substance Use and Addictive Disorders
Neurocognitive Disorders
Personality Disorders
Paraphilic Disorders
Other Disorders

communication disorders (like stuttering). It is important to note that these disorders may begin in infancy or childhood but most are also likely to persist into adulthood.

Schizophrenia Spectrum and Other Psychotic Disorders

Schizophrenia and other psychotic disorders are particularly troublesome because the symptoms are both diverse and extreme. Schizophrenic symptoms involve disturbances in thought, perception, and emotion. Because of this diversity and extremity of symptoms, there is no "standard" set of symptoms that define who does and who does not suffer from this disorder. Indeed, diagnosis involves a range of symptoms, only a subset of which need be present in order for the diagnosis of schizophrenia. The diagnosis of schizophrenia is often arrived at through exclusion. This means that such a diagnosis is typically reserved for use only when all other disorders have been ruled out. There are several reasons for this, including: (a) Schizophrenia is not as amenable to treatment as other disorders that may cause some of the same kinds of symptoms, and (b) the diagnosis, in and of itself, raises severe fears and misconceptions.

Symptoms of schizophrenia are categorized as either positive or negative. Positive symptoms are ones of excess. These can include disorganized speech, disturbances in perception (such as hallucinations), and delusions. Negative symptoms are not as obvious, but this does not mean that the symptoms are in some way less severe. Negative symptoms include flat affect (a lack of affective reactions such as facial expressions), poverty of speech (absence of or only minimal use of speech even though the person is physically capable of speaking) or speech content or both, and avolition (which is a general apathy or lack of enjoyment of life).

Bipolar and Depressive Disorders

Bipolar Disorder can involve cyclical episodes of depression and mania. As the name suggests, depressive disorders involve severe disturbances in emotions. Although the most obvious mood disorders related to mood involve extreme sadness (such as depression), such mood disorders can involve extremes in positive emotions (such as the "manic" phase of Bipolar Disorder now categorized separately) as well. Depressive disorders do involve disturbances in emotion but the symptoms go beyond these emotions. Major Depressive Disorders, for example, involve loss of appetite, disturbances in sleep, and fatigue.

Anxiety Disorders

As you can guess, anxiety disorders involve feelings of fear and apprehension. Like feelings of depression or elation, anxiety is an important part of healthy functioning. For most people, feeling anxious when seeing a snake is perfectly normal. Experiencing such extreme fear of snakes that you refuse to mow the yard, however, is probably cause for concern. With any of the disorders that we will discuss, symptoms in excess are the primary concern.

Fear is considered both healthy and normal in response to stimuli or circumstances that "should" cause concern. Just as it would be considered "abnormal" to be so afraid of heights that you could not climb up on a step stool to get a puzzle off the shelf in the closet, it would also be considered abnormal to not experience any fear when a bear jumps out from behind the trees and grabs you. So, it is not the presence or absence of fear in a situation that determines abnormality but whether those bouts of anxiety and fear are either too extreme given the actual degree of danger or not strong enough given the actual degree of danger. Anxiety disorders can range from generalized anxiety (extreme, unfocused anxiety) to phobias in which the cause of the extreme anxiety is well-known.

Obsessive-Compulsive and Related Disorders

This is a new diagnostic category with the publication of DSM-5. These disorders are all characterized by obsessive thoughts and compulsive actions. Four new disorders have been included in this category: (1) excoriation (skin picking) disorder, (2) hoarding disorder, (3) substance-medication-induced obsessive-compulsive and related disorder, and (4) obsessive-compulsive and related disorder due to another medical condition.

Trauma-and-Stressor-Related Disorders

Posttraumatic stress disorder (PTSD) has now been included in this broader category. Disorders in this new category all involve stress responses either as a result of traumatic events or adjustment-related syndromes.

Dissociative Disorders

Dissociative disorders involve the experience of disruptions in consciousness, identity, or memory, or a combination of these. Such disruptions may involve temporary separations between the individual and his or her memories (such as dissociative amnesia) or more long-term separation between various aspects of the individual's identity (as in dissociative identity disorder). What does it mean to suggest that an individual has been separated from his or her memories? It simply means that the normal, coherent relationship between the various aspects of who a person is and the memories associated with the person has become separated and possibly fragmented in some way.

With dissociative amnesia, the memory loss is quite specific and may involve the temporary inability to recall pertinent personal information that relates to a significant personal loss. An example would be being unable to recall one's name, address, and phone number after narrowly escaping from a fire in which all of one's immediate family has been killed. The more severe dissociative disorders involve more complete separations from memory and identity, up to the most severe dissociative disorder known as dissociative identity disorder (formerly known as "multiple personality"). In order to facilitate treatment of such individuals, the clinician must discover a method for "reintegrating" the aspects of self or memory that have become dissociated. Frequently this will involve an attempt to aid the person in confronting and resolving the crisis or stressful event that activated the dissociation.

Somatic Symptom Disorders

Soma means "body." As such, a *somatoform disorder* refers to a disorder in which the person experiences physical ailments but no physiological cause can be found. The complaints can range from somatic symptom disorder with predominant pain—in which the person experiences extensive pain that cannot be explained by any medical condition—to other somatic symptom disorders in which the individual is preoccupied in a negative fashion with some aspect of his or her appearance. It is important to note that although the cause of pain or concern with somatic symptom disorders seems to be caused by psychological factors, the pain and distress that is caused is experienced by the person as real.

Feeding and Eating Disorders

Eating disorders typically involve disturbances in eating-oriented behavior and in perceptions of body shape, size, and weight. The two most common eating disorders are Bulimia and Anorexia Nervosa. With Bulimia Nervosa, the individual may binge or engage in gross overeating. These binges are followed by purging involving vomiting and/or the use of laxatives and other methods for "compensating" for the food and calories ingested during the binge. With anorexia nervosa, the individual has a severely distorted perception of her or his body image that causes the individual to engage in near starvation in order to achieve a state of bodily perfection that is impossible to achieve. Both of these disorders are found to be more common in countries (such as the United States) where there is an intense focus on bodies that are lean.

Elimination Disorders

Elimination Disorders involve the elimination of urine or feces from the body abnormally, for example, in abnormal ways (such as painting the walls with it), abnormally based on age (such as a 15-year-old still not "potty" trained), etc. The elimination can be either voluntary or involuntary, occur at day or night and be due to medical or psychiatric reasons.

Sleep-Wake Disorders

Although most persons may think of insomnia when considering sleep disorders, there are a whole range of disturbances that fall into this category. These disorders involve a disturbance in the quality (e.g., repeated awakening throughout the night), timing (e.g., the person is unable to sleep during what would be considered to be "normal" times), or the amount of sleep that one gets (e.g., difficulty falling asleep or early waking). These disturbances also include unusual events that happen during sleep (e.g., night terrors or sleep walking). Although some of these disorders are clearly linked to the biology of the brain—such as rapid eye movement (REM)–sleep behavior disorder in which the brain does not send out messages to paralyze the muscles during dream sleep—others such as insomnia may be related more to the individual's psychological state. This grouping also includes three breathing disorders, and circadian-rhythm sleep-wake disorders. The goal of this categorization is to "acknowledge the bidirectional and interactive effects between sleep disorders and coexisting medical and mental disorders" (APA, 2013a).

Sexual Dysfunctions

These disorders typically involve atypical sources of sexual gratification (such as voyeurism and exhibitionism) or sexual dysfunctions (such as premature ejaculation). The theories about the causes of such disorders are as diverse as their suggested treatment approaches. Approaches for premature ejaculation, for example, range from behavior modification techniques, in which the individual is taught to slowly delay ejaculation, to chemical treatments in which substances are used that are expected to maintain ejaculation at least until penetration has been experienced.

Gender Dysphoria

Gender dysphoria involves issues of gender identity. It could be the individual is not comfortable with his or her anatomical sex. To be diagnosed with gender dysphoria, the person must exhibit a persistent and strong cross-gender identification. Usually, gender dysphoria is accompanied by discomfort and dissatisfaction with one's current sex. Individuals may dress and act like the sex they feel is the "correct" sex for them.

Disruptive, Impulse-Control, and Conduct Disorders

Every person has experienced an urge to do something that he or she should not do. But most of these persons will resist the urge to engage in that behavior. Individuals with impulse control disorders, however, are unable to resist the urge to engage in the problem behavior. The most commonly depicted examples in the media tend to be kleptomania, in which the individual cannot resist the urge to steal things even though the stolen objects are not even needed, and pyromania, in which the individual is unable to resist the urge to set fires.

Substance Use and Addictive Disorders

With a substance-related disorder, the individual's occupational functioning or relationships are impaired by the ingestion of substances. Although many people in the United States, for example, drink alcohol, take sleeping pills, or use an occasional painkiller, such use would only be considered "abnormal" when such ingestion interferes with normal functioning. The individual who cannot "face the boss" without cocaine as an upper, for example, probably suffers from a substance-related disorder. More common than either of these problems, however, is pathological gambling. The pathological gambler, who is unable to resist the urge to gamble, will squander huge sums of money that he or she does not have, and may experience even greater urges to gamble when confronting problems in life. The gambling is assumed to be a method the individual uses to attempt to "escape" from those life problems. In an interesting change from DSM-IV-TR to DSM-5, pathological gambling is now categorized under addictive disorders rather than impulse control.

Neurocognitive Disorders

In order to understand this category of disorders, it is helpful to understand delirium and dementia. Dementia refers to a permanent deterioration of cognitive capacity, usually involving memory. The most common causes of dementia are biologically related, such as stroke or Alzheimer's disease. Delirium, however, can be caused by medical conditions or even the ingestion of foreign substances (such as alcohol or illicit drugs). As an additional change brought about by this category, DSM-5 also now includes (earlier versions did not) "Mild Neurocognitive Disorder" (not just "Major"). This has been included in an effort to promote early detection and treatment.

Personality Disorders

According to the American Psychiatric Association, "Personality Disorders are associated with ways of thinking and feeling about oneself and others that significantly and adversely affect how an individual functions in many aspects of life" (APA, 2013c). There are 10 distinct types of Personality Disorders: (1) Paranoid Personality Disorder, (2) Schizoid Personality Disorder, (3) Schizotypal Personality Disorder, (4) Antisocial Personality Disorder, (5) Borderline Personality Disorder, (6) Histrionic Personality, (7) Narcissistic Personality Disorder, (8) Avoidant Personality Disorder, (9) Dependent Personality Disorder, and (10) Obsessive-Compulsive Personality Disorder.

Paraphilic Disorders

This grouping starts with the basic viewpoint that "most people with atypical sexual interests do not have a mental disorder" (APA, 2013d). Diagnosis of a paraphilic disorder means the individual feels personal distress about the interest or has sexual desires that involve distressing, injuring, or killing someone, or forcing someone else to do something he or she would not want to do. This category now also distinguishes between the sexual act (the paraphilia) and a disorder (paraphilic disorder). Examples of these disorders include (1) pedophilic disorder, (2) sexual sadism disorder, and (3) exhibitionistic disorder.

Other Disorders

DSM-IV-TR included many disorder categories designated as "NOS" or "Not Otherwise Specified." DSM-5 attempts to minimize this "catch-all" approach by adding an additional category titled "Other Disorders." Rather than encouraging clinicians to place symptoms into the "closest" disorder category with the NOS designation—such as "anxiety disorder NOS," DSM-5 attempts to keep NOS designations to a minimum but still allow for the fact that not all patterns of symptoms fit clearly into a diagnostic category.

Dual Diagnosis

It is possible for an individual to suffer from more than one of the disorders described in this section. In such cases, the individual may be "dually diagnosed." In order to be labeled in this manner, the individual must meet the diagnostic criteria for both disorders. In other words, the person must exhibit the *symptoms* that would meet the criteria for both of the disorders involved. It is important to mention that many mental health professionals, especially those working with persons with dual diagnoses such as Borderline Personality Disorder and Substance Abuse Disorder, are moving away from using the phrase "dual diagnosis." The movement away from such a term is primarily a reflection of the fact that the term is being used to indicate persons with two medical conditions and not just mental illnesses.

The term *dual diagnosis* may also be somewhat misleading. It is very difficult to know how much of a role one of the illnesses has played in the development of the other. A preferred label may be "co-occurring illnesses." This emphasizes the importance of treating both illnesses and not assuming that one will take care of itself once the other is being effectively controlled. Another term that is used to describe this situation is *comorbidity*. Although comorbidity or co-occurring illness is troublesome, some degree of it is to be expected. If 1 percent of the adult population, for example, suffers from Bipolar Disorder, and over 1 percent suffers from schizophrenia, then statistically we would expect 1 percent of that 1 percent to suffer from both. What is of special clinical interest, then, are categories of disorders in which comorbidity is significantly higher than what would be expected on the basis of chance. An example of comorbid disorders that occur much more frequently than one would expect based on chance is the co-occurrence of obsessive-compulsive anxiety disorder and depression.

The Role of Clinical Judgment

The role of clinical judgment in making decisions about diagnoses and degree of impairment requires considering the degree to which a person's current symptoms differ from his or her previous experiences, and the extent to which his or her ability to manage relationships, work, and daily tasks is impaired. For example, in considering whether a military veteran meets criteria for PTSD, it would be important to know whether the veteran is experiencing frequent nightmares or other reexperiencing symptoms of a traumatic event. If the veteran already had frequent nightmares before joining the military, and there was no increase in the frequency or severity of the nightmares, then the current nightmare complaints may not reflect PTSD. Similarly, we would want to know not only about current sleep quality (number of hours slept, daytime sleepiness), but how current sleep status compares with premilitary sleep status. Thus, a combat veteran with newly developed symptoms of nightmares, sleep disturbance, and avoidance of crowds may meet criteria for PTSD; however, a combat veteran who already had frequent nightmares and sleep disturbance prior to joining the military, with no worsening following combat, should likely have diagnoses of nightmare disorder and insomnia disorder, as pre-existing conditions, rather than a new diagnosis of PTSD.

Clinical judgment is also important in considering the degree of impairment attributable to the condition. A crucial principle in disability evaluations is that "diagnosis does not equal disability"; in other words, someone can be diagnosed with a condition that causes them significant personal distress, but they may function normally in their relationships, school, and work. However, when a previously high-functioning veteran returns from combat and subsequently has marital problems due to increased anger, disintegration of friendships due to feelings of detachment, loss of social activities due to increased avoidance behavior, and multiple job terminations due to newly developed conflict with coworkers, then these impairments may be directly attributable to the PTSD caused by the combat exposure. The clinical reasoning underpinning this is that the veteran had previously functioned well across several domains, but on returning from a traumatic deployment has developed symptoms of such severity that they cause functional impairment in areas including work, family, and social relationships. The observation of this change following the development of the symptoms is incorporated into the clinical judgment about whether a diagnosis is present, and how impairing the disorder may be. This may be contrasted with an individual with a lifelong history of poor relationships, inability to maintain steady work, and other maladaptive behaviors; learning that such an individual was currently having relationship difficulty and unstable employment would not reflect a significant change and so a diagnosis of a new psychological disorder based on this presentation of symptoms would not be warranted.

Conclusion

The DSM is viewed as a changing document. It reflects current thinking about disorders and should not be considered "absolute." This is recognized by the American Psychiatric Association (publisher of the DSM and related materials) who refers to the DSM as a "living document" subject to correction. Some view the DSM and its use as a kind of "cookbook" psychiatry while others see it as a useful tool for sorting through the variety of symptoms associated with mental disorders and illness. We will not judge the DSM, but want you to be aware that it has both its proponents and its opponents.

4

THE CASE OF RICKY G

Schizophrenia

Introduction

The police cruiser was making a routine pass through the backstreets of New York City. "Hey, stop the car," Frank told his partner. Jerry, a much younger officer than his seasoned partner, immediately brought the cruiser to a halt. Frank climbed out of the car and aimed his flashlight toward the rain-soaked cardboard box. The light fell on a bedraggled-looking man. "We've got us a drunk," Frank called to Jerry. Jerry joined his partner in the alley and moved the police cruiser spotlight so that its beam fell on the man they had found. Something about the expression on the man's face suggested to Jerry that he was more than intoxicated. He looked kind of wild.

Frank reached and grabbed the man by the arm saying, "Come on, partner, a night in a warm jail cell will do you some good." The man's reaction startled both of the officers. He yanked his arm free from the police officer and began screaming. "Get them off me," he bellowed. "Get them off me . . . oh God, the bugs are eating my skin." Frank looked at Jerry and both of the men backed away from the gesticulating stranger. "Please help me," the man pleaded. "The bugs will eat my skin if I don't do the bad things the voices tell me to do."

Frank had seen reactions like this before. Sometimes they were drug induced and sometimes they weren't, but he was not going to take any chances. He had learned the most important rules for bringing someone down from such a reaction: You had to speak slowly; you had to speak calmly; and you should not touch the person. "It's okay," he reassured the frantic man. "My partner and I are police officers and we can chase those bugs away." The stranger stopped glancing around frantically and for just a second focused his eyes on the gray-haired officer. Then his eyes started darting around again. "Are, are, are, you s-s-s-ure?" the man asked. "Absolutely," Frank promised. "That's our job."

While Frank continued to talk to the man, Jerry moved very slowly to work his way behind the now much calmer man. Frank moved to stand directly in front of the stranger and looked him right in the eye. The human contact without touching seemed to calm the man even more. While he continued to fix his gaze on the man, Jerry moved in behind him.

Frank explained what they were going to do. "We're going to put handcuffs on you now," he began. "To help keep the bugs away we're going to take you somewhere safe. But to do that, we have to put handcuffs on you. Do you understand?" Frank never broke his connection with the man's still-frightened eyes. The man seemed about to protest, then simply dropped his chin to his chest and put his arms behind his back. Jerry took the signal and very gently placed handcuffs on the now unmoving man's wrists. The officers helped the man into the cruiser and headed for the hospital. Given the state the man was in when they first confronted him, it seemed wise to have him checked out before they took him to the station.

The Diagnostic Interview

After his vital signs were checked by emergency room personnel, Ricky was escorted to a tiny office near the psychiatric section of the emergency room. He waited quietly until two women appeared at the door, gave a perfunctory knock, and entered. The younger one introduced herself:

"Hello. I'm Dr. Morgan, a psychiatry resident here. This is Ms. Johnstone, a nurse's aid." Then, after a brief pause, "What is your name?" Ricky said nothing.

Dr. Morgan carefully noted Ricky's appearance: He was dirty and disheveled. He sat stiffly and abruptly looked away when she tried to make eye contact. He seemed to pay little attention to his surroundings.

Dr. Morgan's formal assessment of Ricky began in a slow, sincere tone of voice: "Do you know what place this is?"

Ricky mumbled, "Hospital."

"That's right, Memorial Hospital. Do you know what day it is?"

After a pause of several seconds, "Tuesday."

"Actually, it's early Wednesday morning, but you're close." From this part of the mental status exam (Siassi, 1984) she concluded that Ricky was oriented to place and time, meaning that he knew where he was and approximately what time it was. Her low-key manner relaxed Ricky slightly, and he began to give brief, cautious answers to her questions. Finally he told her his name. She then asked, "Can you tell me what happened that caused the police to bring you here?"

Ricky's responses were guarded and hesitant, but over the next hour he revealed bits of information that when pieced together indicate he has been in New York for less than 2 weeks, having abruptly left his hometown after his parents tried to obtain a court order committing him to inpatient treatment at a state psychiatric hospital. Using most of the money he had for his bus ticket, he arrived at the Port Authority terminal and managed to find a run-down rooming house in which to stay.

The rooming house was noisy and Ricky was very uncomfortable there. He spent most of the time in his stuffy little room, and as the days passed he began to hear messages coming from the television, even after he unplugged it. When police cars came down the street or a helicopter flew by overhead, Ricky believed they were trying to photograph him. Once he even telephoned the police to tell them that he knew they were working with the CIA to control him.

A CRITICAL THINKING AND QUESTIONING PAUSE

Given the brief description of this case thus far, what questions might you want to ask Ricky in order to pursue a diagnosis? Generate at least three questions (such as, "What do you think you know that the CIA would find so important that they want to control you?"). Keep these questions in mind as you consider the initial diagnosis and suggested treatment options that follow.

A Tentative Diagnosis

Ricky clearly had several symptoms. Among his cognitive disturbances were delusions, which are irrational beliefs (for example, that others are trying to control him and his thoughts), and disturbed patterns of thinking that resulted in Ricky having a difficult time keeping his thoughts "on track" and connected. These cognitive symptoms suggested a serious mental disorder, but they could also have been caused by acute intoxication from substance use or (less often) a nutritional deficiency. In her initial interview, Dr. Morgan asked Ricky about his appetite and his use of alcohol and other substances. He refused to answer these questions, so she decided to wait, rather than press him, knowing that the toxicology screens would suggest if substance use or nutritional deficiencies might account for Ricky's symptoms.

To evaluate other more remote possibilities, such as cerebral stroke or tumor, she asked Ricky if he had had any noticeable feelings of nausea, headaches, recent falls, or blows to the head. She also asked him for his parents' phone number so she could contact them right away. Dr. Morgan expected that enlisting their help would make it much easier to arrange adequate care for Ricky once he left the hospital. However, Ricky refused to give her any information about his family.

Ricky also appeared to be experiencing hallucinations that were at least visual and auditory in nature. You will recall that Ricky was making statements about "bugs eating his skin" if he did not do the bad things the voices told him to do. Although these symptoms appeared quite dramatic and unusual, they may have indicated a broader problem that Ricky was having with processing sensory information. This possibility will be covered more thoroughly in the Biological Perspective section later in this case.

Let us examine Ricky's delusions in more detail. A key feature of Ricky's delusions were their suspicious quality, including "ideas of reference." With ideas of reference, everyday occurrences and situations are assumed to have special meaning. One such example might be having someone assume that a Coca-Cola commercial proclaiming, "Coke—It's the real thing" means that the people in the room can be trusted but others cannot. An example of this in Ricky's case was his belief that police cars and helicopters were in the neighborhood because of him. Dr. Morgan questioned the evidence for these beliefs, testing whether Ricky's thinking is sufficiently chaotic that he would abandon these ideas in favor of other completely different notions. Ricky stuck by his story, however, and as she waited for the medical results, Dr. Morgan decided to evaluate the appropriateness of schizophrenia as a diagnosis.

For a diagnosis of schizophrenia, the patient must show continuous signs of disturbance for at least 6 months and demonstrate two or more of the following: delusions, hallucinations, disorganized speech, disorganized or catatonic behavior, negative symptoms, and social or occupational dysfunction. At least one symptom must be delusions, hallucinations, or disorganized speech. Ricky described hallucinations, and his beliefs about strangers trying to control him are almost certainly delusional. Although Ricky's responses were guarded, Dr. Morgan was able to infer that he had been gainfully employed in the past but had not worked for some months, suggesting social and occupational functioning markedly below the level he achieved previously.

Although Ricky's account of his problems at home and difficult time in New York suggest recent episodes of intense anxiety and agitation, there was no evidence that he experienced major depression, manic episodes, or mixed bipolar symptoms or fluctuating moods. From all of this information, Dr. Morgan arrived at a tentative diagnosis of schizophrenia based on Ricky's frequent auditory hallucinations and his preoccupation with delusions of external control over his thoughts and behavior. Following DSM-5, she rated the severity of each of these symptoms as 3 on a scale of 0–4, and also noted that at this point there is very little evidence of severely disorganized speech, disorganized or catatonic behavior, or flat or inappropriate affect. From what Ricky has told her, Dr. Morgan infers that his symptoms have persisted for at least 6 months.

When using DSM-5, it is important to try to understand the person's cultural background and identity as these might be related to the symptoms. Ricky's race and ethnicity appeared similar to her own, so Dr. Morgan decided to ask him whether his thoughts and perceptions have anything to do with his religious and spiritual beliefs, or those of his family. Again, he refused to answer.

Finally, having insufficient information from Ricky about any past episodes of schizophrenia, she completed her tentative diagnosis of schizophrenia by adding the term "acute," but did not indicate whether this was Ricky's first episode or instead the latest of multiple episodes he has experienced. In Dr. Morgan's mind, Ricky's symptoms were serious enough, and the nature of his illness was clear enough, that she did not need to keep him off of medication. She asked him what medications he had used in the past, and with her help, he identified some antipsychotic medications. He accepted her decision to have him resume one of these medications.

Ricky's symptoms fit the diagnosis of schizophrenia very clearly, but it was important that Dr. Morgan get to know him as an individual. With this in mind, she renewed her efforts to contact Ricky's family, hoping to pave the way for Ricky's return home. Again, Ricky refused to provide any useful information. A few days later, Dr. Morgan had no choice but to have Ricky transferred to the Creedmoor Psychiatric Center, one of New York's state hospitals for people with mental illness.

Ricky's History

As Ricky's parents would later explain, he had a normal childhood and everyone in the family got along well. Ricky was involved in all the things that boys do, such as Little League baseball and Scouts, and was a solid B student all the way through high school. He played the clarinet in the high school band, had several after-school jobs, went to dances, and seemed to enjoy friends in a normal way for a teenager. Toward the end of high school, his parents noticed some problems but thought it was just typical teenage anxiety. During the second semester of his senior year of high school, his parents noticed some suspiciousness and odd statements, but they dismissed these signs also, believing that Ricky was simply anxious about graduating from high school and nervous about going to college.

Ricky went to college in another state and did not know anyone at the school when he arrived. The first month there, he seemed a little mixed up and called home frequently, but again his family thought it was just an adjustment problem and he would get over it. Before long, he became good friends with his roommate, Chris, who was from India. However, Chris introduced him to LSD, marijuana, hashish, mescaline, and other drugs. Ricky tried LSD, had a terrifying experience, and was placed in the university infirmary. His friends assured him that the best way to get over a bad trip would be to try LSD again. However, he tried it again and once again had a psychotic episode and was placed in the infirmary.

Ricky managed to complete his freshman year, but when he came home in June, he was extremely thin and quite nervous. After much questioning, he finally told his mother about the drugs and confided that he was worried about losing his mind. They first approached their family physician because, as Ricky's mother often explained, "We are the kind of people who always start by consulting our doctor." The doctor talked to Ricky and, unable to learn much from him, referred the family to a neurologist. The neurologist examined Ricky but found nothing wrong, so he suggested seeing a psychiatrist.

Ricky couldn't get an appointment with the psychiatrist for 6 weeks, so he sat around the house and slept a lot. After the psychiatrist had interviewed him for about an hour, he recommended that Ricky be evaluated at the local general hospital, which had a wing for the treatment of psychiatric patients. His mother thought the doctors would prescribe a medication and he would be better in a few weeks or even a month.

Ricky stayed for only a week, and although he showed little response to treatment, the staff did not believe he was psychotic enough to require hospitalization. When he returned home, Ricky insisted there was nothing wrong with him and refused to take any medication. When his mother went to do his laundry, she found that Ricky had been hiding much of the medication he was supposed to have taken in his dirty laundry. In addition, he either ate ravenously or refused to eat anything. He withdrew socially, spending less time interacting with friends and family, and more time in his room playing his stereo. He often slept during the day and stayed awake most of the night listening to loud music. Sometimes his family could hear him scream at someone, but they were sure there was no one else in the room.

His sisters' friends wondered what was wrong with him; their brothers, who were the same age, were out doing things. Once in a while, Ricky would sit with them and try to participate in their conversations, but he couldn't keep up. It seemed that it took him too long to grasp what people would say and then think of something to say back. It was as if he were playing a tennis game in slow motion, but everyone else was playing at regular speed. The conversation just went too fast. His inability to participate in conversations added to the embarrassment his sisters felt.

As time passed, Ricky behaved more and more strangely. When he went out, he would dress "incognito," he would say, wearing sunglasses and a hat and sitting very low in the seat of his vehicle. He wore golf gloves even though he never played golf—and, in fact, he slept with the gloves and his socks on. At times, members of the family would find him standing in front of the mirror patting different places on his face. When he had a chance at the full length mirror in his sisters' room, they would see him look into the mirror and pat different parts of his body.

At home, he would sit in the living room and stare right past everyone. He had very little contact with former friends and became more and more argumentative with his parents. As these arguments became more heated, Ricky's younger sister feared that he might injure one of their parents or even perhaps kill them. Once he called her down into the basement where his bedroom was, and told her that he quit skydiving lessons (which in fact he had never taken) because he knew his mother and sister were trying to kill him and he thought they would pay someone to damage his parachute.

Eventually Ricky began to look for a job, but couldn't seem to find anything satisfactory in his home town. He decided to move to California, where he knew someone who was attending a university there. Ricky found work as a janitor, and later worked in a fast-food restaurant, but after 6 months, he returned home saying that some people out there were after him.

Ricky decided to reapply for college and was accepted at an in-state university. He enrolled there, but seemed to have a lot of difficulty. Soon his family stopped hearing from him, and there was no answer when they phoned his apartment. After they left urgent messages at various university offices, an official from the school called them to say that Ricky had been arrested and that he was in jail. He had fired a gun in his apartment. He didn't fire it at anyone, but fired it into the ceiling, saying that the planes overhead were buzzing him and bothering him.

The police, realizing that this was probably a psychiatric problem, decided to take him to a psychiatric clinic in town, but on the way, he assaulted one of the guards by biting him on the hand. Because of this, when they got to the clinic, the intake staff said he was too dangerous in his present state and refused to see him. The police had no choice but to put Ricky in jail.

Ricky's father accompanied him to court and got the charges dismissed on condition that Ricky return home and receive psychiatric treatment. He was admitted to a state psychiatric hospital 2 weeks before Christmas. Christmas that year was very hard on the family. Ricky's sisters didn't want to go see him because they were frightened by all that he had been doing and what was happening to him. At that time, the typical medication regimen initially entailed high doses of powerful medications that were gradually tapered over time. When his parents visited, Ricky didn't look or act like the son they knew. He was hospitalized for 3 months. He was somewhat improved after 6 weeks of hospitalization, at which time the staff psychiatrist told the family that Ricky's diagnosis was acute schizophrenia.

The family felt terrified about this diagnosis. What was schizophrenia? They looked for books about it at the library. Unfortunately, much of what they found was old and featured outdated theories that schizophrenia was caused by bad parenting. The family not only felt overwhelmed with the suffering that Ricky was experiencing, but also tremendously guilty and inadequate.

After 3 months at the state hospital, Ricky returned home. He was supposed to continue taking powerful phenothiazine medications to blunt his delusions, but he disliked their troublesome side effects (dry mouth, constipation, blurred vision, and fatigue) so he stopped taking them without telling his parents. Within 2 months, his psychotic symptoms began to return. He believed the doctors, and even his family, were plotting against him and helping the CIA to control him; his family was trying to poison him, he thought, and he would eat only things from cans he had seen opened.

One time there was a dishcloth lying on the sink with some food on it. When he saw it, he said, "Those are bugs! Those are giant bugs!" He took the family dog and ran upstairs, refusing to eat with the family. He took plastic from dry-cleaning bags and covered up his bed because he thought his mother was putting poison in the washing machine instead of detergent. He thought that she was not only putting poison in his food, because it tasted different, but also he thought she was poisoning the dog by putting poison in the dog food. He believed that he was designated to save the dog. He became very delusional, was afraid to be around people, and started carrying large rocks in his car in case he had to confront someone.

Things came to a head when one day Ricky told his mother he'd have to kill her because people driving by knew that she was a bitch and was poisoning him and his dog. He told his mother that the people in the car said that he was worthless crap, but he could really be somebody important if he killed his mother. He put his hands around her neck. She ran out the door and was able to get away from him. After a long time, she was able to get him to leave the house. This unfortunate incident illustrates an important finding of research on the relationship between schizophrenia and violence: People who are acutely ill with schizophrenia and other serious mental disorders are sometimes dangerous to themselves or others, especially if they have histories of past violent behavior and have been abusing alcohol or other drugs (Elbogen & Johnson, 2009), but the people who are most at risk besides themselves are their own family members or friends, not members of the general public (Steadman et al., 1998).

Mental illness, in and of itself, does not make someone violent who would not normally be violent. In addition, most persons with mental illness never become violent. So, how do we reconcile this information? If someone is hearing voices telling them to do bad things, it is possible this person would, ultimately, do such things. Many persons without diagnosable mental illnesses are or become violent. It is important to keep such things in perspective in order to avoid the temptation to assume that persons with mental illness who are exhibiting symptoms that could be labeled as "unusual" are, by definition, dangerous. Clearly, this is not the case. Research suggests individuals with mental illness who are in treatment are no more violent than the general population. In fact, people who are mentally ill are far more often the victims of violence than perpetrators of violence.

Given the extremity of Ricky's behavior, and believing that Ricky must have medication in order to improve, the family obtained a court order to force treatment. Two police cars and one state trooper arrived at the family home. The police read him his rights and had him empty his pockets. Ricky made a weak attempt to resist, and the officers immediately threw him to the ground and pinned his arms tightly behind his back. Ricky was terrified and began screaming as they tied him up and pushed him into the police car. This ordeal was traumatic for everyone, including the police.

After a brief stay in the local mental health center's inpatient unit, Ricky was placed in one of their group homes. Because of his court-mandated treatment, Ricky received medications through injection. He hated the needles and always complained. A year passed, and Ricky moved out of the group home and into his own apartment. In the confusion that followed several staffing changes, the mental health center lost touch with him and allowed the court-ordered treatment to lapse. The next time Ricky saw the psychiatrist, he complained as usual about not wanting to take his medication, and the doctor said, "Well, you're not on commitment any longer, so I can't force you to take it." Ricky immediately chose to discontinue the medication.

Not long after that, Ricky became involved with a religious cult in a nearby town. Because he was no longer court-ordered to receive treatment, he decided to move with some members of the cult to Colorado. In an effort to recontact Ricky, staff from the mental health center eventually learned of his whereabouts, but because of confidentiality, they could not give any information to his family.

After 6 months in Colorado with no medication, Ricky was becoming very psychotic. The cult members became concerned about him and called his family, who advised them to contact the local mental health center and tell them he was mentally ill and needed to be on medication. The cult members kept his car and all his belongings and bought him a one-way plane ticket home. At this point, Ricky's parents sought to have him committed involuntarily to the state hospital. Before they could do this, however, he left for New York.

Therapies for People With Schizophrenia

Through the efforts of his family and volunteer members of the National Alliance on Mental Illness (an interesting story that Ricky's mother narrates later in this chapter), and with the assistance and encouragement of the Creedmoor staff, Ricky returned home. In the year and a half since he stopped treatment there, the local mental health center had reorganized its community-based services and now offered some progressive new programs. Most people who are like Ricky will need some kind of treatment and support for the rest of their lives. Ricky's schizophrenia is not curable in the same way that taking an antibiotic clears up an infection, or setting a broken arm properly heals it completely. However, the mental health center had begun providing services designed to help manage his illness and some of the problems associated with it.

Given all of his recent difficulties, the mental health center first admitted Ricky to a special group home that is heavily staffed, called the Sub-Acute Center. All eight of the residents there had recently been inpatients at a psychiatric hospital. They did not have as much freedom as at the usual group home, but more freedom than they would in the state hospital.

The Sub-Acute Center and other new services were developed partly because traditional treatments, such as individual psychotherapy, are not very effective for people with acute schizophrenia. Ricky was too suspicious to trust the therapist and was often not convinced he needed treatment.

As for medications, Ricky has taken drugs with the trade names Thorazine, Navane, Haldol, Tegretol, Prolixin, and Eskalith, all of which worked some of the time. His psychosis, hallucinations, and hearing of voices would diminish, but the anxiety and fears were almost always there, almost paralyzing him.

The biggest problem with medication was the side effects. Some of the adverse effects Ricky experienced were weight gain, dry mouth, frequent urination, constipation, diarrhea, tiredness, and stiff joints. The medications also affected his vision. He always seemed to think he needed new glasses. With one of the medications he took, he started to show involuntary movements of muscles in his face and mouth that looked like the beginning stages of tardive dyskinesia, a serious neurological problem, so that medication was stopped.

Eventually, on his doctor's advice and with his family's support, Ricky agreed to try clozapine (Clozaril), an "atypical" antipsychotic medication. Regular blood counts were required, so his blood was drawn every week. Enough medication for 1 week was given—a small dosage to begin with and then a gradual increase, eventually up to 600 milligrams a day. For several months Ricky experienced an excess of saliva, a red nose each morning, and bed wetting, but his schizophrenia was much improved.

In the beginning, his family had to drive to a private lab for blood work every week to get the blood count, go to another part of town to see the psychiatrist, and then drive to a drugstore in another town that was approved to carry Clozaril. After several months, his psychiatrist was able to have the blood drawn and give the Clozaril, all in one visit. Ricky's family was very supportive of his therapy. His parents drove him to the doctor every week because his history of several car accidents meant that his parents' insurance wouldn't allow him to drive their car. Ricky had gained weight and slept more than before, but his family was grateful for Clozaril and believed that it gave them new hope.

Because of the escalating costs of inpatient treatment and other considerations, the mental health center's newer programs for persons like Ricky place increased emphasis on comprehensive supports in the community. With medication keeping his worst symptoms under better control, a case manager from the mental health center worked with Ricky to develop a plan for managing other aspects of his illness. Working with other staff on an integrated "treatment team" as needed, they also enlisted his family's support for help in identifying and monitoring prodromal symptoms (such as increased suspiciousness, or isolating himself from others) that may signal an impending relapse. His case management services are designed to help him manage his illness so that rehospitalization will not be necessary. These services also reduce the risks he might otherwise face of homelessness, victimization, substance abuse, social isolation, and suicide.

For several months after he returned from New York, Ricky lived with seven other clients of the mental health center (from the Sub-Acute Center mentioned earlier) in a group home with on-site supervision 24 hours per day. In this home, Ricky was expected to take responsibility for keeping his room (shared with another client) clean, and do chores that helped to keep the home clean and safe. He also took his turn in the kitchen. There were outings most days, such as grocery shopping or to the mental health center day program. At least once per week, there was a special outing, such as to a movie in town or a sports event.

Ricky's treatment during this period included group therapy. Since people with schizophrenia usually have difficulty with social interactions, a protective, supportive group experience was believed to help them acquire and practice skills in verbal communication and reality testing that would make reintegration into normal life easier. Group therapy is also a place where people like Ricky can get information and advice on managing the side effects of their medication.

Some residents of the home also participated in Behavior Therapy programs directed at improving their social skills and self-care behaviors (e.g., personal hygiene). As they demonstrated improvements, these patients were rewarded with privileges (it is assumed that their increasingly more adaptive responses will lead to increased rates of natural reinforcement). While such behavioral interventions are not direct treatments for the illness of schizophrenia, they may improve a patient's day-to-day functioning. Many people who are not seriously mentally ill use behavior modification, such as dieting or undertaking fitness regimens, to make changes in their behavior. Use of these approaches does not assume that the problem behavior was originally caused by faulty learning.

As Ricky's symptoms diminished and his interest in normal everyday activities resurfaced, he left the group home for a supervised apartment. Given his history of psychotic episodes, hospitalizations, substance abuse, and legal difficulties, his case manager thought Ricky would be a good candidate for comprehensive, team-based services. These involved intensive, individualized support to individuals with schizophrenia or other severe mental disorders to prevent or reduce the need for hospitalization and to increase the person's quality of life in the community. The services were designed to take advantage of Ricky's strengths (e.g., above-average intelligence) and emphasize the use of natural supports such as his family. The team focused directly on basic living skills, medications, finances, transportation, and advocacy to help Ricky obtain needed services from other agencies (such as Social Security Disability Income, to which he is entitled because of the many jobs he has held).

The team did its best to make sure Ricky continued taking Clozaril (to the point where they began transporting him to the pharmacy as well as to appointments with the psychiatrist), and stayed away from alcohol or other substances. Ricky disliked taking a bus to the mental health center, so when necessary, Ricky's interactions with members of the team occurred at his apartment or in other everyday community settings.

The treatment team also worked with Ricky and his family to evaluate options for his further vocational or educational development. Like many people with schizophrenia, he had adequate skills for competitive work, but without active support, he has a tendency to lapse into inappropriate dress and hygiene, lack of dependability, and poor problem solving. Although Ricky has had many jobs, most were brief and represent the bottom of the employment hierarchy (i.e., fast-food restaurants and janitorial work, known as "food and filth" in the lingo of vocational rehabilitation).

Ricky first attended the Job Club, a voluntary program designed to improve his readiness and preparatory skills (resume writing, developing job leads, practicing job interviews). From there he moved to Transitional Employment, which offered short-term, practical work experience inserting advertising supplements into newspapers. Ricky adjusted reasonably well to this part-time work, but after 3 months, he decided that what he really wanted to do was return to college. He had been a good student in high school and completed a full year of college credits. With the right support, he believed he could earn a college degree.

The treatment team helped him obtain information about reenrolling at the state university and worked to prepare him for coping with the stresses of school life. They referred Ricky to another mental health center near the university that had recently started a supported education program to help people with disabilities who want to study at the university. In addition to giving direct support to his educational efforts, staff members at this agency helped Ricky with housing, advocacy, crisis intervention, and other services as needed. They also encouraged Ricky to attend meetings of a self-help group made up of other young adults with serious mental illnesses.

Ricky's long-term prospects are far from certain, and another serious relapse is always a possibility. More and more people are recovering from this illness to the point they are able to support themselves. There must, however, be community support for those who will need continuing care. Even though it has been grim for Ricky and his family, and others in similar circumstances, we must believe that with many of these cases, there is hope for taking steps toward recovery. Ricky seems to have taken some of those steps and, for the first time since he left home for college, he is starting to feel optimistic about what lies ahead.

A Biological Perspective on Schizophrenia

You are learning about the different illnesses that are of interest to students of abnormal psychology. Schizophrenia is an illness that until the mid-1980s was believed to be caused by poor parenting and faulty family dynamics, even among many professional care providers. Now, even though the exact cause is not known, there is strong scientific evidence to support an etiology that is rooted in neurobiological considerations (Schultz & Andreasen, 1999). It is not our goal here to review all of the evidence that has been brought forward to support different theories related to the causes of schizophrenia. The diagnosis is based on the presence of a certain number of identified symptoms. Most of what we will discuss is more generally related to schizophrenia and the biological implications for those who suffer this illness. Our primary goal is to help you understand the effects of the biological implications of the illness, whether these relate to possible causes, effects, or treatment.

Schizophrenia is classified as a thought disorder, but it appears to affect more than the logic of Ricky's thinking. There is interference in the processing pathways of the brain. To understand this, it helps to know that sensory information comes into the brain from an elaborate input system beginning with one of the sensory organs (eye, ear, skin/muscle/joint receptors, taste buds, or the olfactory membrane of the nose). All sensory messages move across neurons to the parietal lobe of the cerebral cortex and can be processed for understanding by the person and converted into motor output (i.e., behaviors). In a person with schizophrenia, there are "glitches" or mismatches of the neuronal circuitry in the processing pathways that scramble the input and affect the output. The person can no longer trust the sensory information that comes to her or him, and the person loses his or her ability to "test" reality accurately.

A CRITICAL THINKING AND QUESTIONING PAUSE

Take time at this point to go back and reread Ricky's story. Note each instance that Ricky's behavior indicates that his sensory system is "playing tricks" on him. Some are subtle. See if you can find one or more for each sense.

Because there are so many ways for a biologist to go in such a broad subject as schizophrenia, let's focus on some possible biological perspectives that center on specific questions that one might ask about this particular family. Two of these are: (1) Does schizophrenia run in families? (2) Does gender play a role in the incidence or prognosis for schizophrenia, and who is more likely to have schizophrenia? Take a minute to consider this family to make a preliminary educated guess at possible responses.

The answer to these questions appears to be "it depends." Schizophrenia affects approximately 1 percent of the population. However, once there is a person with schizophrenia in a family, the chance that a first-degree relative will develop schizophrenia is much higher. Though two of the authors of this work were taught that concordance rates were quite high—10 to 20 percent with a first-degree relative, perhaps 40 to 60 percent if both parents have schizophrenia, 10 to 20 percent for fraternal twins, and upwards of 80 percent risk if one member of an identical twin pair develops schizophrenia—some current studies suggests the rates, though still quite high, are not as high as these numbers suggest (e.g., Hyman, 2008). Even if these newer studies showing concordance rates that represent a ninefold increase in the risk of schizophrenia for first-degree family members are accurate, the reality is that this percentage increase in risk, though lower than more traditional estimates, still indicates that genetics or family predisposition is an important factor in understanding schizophrenia. There are multiple issues at play here. First is the issue of concordance—which is defined as "(in genetic studies) the degree of similarity in a pair of twins with respect to the presence or absence of a particular disease or trait" (dictionary. com). This is different, however, from the second issue, which is one of "heritability." This is defined as "capable of being inherited" (dictionary.com). The difference is important in that heritability might suggest the use of genomic studies that focus on a few or single families to find ways to get at "real world" evidence (blood tests, functional magnetic resonance imaging, or magnetic resonance imaging) to diagnose, treat, and follow the course of patients.

It has been known for years that females are often protected against the ravages of schizophrenia. Over a lifetime, the number of women who develop schizophrenia is approximately the same as for men. However the onset in women is later, and the course seems less severe. A paper by Glantz and Lewis that was published in the Archives of General Psychiatry in 2000, offers insight into these questions. The authors remind us that male brains are larger than female brains due to the fact that males have more neurons. However, females have more dendritic connections than males. Loss of neurons leads to the symptoms of dementia. Loss of dendritic connections leads to a loss of ability to communicate and relate to others. One implication of these differences is that while women, with fewer neurons to spare, may be more susceptible to dementia, they may tolerate the assault of schizophrenia on the dendrites more successfully than men do.

As Ricky loses his ability to connect with his surroundings accurately, he also loses his trust in people. He doesn't know whom to trust. It is difficult for him to "read" facial cues. When he cannot tell from a person's face the signals that the person is sending, he cannot tell whether the person is about to become angry or critical, and he cannot afford to take a chance on having a "blow-up" occur. The brains of persons with schizophrenia seem especially likely to interpret criticism, loud noises, or unexpected movements as a threatening situation. Imagine Ricky's difficulty, then, when the police forcibly removed him from his parents' home.

Other sensory mix-ups are also troubling. If his food smells and tastes different, it occurs to Ricky that the person who prepared it may be trying to poison him. If clothes and materials he uses smell different, perhaps they contain poisonous substances. He may see things that other people don't see, such as bugs or worms in food or on furniture. He may hear things that other people don't hear, such as voices that give him instructions, or secret messages in songs that are played over the radio. He may feel things crawling on his skin.

Most of all, his proprioceptors that tell him where his body is don't work right. He loses his sense of body boundaries and can't tell where he ends and the rest of the world begins. Some people with schizophrenia report that it isn't just the body that seems to have a loss of boundary perception, but that there is a feeling that thoughts and words are also without bounds.

A neurotransmitter that seems to weave a path through the problems that persons with schizophrenia have is dopamine. The portion of the brain that produces large amounts is the substantia nigra. The brains of persons with schizophrenia either produce more dopamine than required for normal functioning or have receptors that are exquisitely sensitive to the dopamine. Dopamine has several functions in the brain that are of interest in studying its role in schizophrenia. It inhibits prolactin, a hormone found in both males and females that plays a role in pregnant and postpartum women developing the ability to produce milk for lactation. Therefore, when dopamine is inhibited (as is accomplished by the dopamine receptor–blocking action of most antipsychotic medications) breast tissue can become enlarged (in both men and women), and some women may even lactate.

Dopamine is also related to frontal lobe functions. Planning, judgment, orientation, and short-term (also called working, or scratchpad) memory seem to rely on appropriate amounts of dopamine with receptors for dopamine that are also appropriate. The primary motor area is also in the frontal lobe. Interference with dopamine or dopamine receptors can alter movement. Persons who are treated for schizophrenia often suffer side effects that resemble the symptoms of people who have Parkinson's disease. When a medication is given to counter these side effects, the person's vision, digestive processes, and sexual functioning can be affected as well as cognitive function. For these reasons, many refuse to continue medication.

As technologies improve, research scientists have struggled to focus on both the heritability of schizophrenia and on ways to make more accurate diagnoses, and on ways to follow treatment outcomes. A 2009 paper by Stober and colleagues make clear that the complexity and multifarious nature of psychoses associated with the group of disorders that have been called "schizophrenia" prevent us from determining a "simple and logical biologically based hypothesis for the disease group." However, the paper provides an excellent overview of the concept of markers and follows several hypotheses associated with schizophrenia in both the brain (given that schizophrenia is primarily a brain-based illness) and even possible markers in the periphery. The authors describe biomarkers as biochemical, physiological, or anatomical traits that can be used to diagnose and follow the treatment of an illness such as schizophrenia.

One of the finest contributions of this paper is the review it provides of a number of the hypothetical theories regarding the nature of schizophrenia. Among them are the hypotheses related to dopamine, glutamate, brain morphological markers, functional brain systems and currently accessible analytical systems such as immune factors, lymphocytes, platelets, and functional genomics.

The authors of a more recent review article are careful to develop an understanding of "the genetic architecture of schizophrenia" before they focus on de novo and rare mutations that implicate more specific biological synaptic pathways in the disease process of schizophrenia (see Hall, Trent, Thomas, O'Donovan, & Owen, 2015). The article emphasizes the fact that there is growing agreement among scientists that schizophrenia displays heritability and that there is a need for genomic studies to further understanding of the illness. The authors describe findings that indicate patients with schizophrenia had enriched de novo mutations in the glutamate receptor (particularly the N-methyl-D-aspartate receptor) signaling complex, the fragile X mental retardation protein complex, and the voltage-regulated calcium channels. In these studies, schizophrenia patients were found to have enriched de novo mutations in genes belonging to the postsynaptic density at glutamatergic synapses, particularly components of the N-methyl-D-aspartate receptor signaling complex, including the PSD-95 complex, activity-regulated cytoskeleton-associated protein interactors, the fragile X mental retardation protein complex, voltage-gated calcium channels, and genes implicated in actin cytoskeletal dynamics. While the outcome of studies such as the ones presented in this review article do not give greater ability to diagnose, treat, and follow the progress of persons with schizophrenia, they do provide stepping stones of understanding and hope that in the near future we will be able to do so.

Interviews With Family Members

Because of their importance in Ricky's life and in his struggle with schizophrenia, we decided to end this chapter by having members of Ricky's family explain what his mental illness has meant to them. We begin with Ricky's sister, speaking a few years ago at the time Ricky's schizophrenia was most acute. After that, Ricky's mother and one of his nephews each look back on the family's experience of schizophrenia from their vantage point today.

Ricky's Younger Sister

Growing up we had a great time. My family was very close and we did a lot of things together and had a very normal childhood. However, when I was in the eighth grade I remember that Ricky started taking showers that lasted for hours. I couldn't get into the bathroom, and so I would shout at him. He said something about washing the squigglies off that were crawling all over him. I thought that maybe he was kidding me, but he really didn't sound like it.

Then one day during my sophomore year of high school, my dad came to pick me up and I knew something was wrong. He told me my brother had overdosed on LSD or something and was in the hospital. That was the beginning of Ricky's—I guess—mental illness days. It was probably the day we lost him, and I can't say we never got him back, but he hasn't been the same since.

His hospitalizations were very trying times. My parents would assign people to be my parents for the night at the swim meets and at the ball games, while they were with Ricky in the hospital. I wouldn't want to be going through what he's going through. We were always sitting on the edge of our seats not knowing what was going to happen next. It was pretty scary, I mean, the yelling to try to get rid of the voices, and the playing music loud, and the listening to my brother tell my mom and my dad that he hated them and, you know, that they were against him, and I couldn't understand that because they did everything they could to be there for us. I mean they were definitely parents that lived for their kids to be happy and whatever, and then, you know, once I started asking questions, I figured that was part of the illness and not that he really hated them.

Holidays were really hard. I think Ricky really psyched himself up for them but then it was, you know, a let down. If he wanted to go to the bedroom and lie down all Christmas day, he would, but we missed him. Bringing friends over to the house wasn't always easy, but my parents still had us do it. You know, if we're smiling sometimes, he asks if we're mad at him. It's kind of sad because I don't want him to think we're mad at him, but that's just part of the illness.

Sometimes, his behavior might have seemed funny, but it really wasn't. Ricky actually bought clown makeup and painted his face with clown makeup that he wore in public sometimes, but I knew he wasn't trying to be a clown. He just looked foolish. I was embarrassed.

When he was in the hospital, there were some rules that I didn't appreciate. First of all, the nurse never brought up the word schizophrenia—I had to, and she tried to avoid even saying anything about it. When you phone the hospital, they say that if they have someone there by that name, which they don't know or they can't tell, they'll have them call me back. Well, I'm sure they don't do that with their heart attack patients or their cancer patients. The stigma of mental illness is still so strong, and if it's there in the psychiatric ward at the hospital, then we've got a long way to go.

For most of the time since Ricky got sick, I thought there was no one else in the world that was experiencing what our family was experiencing. I felt very isolated and very alone with what had happened in my family. . . . I always dreaded going home on vacations or breaks because of what I was coming home to. Like I said, my brother is extremely difficult to be around. He can be very mean and just do bizarre things and can be impatient. It was very unpleasant to go home and it always made me very sad when people were anxious to go home to visit their family over breaks in college. I just absolutely dreaded it but could never tell my parents and always had to act like I was happy to be there when I really wasn't.

The future is hopeful and the future is bleak. Mom goes to NAMI meetings. She helped organize a local affiliate when a man from NAMI named Phil helped us find Ricky and bought his ticket to get home. I'm still amazed that the only way Phil would let us repay him was for us to make a donation to NAMI.

Mom says that in some places the NAMI affiliates are large enough to have a special group for siblings and for consumers like Ricky. That would be cool! NAMI has helped Mom to understand a lot about schizophrenia, and she helps us understand. The thing that helped most was that NAMI has let her know that none of us as Ricky's family did anything to cause his illness.

At one point I had thought maybe because I teased him a lot, it had something to do with making him sick. A sister can make life miserable for a brother if she tries hard enough. I told Mom and Dad that it had to be their fault, because I wanted the horrible thoughts that I was having that I might have caused it to go away. All of us feel better knowing that schizophrenia is a neurobiological disorder, and that we didn't cause it. There are things that we can do to make life easier for Ricky, but we didn't cause him to get sick. Mom says now we need to advocate for a better system of care.

I've watched my brother be sick for six years and go through different medications and wonder drugs that just haven't worked for him, which is kind of sad. Right now, he's the best he's been for some time. Maybe one day he'll be even better. One day the system might work . . . really.

Ricky's Mother

When I found out you were going to interview me, I jumped up and down, literally! How our lives have changed!! I know that must come as a surprise to you because we have two grandchildren with schizophrenia, and I would be the first to say that it is a tough situation to face. No one would wish any disorder for any of their children or grandchildren; but after what we went through with our son, Ricky, we know how much better life is now for those who have schizophrenia and their families. I was interviewed eight years ago. I saved a copy that the nice man who interviewed me about our situation with Ricky gave me. Today, eight years later, I get to tell you how things have changed for us as grandparents of Ricky. Please let me read you that interview eight years ago. Then I will tell you how much things have changed.

Almost from the beginning Ricky's illness took control of our lives and our home. It was all we talked about and all we thought about, and we were all under a great deal of stress. Every time the phone rang while I was at work, I thought it was going to be something about him. Every time the phone rang at home, I thought it was going to be something about him. So, our family was under a lot of stress because we didn't understand what was happening to him, we didn't understand his illness.

Placing the blame for the illness was easy to do. I blamed my husband, he blamed me, and our daughters blamed both of us. Ricky also blamed the city he was living in and always thought that if he moved to another city, he would get a fresh start, make new friends, and no one would know him, and that his problems would go away. He always talked about going to New York and starting over, but we never expected him to actually do it.

We as a family had some counseling at the hospital. Most of the blame seemed to be directed at me. Some of the therapists asked what I had done to him as he was a little boy and as he was growing up. So, I had a lot of guilt and I think my husband did, too. My husband and I had a lot of disagreements about our son and his illness and we yelled at each other. We shouted at each other.

He's been mugged, he's been robbed, he's had people trash his apartment and damage the place to the tune of about $2,000. He was thrown out of one apartment because of the damage that his friends who were drinkers and drug users caused. He's still paying for those damages. He was taken to court. A judgment was entered against him, and that money is being taken out of his Social Security Disability until it's paid off. Someone else wanted to borrow money from him, so Ricky gave him $100 and the person wrote him out a bad check. He was stuck with the bad check and was taken to court again. He was handcuffed and shackled as he was taken from a local hospital to a state hospital. Ricky said it was the most humiliating thing that had ever happened to him, and he still has nightmares about it. I can imagine the consternation of people who have heart attacks or cancer if they were ever treated that way.

The real break that we got was when Ricky was in New York. I was frantic not knowing where he was and knowing he was so sick. It wasn't just that the girls and I were at wit's end, but Dick became a person he wasn't before. Ricky wasn't there to stir things up, but there was no peace for Dick either. I could tell that he was worried sick about Ricky. He would get so angry. He'd yell and throw things, and then would get depressed and quiet. It was almost as hard to take as Ricky's behaviors. I think that when a father feels something is going wrong, he should be able to "fix" what is broken, but dads like this just get frustrated when it's a missing son and a broken brain.

At first, I yelled at Dick, but then realized that just made everything worse for all of us. I cried and prayed. That at least helped me stay calmer and stop yelling back. But one night I heard Dick sobbing in bed when he thought I was asleep. I hadn't heard him cry before, even when he was badly hurt in an accident, or when his father and his sister died. That experience made me take the biggest step of all. The next morning I got out the phonebook. The mental health center seemed to have given up on us, and so the Mental Health Association was the only place I thought I could call for help. The woman I talked to was very nice. She gave me the number of an organization called NAMI, which stands for National Alliance for the Mentally Ill.

The NAMI volunteer I talked with just listened to me at first. The only things I knew about her were that her name was Gloria Anderson and her son had schizophrenia. I tried to tell her everything that we had been through, and before long, she understood it all so well, she was finishing my sentences for me. When I finally paused she said "You need to know that you are not alone." She told me that she talked with a number of families who have loved ones who suffer with schizophrenia and that it is a very common illness. That shocked me. At times, I felt that maybe we were the only family in our town who had ever dealt with this.

She told me that there were many ways that NAMI could help with support groups and education, but it seemed to her that the first problem that NAMI could help us tackle was finding Ricky. She asked my permission to give information about Ricky to NAMI's Missing and Homeless Network. She said that if I could provide a picture of Ricky, they would circulate it along with any other information we provided. She also asked whether I had any ideas where Ricky might go. I told her the two places that fascinated him most were Washington, DC, and New York City. Gloria laughed and jokingly replied that I didn't have to give her "easy" ones, because those are both huge cities! But she promised to contact all of the local affiliates in those two cities with information about Ricky.

And that is just how we found him. A man named Phil in New York who is a NAMI member and had a son just Ricky's age saw the picture and the description. He said when he first saw the picture, it looked so much like his son, Terry, that he stared at it for a long time. Terry committed suicide last year, just as he seemed to be getting better. Phil went to the state hospitals and told social workers who would talk to him about Ricky and left his picture with them. They couldn't give him any information because of confidentiality laws, but they took the picture and information and promised Phil that if they came across such a patient, they would give the patient Phil's number, see to it that Ricky got permission to make the call (even if he had lost his telephone privileges), and encourage him to call Phil. Eight days after he left the last flyer, Ricky called Phil. Phil went to Creedmoor that day and told Ricky his family was looking for him. When Phil asked Ricky if he wanted to go home, Ricky just nodded, yes.

We know some people who have schizophrenia are well enough to work full time. Several are married and seem to live happy lives. Ricky just hasn't done that well. He would love to have a real girlfriend, but even though he's back in college, his interpersonal skills just aren't good enough to maintain that kind of relationship. He has talked about only being able to get sex by paying for it. I know that a mother shouldn't talk this way but I am grateful when he is getting along well enough to do that.

As long as Ricky has taken medication that works, and as long as he does take it, he's pretty well able to take care of himself and maintain some normalcy. But, in fairness to Ricky, there have been times that he has taken his medications and still exhibited symptoms in spite of it. That's really hard, because everybody, except those of us who know that, accuses him of being uncooperative and he's not.

We are afraid to have him try some of the newer atypical medications because Clozaril is working at least somewhat. We have been advised that changing can be risky, unless he returns to the point that he was at without the medication even though he is compliant. Life is tenuous. But with NAMI, the possibilities of more appropriate medication for Ricky in the future, and the new supported education program he's part of, we now have hope that we never had before.

My Story Eight Years Later

So many things have changed . . . some are small and some huge, but all make a difference in our lives. We saw some of these changes make life better for our Ricky. Our second experience was with our grandson Kevin, one of a set of identical twins. We had some concerns as Kevin and Ken grew up because of Ricky, but they did well in school and got along with each other. They decided to attend different colleges and both started out really well, but things started going wrong for Kevin midway through his sophomore year. He acknowledges that he did some things that were not in his best interest. He doesn't share all that he means by that, but I would guess that it included alcohol or worse. Kevin ended up coming home before the end of his sophomore year. Going home from college worked out very well for him. He started going to the community mental health center that not only provided for his medical needs, but also he was wise in taking part in all of the social opportunities they offered. They had a clubhouse where he met his wife. It has been a wonderful match for both of them.

I would also like to note another big change since Ricky was first diagnosed and treated. Mental health center treatment teams now collaborate more effectively with physicians and nurses to integrate psychiatric care with primary health care. This collaboration makes a big difference given that sensory experiences can be different for people with schizophrenia and they may not identify and describe physical symptoms in a way that the physician is familiar with. Physical symptoms of serious illness that are inadequately described by the patient may be dismissed by the physician as simply signs of psychosis. Integrated care enables mental health treatment teams to facilitate more effective participation of consumers in the diagnosis and treatment of their medical conditions.

Our most positive experience has come with Rich. It seems so strange that his greatest break came because he was so young when schizophrenia raised its ugly head. I know that you have arranged to have him tell his story, so I will not rob him of his chance to share. What I am thrilled to talk to you about is how life has changed for Dick and me.

I have remained active in both of the organizations that helped me so much when I was struggling with Ricky's situation. Both have changed their names and the scope of their services have changed a bit also, but both are invaluable to both those who have the illnesses and their families. The Mental Health Association is still MHA, but now it stands for Mental Health America. I have been especially involved with MHA and their involvement in legislative issues. The Alliance for the Mentally Ill (AMI) is now The National Alliance on Mental Illness (NAMI). That wonderful organization still provides support, education, advocacy, and a strong interest in research. Although the treatment program that was so helpful for Ricky is no longer strongly connected to NAMI, other programs have become a stronger part of NAMI. Dick has become immersed in the CIT-NAMI program. The letters stand for Crisis Intervention Team. The program is a national one that is based on a program started in Memphis, Tennessee. It involves 40 hours of special training for experienced police officers. The TEAM in the T of CIT refers to the working together of the police, agencies providing treatment for persons who have these brain-based disorders we call mental illness and NAMI whose consumers (members with one of the illnesses) and family members are immersed in decision making, planning, training sessions and leading training sessions. CIT is successful because the police officers are skilled in evaluating the situation, deescalating the situation and taking the person to the appropriate treatment facility. The facility agrees to having the officer back on duty promptly and to follow the person through a program that will provide stable treatment to keep that person from becoming one who gets caught in a revolving door system.

Dick has come to life through CIT. He told me one night that as much as he hated all that Ricky and our family went through, he feels as if it has prepared him to be a part of "fixing" things. He was so distraught with Ricky's situation because there was nothing that he could "do" to feel he was making things better. Now he realizes that he is in a perfect position to make a difference in a number of lives. It is not a small thing.

Ricky's Nephew Rich Speaks

Yes, sir! You asked what to call me and the best answer I can give you is Rich. That's what they call me at work and called me all the time that I was in school. Most of my family calls me Richy, and my wife calls me Richard. She comes from one of those families where they don't use nicknames. Secretly, I like it best when she calls me Sweetheart. But I am talking in circles. So we can stop there . . . and start here with my name. I am Rich, and I would be happy to speak with you about having schizophrenia. I present often for both Mental Health America and NAMI. It isn't so much that I am proud to be their poster person as it is that I want to help people understand what it is like to live as a person with schizophrenia.

You see, I am a lucky one! I come from a family where many of the boys and men have schizophrenia. Not all have the luck that I have, you see, I am a lucky one. But I am talking in circles. So we can stop there . . . and start here with family. My family did not know about all of them until my uncle Ricky had lived with schizophrenia for 10 years or so. Then my mom and grandma began to find out about second and third cousins, along with men from generations in the past who may or may not have been diagnosed, but they sure did have the symptoms. There is still a strong stigma when it comes to schizophrenia, but it is not like it used to be. People simply sheltered family members who acted differently; and if they were too difficult to live with, they were sent to State Hospitals where they were often forgotten.

When it comes to me and my generation, things are better. My cousin, Kevin, has schizophrenia (even though his identical twin, Ken, does not). That makes them good candidates for research programs. Kevin and I both have college degrees, both are married, and both have strong family support.

When I was a kid, my dream was to be a pilot. I'd see the airplanes in the air and can still remember having my dad explain that people were inside them. He told me that some people even learned to fly them the same as some people learn to drive a car. I knew then what I wanted to be. Well, that did not happen.

I graduated from high school with some special help after I had my first break during my sophomore year when I was barely 16 years old. After that, the counselors suggested other programs for me. I must acknowledge that no one ever told me that I could not be a pilot, but I went to a college with special programs for persons who have a mental illness. As I said, they did not tell me that being a pilot was inappropriate, but I ended up with a degree in English with a minor in history. I am happy with that. I met my wife, Beth, there because she is a physical therapist who volunteered in the tutoring program that provided readers and proctors for written and oral tests. Her brother has schizophrenia, so she looks for ways to help where she can. We hit it off right away, which meant she could no longer proctor my tests. She said it would not be ethical. We married the week after I graduated. Not everyone with schizophrenia is likely to get married, I am married but not too many with schizophrenia end up getting married. But I am talking in circles. So we can stop there . . . and start here with our life.

The college had a placement program and I was able to find a job in a library that fits me well and pays well enough for me to share the load in supporting my family. Beth works for an agency that provides services for special needs children from birth to 3 years of age. Life is good for us.

You know, I heard a story on the radio about a person with schizophrenia who wanted to date. He talked about trying to find dates online. I spend a lot of time suggesting to people who have schizophrenia that it pays to be very careful about what to get involved with online. It is difficult for us to know who to trust, and there are a lot of people out there on the Internet who simply cannot be trusted. A lot of our people try to find dates or meet dates in bars. I hesitate to "preach" much about that, but it is not an appropriate place either. Alcohol and schizophrenia don't mix well—but I usually wait until I know someone really well to move on to that topic. [See Hedrick, 2015.]

My grandpa used to tell Kevin and me that it would be better for us to date where the most appropriate mates for us are. We listened to him. Both of our wives knew all about schizophrenia when we met them. I told you how I met Beth. Kevin met his wife at the community mental health center. She has panic disorder that is very well controlled with medication, but she has close family members who have depression and/or bipolar illness. She learned about schizophrenia from friends that she made at the community mental health center.

So by now you are wondering what is not too good about having schizophrenia. Good is hard to define. Not everything with schizophrenia is good. But I am talking in circles. So we can stop there . . . and start here with what is good. I always tell the truth, so I will tell you that if you have a choice about what disorder to have, I advise you to pass on this one. It is tough to live with. The biggest problem is not knowing who or what to trust. That is one of the most important things for Kevin and me. From my earliest memories, I heard Grandpa explain to us how our family was different because of Uncle Ricky. Grandpa said that everyone in our family is careful not to lie because Uncle Ricky needs to know that we will only tell him the truth. We don't have to be perfect. We can make mistakes and be wrong, but we are not allowed to tell even the smallest white lie. When other kids had parents who made big footprints in the snow and left cookies out for Santa (which my grandpa said was fine for other families to do), our parents talked about a Saint Nicholas who did nice things for kids and wore a red robe, so lots of people dress up in red outfits and act like Saint Nicholas. We also knew it was not the Easter Bunny, but it was our parents who hid the candy and colored eggs.

That really helped Kevin and me a lot after we got sick. Both of us knew deep down that our family did not tell lies and we could trust them even though the schizophrenia worked hard on us to try to convince us otherwise. The doubts and the hallucinations are damning. The voices are in your face all the time; but even worse sometimes is that the same "wicked witch" that swears at you and threatens you and calls you all kinds of bad names, does a change of pace and tells you how good you are and how she wants to treat you really nice. Not knowing what to expect is the worst.

I have problems with other sensory distortions. Beth has had to stop me several times from throwing perfectly good meat out because it smells rotten to me. Bless her soul, she didn't get angry or yell, she simply explained very quietly and calmly to trust her to know when the meat was rotten. She did go so far as to say my nose was playing tricks on me, and we could save a lot of money to trust her about the meat. I do.

Sometimes, I can tell that the voices are not real, but not so with the delusions. I know that I am not President Clinton's godson because people I trust say that I am not. It is hard to explain to you, but I still know that I am his godson. He told me so. I have just learned not to talk to people who do not understand schizophrenia about it. You seem to understand these things. It is okay to let you know.

I take the medicine although sometimes I feel that I really do not need it. Grandma has been really helpful there. She explained what a big word "anosognosia" means. People who have had certain right-brain strokes, she says, do not get messages back to the brain to help them know that they cannot move the left side of their bodies. It isn't denial in the classic sense of the word, it is an internal communications system breakdown. Another serious problem is that someone can be sincerely unaware that he or she has a disorder. Grandma said that she could not tell when her blood pressure started going up. At first, she thought that there was something the matter with the instrument used to take it. Her second thought was that the person taking her blood pressure made a mistake.

That is not as serious as anosognosia, but it adds to the problem of why people do not take their medication. Many people do not take the medications that would help them recover from illnesses or disorders that they have. They have many reasons for not taking the medications. The way that is different for those of us who have these brain-based disorders that we call "mental illnesses" is that the consequences of our not taking the medications that we need can put others in danger to a much greater extent than many of the other disorders.

Thank you, Sir, for giving me a chance to share. We have come a long way from where we were when my Uncle Ricky became ill, but we still have a long way to go. As I told you, Kevin and I are the lucky ones. I dream of a day when schizophrenia as we know it is a "thing of the past."

5

THE CASE OF BARBARA M

Major Depressive Disorder

Introduction

"Mom, you've got to see someone," Susan stated.

"I agree," Stan concurred.

"I'll get through this on my own," Barbara promised. *"It's just harder right now because it's been almost a year. People say the anniversary dates are the hardest. That's all this is, I guess."*

"You didn't handle this any better three months ago than you are now, Mother, so don't tell me that it's just an anniversary thing. I think you went back to work too fast after Dad died and you did not take enough time to really grieve. That's why you're still having so much trouble. You can't hide it. Stan and I have talked about it. Any time either of us comes over to visit, you've got tears in your eyes. It doesn't look like you've been eating very well. Sally says you haven't gone out and done anything with her for months now. You can't just hole up in this house and pretend that things will get better. Dad is dead; that won't change. But you're alive and Stan and I want to keep it that way. If you won't see someone for yourself, see someone for us. Please?"

Barbara M is a 56-year-old insurance claims processor. She was married for 30 years, and has two grown children. Her husband, William, died of cancer 11 months ago. Although his death was not unexpected, the impact of his declining health over several years took an emotional and physical toll and had a severe impact on Barbara's productivity at work. She took 3 weeks off immediately after William died, but found it hard to return and be as energetic and efficient as she was previously. Her supervisor was initially concerned, and later began to lose patience with Barbara, insisting that she talk with someone at the firm's Employee Assistance Program (EAP). With a referral from the EAP staff, and at the urging of her children, Barbara made an appointment to see a psychologist.

The Diagnostic Interview

Dr. Davidson, the psychologist, began his assessment by asking Barbara questions about the past several months. She described how most of the time in the last year she has felt tired, yet is unable to sleep soundly most nights. Because she lacks the energy to manage the preparations, she has stopped inviting coworkers and other friends over for social occasions. Lately she has become more forgetful around the house, and she also reports that in her most recent review, her supervisor claimed Barbara had difficulty concentrating and was indecisive at work.

At the time of the interview, Barbara remained upset about William's death, still had frequent crying spells, and felt inappropriately guilty about the fact that she continued to work during the later stages of his illness rather than spending all of her time with him. There were things she had wanted to tell him, but his illness often made it difficult for them to talk. When she returned to work several weeks after he died, the demands of her job seemed much greater to her. In fact, a new information system had been installed, and the senior management made it clear that significantly higher productivity was now expected of everyone in Barbara's workgroup. Barbara learned to use the new system, but completed her assignments more slowly than did most of her coworkers.

Clearly Barbara was suffering, but Dr. Davidson's job was to search beneath what is most easily visible (her symptoms) and try to determine the most effective way to conceptualize and understand her suffering. Was Barbara simply showing the features of someone who is bereaved, such that merely giving her more time will be sufficient to bring about recovery? Dr. Davidson concluded that Barbara's response was not uncomplicated bereavement, wherein diminished functioning generally persists for no more than 2 months, but a more serious and prolonged interval of dysfunction.

This assessment is important because DSM-5 asks the diagnostician to consider the possibility of Major Depressive Disorder in a bereaved person who displays intense sadness, poor concentration, insomnia, and guilt. Dr. Davidson noted that Barbara's feelings of emptiness and loss worsened with thoughts or reminders of her husband, but what seemed even more significant to him was the persistence of Barbara's depressed mood over almost a year and her lack of happiness or pleasure even when her mind was engaged in other activities. She reported no recent instances of happiness or humor and considerable self-criticism and feelings of worthlessness, making him confident that her diagnosis was major depressive episode.

However, was Barbara experiencing what could be called a temporary "state of crisis"? Some features of her situation were consistent with the crisis concept. For example, she has experienced a significant stressful event, and appeared to have inadequate support to enable her to recover. Another feature relevant to using a crisis intervention approach in this case is that Barbara's history indicated that a return to the level of functioning she exhibited before William's death was a reasonable goal. What was not consistent with the notion of crisis, and thus with a prescription of crisis intervention as an appropriate treatment, was that the stressful event happened almost a year earlier, and the onset of somatic, cognitive, emotional, and behavioral disruption following the event was not sudden.

Assessing whether psychological dysfunction following a significant event indicates a time-limited crisis or a diagnosable disorder is part of the initial interview process. Dr. Davidson evaluated the history of Barbara's symptoms (onset, degree of disruption of her day-to-day activities, whether or not she ever experienced these symptoms before) and also her sources of support (family, friends, coworkers, previous experiences in therapy). He also asked about Barbara's recent medical and psychiatric history, and interviewed Susan, Barbara's daughter, to obtain additional information directly from her. Susan was concerned enough about Barbara to see that she needed help, and influential enough that Barbara followed through with the difficult step of going to see Dr. Davidson. Susan was also an important resource for her mother during her months-long effort to recover.

Dr. Davidson also conducted a mental status exam (see Chapter 2). In the informal portion of this exam he studied Barbara's appearance, the content of her thoughts, style of speech, manner of relating to him, and suicide potential. She was drawn and weary, and made little eye contact with Dr. Davidson. Her speech was slow, and was punctuated with frequent long pauses. In the formal mental status exam, he evaluated Barbara's reality orientation (to person, place, and time), and her memory and ability to concentrate.

Utilizing the CAGE Technique to Assess Substance Use

Two other specific assessments were relevant—Barbara's history of alcohol and other drug use, and her current risk (and past history) regarding suicide. In reviewing how she has tried to cope since her husband's death, Dr. Davidson asked Barbara what she drank or used to help her cope, including prescription medications. His question was phrased in this way (rather than "Do you drink?") to make it easier for Barbara to acknowledge using alcohol or other substances if in fact she did. If Barbara acknowledged any use at any time in her life, Dr. Davidson had her characterize as best she can specific quantities and frequencies of use, since different people's understanding of what "a little" or "a lot" means can vary a great deal. Dr. Davidson remained alert for signs of underlying anxiety, defensiveness, or hostility from Barbara regarding these questions.

Barbara acknowledged regular drinking, often by herself, for most of the months since her husband's death, prompting Dr. Davidson to inquire further: "Have you ever felt you should cut down on your drinking?"

"I'm not sure," Barbara replied [long pause], "I guess I might sometimes have wondered about that."

Dr. Davidson continued, "Has anyone ever annoyed you by criticizing your drinking?"

Barbara pauses again, and then replied, "No, I can't recall any comments from others about my drinking that I found annoying."

"Have you ever felt bad, or perhaps even guilty, about your drinking?" Dr. Davidson asked.

Barbara sighs. "No . . . I've sometimes wondered whether it was a good idea to drink by myself, but I never had more than one or two drinks when I was alone and . . . don't remember ever feeling guilty afterwards."

The doctor continued, "I'd like to ask one further question about your drinking at this point—have you ever taken a drink first thing in the morning to steady your nerves or get rid of a hangover?"

Barbara gave a weak smile. "No, I've never had any alcohol before afternoon or evening at the earliest."

The questions Dr. Davidson asked are often used by clinicians to assess the likelihood of substance abuse (Ewing, 1984). The CAGE acronym is a summary reminder to the interviewer to ask if the individual ever felt the need to "cut down" (C) on his or her drinking, if the drinking ever "annoyed" anyone (A), if drinking ever made the individual feel "guilty" (G), and if the individual ever felt a need to drink early in the morning, have an "eye-opener" (E). The more "yes" answers the person makes to these questions, the greater the likelihood he or she has a problem with alcohol abuse.

Barbara clearly answered "no" to all but the first question, and her answer to that one was not "yes" but instead that she was not sure. Had she clearly answered "yes" to any of these questions, Dr. Davidson would have gone on to ask Barbara whether she ever thought she might have a problem with alcohol, or any other drug, whether anyone else ever suggested she might have a problem, and whether she had ever received treatment for such a problem. With the answers she gave, however, he concludes for the moment that Barbara probably does not have a problem with alcohol.

Assessing Suicide Risk

Assessing suicide risk in the initial interview is important because suicide is the seventh leading cause of death overall in the United States, and is preventable. The risk of suicide in Barbara's case is higher than in some other cases because she is an older woman. There is widespread publicity and attention given the tragedy of teen and young adult suicide. The loss of a life with so much left to experience, and the fact that there are fewer other reasons for death among younger people, cause suicide to rise near to the top in ranking causes of death in the age group. While we have no desire to draw attention away from this tragic fact, this case also provides an opportunity to illuminate the very real fact that the actual risk of suicide is statistically greater for older people who also die for many other reasons. Younger people have fewer different kinds of diseases and disorders.

Furthermore, even if Barbara were to deny thoughts of suicide right now, the long-term issue of suicide risk is not settled because she lives alone and may have many opportunities to neglect her health, nutrition, medications, or otherwise "give up on life."

Exploring the Suicide Issue Further

Dr. Davidson was very much concerned because Barbara appeared to meet the DSM-5 criteria for major depression, where the risk of suicide may be as high as 15 percent, especially if the person displays anger, agitation, or hopelessness. He did not avoid the topic of suicide but instead approached it directly, asking "Have you ever felt so down that you thought about hurting yourself, or perhaps even about suicide?" Barbara acknowledged having had such thoughts when times were bad, and Dr. Davidson probed the details of these thoughts and what Barbara did in response to them. Careful questioning is very important here, because one or more previous suicide attempts dramatically increases her current risk. When Barbara explained that on one or two occasions she thought about overdosing on pills, he probed, "What kinds of pills? Do you have these pills now?"

Dr. Davidson asked so many specific questions because the most important predictor of acute suicide is an organized plan. A plan that is detailed, specific, and well thought out is riskier than one that is vague. A plan with a more lethal method (such as using a firearm, or jumping from a high place) is riskier than one which is less certain to succeed (such as overdosing on pills). If Barbara currently has the means available to carry out her plan (e.g., she has pills that could produce a fatal overdose), the situation is riskier than if the means are not currently available. A plan that would make rescue unlikely (e.g., she intends to take the pills at home late at night and disconnect her phone) is riskier than one where rescue is likely.

Other characteristics that increase suicide risk are dependence on alcohol and loss of rational thinking, especially following recent stress. Dr. Davidson was careful to let Barbara explain how stressful her situation was, because what he might consider manageable might be overwhelming to Barbara: What matters most is Barbara's perceptions of how stressful her life is, not Dr. Davidson's perceptions of how stressful Barbara's life is. The amount of stress someone is under can escalate over time. In Barbara's case, for example, distress over her husband's death had caused her to perform poorly at work, which was a second major source of stress.

Dr. Davidson was concerned about Barbara's social isolation, and probed, "Who is available to help you? Who are you currently in touch with?" Barbara had friends at work, but was uncomfortable seeking support from them because she would have had to reveal how difficult everything had become for her and this might have caused them to question whether she could still do her job well enough. At the time, her support system consisted primarily of her children— Susan and Stan—and Marcus, a close friend of the family. Both of Barbara's children lived out of town, so the role they could play in the therapeutic process was somewhat limited. Nonetheless, their input, guidance, and support were needed.

With her consent, Dr. Davidson also made sure that Barbara's children knew how serious her condition seemed to be. Barbara and William had socialized with Marcus and his wife for years. Marcus' wife died several years before William. Because Marcus withdrew somewhat after his wife died, and Barbara stopped socializing when her husband died, the two of them have had only brief conversations in recent months. Dr. Davidson gained permission from Barbara to contact Marcus and bring him in for an interview. Marcus could provide some insight into Barbara's situation and could also be an important part of the support network Barbara needed as she rebuilt her life.

An Interview With Barbara's Daughter, Susan

I guess Stan and I suspected Mom was having troubles when she started to have problems at work. Even while Dad was going through the cancer treatments, Mom always found a way to go to work and do her job. I think having the job to focus on made her feel hopeful. Or at least it kept her mind occupied.

A couple of months ago, though, she started to seem less and less enthused about work. She never talked about it positively at all. Mom has never been the pessimistic kind, but she started to get down on everything. The new computer system was no exception. Usually, Mom would respond with vigor when the company brought in a new system. It was like she was bound and determined to tackle that new system and not let the change disrupt her ability to keep the office running smoothly, but this time, she complained about everything. She also started to second guess herself and that was way out of character.

What I mean by this is she started to doubt herself. She would say things like, "maybe I've just gotten too old to learn another new system," or "the newer employees are more highly educated than I am." Stan noticed those comments right away, too. But we also noticed her withdrawing more. She never called her friends to go out or come over. Whenever one of them would call her, she would always find some way to politely excuse herself out of whatever social event they were inviting her to.

Stan and I talked and we kept comparing our "Mom notes." When we both began to notice and worry about the same behaviors, we knew it was time to sit Mom down and convince her to talk to someone. It was one of the hardest things I have ever had to do. I just hope whatever she and the doctor decide to do will help.

The Initial Diagnosis

For a diagnosis of major depression, the DSM-5 requires that, during a 2-week time interval, Barbara display five or more specific symptoms that amount to a change from previous functioning. At least one of the five symptoms must be either depressed mood or a significant loss of interest or pleasure in previously rewarding activities. Barbara's difficulties satisfied either of these. Other specific symptoms she experiences on a daily or almost-daily basis include sleeping too little; feelings of fatigue, slowness, or lethargy (noticed by her supervisor); inappropriate feelings of guilt and worthlessness; difficulty concentrating; indecisiveness; and some suicidal ideation. These symptoms were severe enough to cause significant distress to Barbara and to disrupt her social and occupational functioning. (Among the DSM-5 symptoms of depression that are absent in Barbara's case are significant weight loss or gain and feelings of agitation or restlessness.)

In a later interview, Dr. Davidson asked questions designed to reveal or rule out dysthymia (a chronic but usually less severe mood disturbance), seasonal mood disorder, and bipolar mood disorder. With respect to this last possibility, Barbara showed no evidence of having experienced a manic episode—being excessively grandiose, talkative, having racing thoughts, and so on—either recently or at any other time in her life. She also showed no signs of substance abuse. Dr. Davidson inquired about possible earlier episodes of depression. It turned out that Barbara's mother died of cancer when Barbara was in adolescence. Part of the difficulty for Barbara at that time involved feelings on her part that her relationship with her mother could have been better, and she faulted herself for not doing more to be a better daughter.

Dr. Davidson asked Barbara to make an appointment with her physician, Dr. Norton, for a more complete assessment of her medical condition, possibly including a physical exam. Barbara agreed to sign forms authorizing Dr. Davidson and Dr. Norton to communicate with each other with respect to her depression. Her physician's role is important: Problems such as hypothyroidism and diabetes can be related to depression, and cardiovascular conditions (e.g., heart arrhythmias) can influence whether Barbara should be prescribed an antidepressant, and if so, which one.

Dr. Norton was also to evaluate Barbara's current and past use of medications. Some antidepressants are powerful and interact with other kinds of medications, which means that two or more kinds of medications in the patient's body create unintended side effects. These effects will, at best, make Barbara uncomfortable (and possibly inclined to stop taking one or more of the medications) and, at worst, could be very harmful.

Viewing Depression From a Biological Perspective

Whether depression is largely due to life events (as appears to be the case in Barbara's situation) or instead is an overwhelming experience having little or no connection to life events, the biologist is likely to ask questions that relate to the structure and function of the human body, especially the brain. Another important question is, "What makes people physically vulnerable?" Often the answer to this question lies in the person's genetic makeup.

Life scientists attribute the symptoms of major (overwhelming) depression to an imbalance of neurotransmitters in the brain, especially serotonin (5-HT) and norepinephrine (NE or NOR). In some people, these imbalances simply seem to happen without any apparent changes in life-events. There have been a number of efforts to associate specific genetic differences combined with social adversity to the expression of Major Depressive Disorder. A study reported in 2006 (Surtees et al.) presents the complexities that make replicating any of these studies very difficult. However, there are indications that genetics might be a factor because the incidence of depression appears to occur more than twice as often in persons who have relatives who suffer from depression.

Although people have commented over the centuries that melancholy or depression seems to run in families, it has only been since the early 1900s that systematic studies began to determine that mood disorders, such as depression, are familial. Since World War II, scientists have had access to adoption records of twins affected by illnesses with genetic components. A 1996 study was made possible by the fact that a Danish twin register identified twin pairs of which at least one of the twins had a mood disorder (either depression or bipolar illness). Results indicated that there was a significant increase in the occurrence of mood disorder between biologically related participants (Wender et al., 1996).

Neurotransmitters

As we have learned before, neurotransmitters are chemical messengers that carry electrical activity from the terminal end of one nerve cell across a gap called the *synapse* to the specific receptor on either the next nerve cell or a muscle. The resulting depolarization begins a new electrical signal on which the second nerve or the muscle acts.

In the brain, there are two main excitatory neurotransmitters, called *glutamate* and *asparate*, and two inhibitory neurotransmitters called *gamma-amino butyric acid* (GABA) and *glycine*. There are three other neurotransmitters that can either excite or inhibit and seem to interact with the "basic four" in such a way as to modulate them. Thus they are often referred to as *neuromodulators*.

With persons such as Barbara who exhibit symptoms of depression, the major neurohormone of interest is serotonin (5 hydroxytryptamine). Serotonin is synthesized from tryptophan and is associated with a wide network of nerve fibers arising from the raphe nucleus, a structure that is connected to the limbic system (the seat of the emotions). Serotonin is strongly implicated in mood.

Serotonin also has an interesting relationship to muscle function. Motor output, such as is exhibited in the REM phase of sleep, is less when the serotonin system is less active ("silent"). Repeated tonic motor activity seems to increase serotonin release. Jogging or bicycling can "rev up" serotonin release. It is hypothesized that the ritualistic behavior of persons with obsessive-compulsive disorder may be due, at least in part, to an effort to self-medicate by increasing serotonin release.

Note that a portion of Barbara's treatment consisted of taking a medication that selectively works on holding serotonin out in the synapse (gap) rather than allow it to be taken up by the nerve fiber. Such an agent is called a *selective serotonin reuptake inhibitor*. These agents traditionally have been called *SSRIs*. The advantage that the SSRIs offer over the more traditional agents is that their specificity for serotonin eliminates the side effects associated with agents that affect the functions of norepinephrine and dopamine as well as serotonin.

Because the neurotransmitters carry the signal in chemical form across the gap (or synapse) between neurons to initiate a new impulse on the second (post-synaptic) neuron, it makes biological sense to hold the transmitter in the gap longer to permit the receptors on the second neuron to receive or experience binding of the transmitter. Three mechanisms underlie the action of medications that effect such prolonging of the transmitter in the gap.

1. *Monoamine-oxidase* (MAO) is an enzyme that degrades or breaks down transmitters, especially norepinephrine (NE). Therefore, if we can give a medication that inhibits MAO, more neurotransmitter remains longer in the gap. The problem with MAOs is that they are not very specific and thus cause a number of unwanted side effects. The MAO inhibitors also may create dangers when certain dietary restrictions go unheeded.
2. *Tricyclic Antidepressants* (TCA) limit the uptake of neurotransmitters such as NE and serotonin, but they also limit the uptake of other neurotransmitters that appear to play little or no role in depression. Thus, some people may suffer unnecessary side effects.
3. *Specific Uptake Inhibitors*, which include SSRIs, Serotonin/Norepinephrine (Re)uptake Inhibitors (SNRIs), and the Serotonin 2 (5-HT)–receptor antagonist. SSRIs selectively inhibit serotonin uptake; SNRIs selectively inhibit the uptake of both serotonin and norepinephrine; and the Serotonin 2 (5-HT)–receptor antagonist works at two sites to make only serotonin more available in transmission.

Imaging

Imaging continues to improve. Along with that progress comes increased understanding of structural differences in the brains of persons who have brain-based disorders such as major depression. A 1999 study used computer-assisted three-dimensional cell counting to support earlier findings that there is decreased volume in the frontal cortices of persons with Major Depressive Disorder. The authors pointed out that the decrease was one of density in both glial and neural cells rather than a decrease in number of these cells. In other words, the cells shrank. Although there were some participants in the test group who had not been treated with antidepressant medication who showed the same decreased volume, the article states clearly that further studies will be necessary to confirm that these results are related directly to the Major Depressive Disorder rather than the use of antidepressant medication (Rajkowska et al., 1999).

Thyroid Function

Thyroid function is essential to regulating body metabolism and is also a critical factor in maintaining normal functioning of the central nervous system. There has long been evidence that enhancing thyroid function has been successful in treating mood disorders, including depression. Now that methods for imaging the brain are available, evaluation of the complex relationship between the brain and thyroid activity has begun and is beginning to be applied to understanding pathophysiology and treatments.

Another treatment for depression that does not involve medication is ECT. In this form of treatment, an electrical stimulus is used to produce the same kinds of changes in brain functioning that medications effect without the side effects of the medications. Not all synapses are dependent on neurotransmitters. There are neurons in the body, especially in the brain, that are closely enough aligned that the ion current flow (electrical connections) can take place from one neuron to the other. Some of the pathways also seem to support bidirectional transmissions. Whether for these or other reasons, there appear to be benefits for many persons who suffer serious depression in delivering an electrical stimulus to the brain via carefully placed electrodes or bands.

This kind of therapy is not new, but traditionally, it was problematic for several reasons. For example, many patients experienced sprains and other injuries while convulsing from the electric shock. Such injuries have been reduced by the careful use of anesthetics, muscle relaxants, and more carefully controlled levels of electrical stimulation. Many persons who have not responded well to other forms of therapy report positive outcomes with ECT. Despite these advancements, ECT is usually used only when an individual has not responded well to other forms of treatment.

Recent research suggests the development of new neurons in the hippocampus is necessary for mood control and may explain the efficacy of antidepressant medications. The hypothesis surrounding this new finding—neurogenesis—has been suggested as raising hopes that mood disorders might one day be treated by stimulating the growth of new hippocampal neurons (see Eisch & Petrik, 2012). Though quite interesting and exciting, these findings are not inconsistent with the biological information already provided. ECT might, for example, be effective in some cases due to stimulation of the hippocampus. In addition, the neurotransmitter information provided in this chapter would certainly relate to the findings of the development of adult-generated hippocampal neurons. It is too soon to determine if these findings will lead to the development of new treatments for mood disorders, but they certainly are worth sharing as we consider biological possibilities of both the development and treatment of Major Depressive Disorder.

A CRITICAL THINKING AND QUESTIONING PAUSE

Having read the comments from a biologist about Barbara's story, take time to reread all that you have learned about Barbara, her illness, and the treatment of her symptoms. As you reread, make your goal one of noting those places that comments from the biologist have enhanced your understanding of the information.

Treatment Considerations

Fortunately, Dr. Norton reported that Barbara is not suffering from any serious or chronic problems aside from depression. However, her depressive symptoms are severe and persistent enough that medication is warranted. Given that this was her first episode, and there appeared to be no comorbid illnesses or medical complications, several different medications are available that are potentially equally effective. Dr. Davidson agreed with this plan, and assuming Barbara cooperates fully in taking the medication, the likelihood she will recover from her moderately severe depression is about 70 percent.

With no previous history of pharmacotherapy for mood disturbance, it is not clear in advance which medication will prove optimal for Barbara. Had there been a family history of mood disorder and a medication that was found to be helpful in those cases, this medication would be a logical choice for Barbara, at least at first. Aside from a medication's demonstrated effectiveness in treating symptoms of depression, and Barbara's personal or family history, the choice of medication is based on side effect profiles among the various alternatives (i.e., the extent to which increased confusion, dietary restrictions, dizziness, or suicide risk would be problematic for her) and her expected level of cooperation with the regimen (which may be a function of side effects and cost).

Among the medications Dr. Norton considers are SSRIs. These include medications with trade names such as Luvox, Paxil, Prozac, and Zoloft. An advantage to these medications is that they have about the same effectiveness and latency to onset as other medications that are less selective, but fewer side effects and lower risk of harmful overdoses. The choices among the older antidepressants are "tricyclic" medications (Elavil, Tofranil) and MAO inhibitors such as Marplan and

Nardil. These older antidepressants have more side effects (such as weight gain or the need for dietary restrictions), and overdoses can be lethal. People differ in their responses to different medications. Some individuals start to improve as soon as a week or two after starting the medication, but others may not respond for a month or more, so it was important to be patient with Barbara's response to medication. Dr. Norton first prescribed a low dose: 20 milligrams of fluoxetine (Prozac) once per day. Barbara lives alone, and he was concerned that the medication she take not pose a risk if she were to develop serious side effects or become suicidal. If Barbara showed no response after 2 months, he might have increased the dose. If her response was still insufficient, his strategy would likely be to try a different medication.

Other Treatments

Dr. Davidson used an entire 50-minute session to explain several additional treatments to Barbara and to answer her questions, because he wanted her to make an informed decision about these further options. Dr. Davidson's plan regarding treatment options for Barbara was based on her specific symptoms and also her resources. Barbara's prior (or "premorbid") adjustment was good; she had no serious medical problems; and some support resources are available, although these may need to be boosted.

ECT can be helpful for major depression. Dr. Davidson asked Barbara if she would like to talk to a psychiatrist about ECT. She was very reluctant, and after some discussion, Dr. Davidson supported Barbara's decision not to try ECT right away. Her need for relief was not urgent. Her immediate risk of suicide was not very high, and she was not showing serious psychotic features (such as extreme withdrawal and uncommunicativeness) that might interfere with her ability to cooperate with other aspects of treatment. ECT might have been reconsidered if Barbara failed to respond to other treatments, if she found the side effects of antidepressant medications intolerable, or if she became suicidal.

Among other options, Interpersonal Therapy is well-suited to individuals whose depression is related to interpersonal losses, to those who are socially isolated and have work-related problems, and to those who experience both of these difficulties. It focuses on recognizing the significance of major losses and developing the necessary coping skills to recruit new support resources. Another option Dr. Davidson discussed with Barbara was Cognitive Therapy, an approach that has become well established in recent years. Cognitive Therapy would focus on Barbara's negative thoughts and perceptions, and how these inhibit active efforts to cope. The person with depression perceives severe negative outcomes that are due to bad experiences, inappropriate expectations, or both. The negative outcomes were explained in terms of "internal attributions," meaning that Barbara saw her difficulties in adjusting to William's death and the problems she was having at work as entirely her fault.

Negative internal attributions promote self-defeating social comparisons (i.e., comparing oneself with others who appear more effective), leading to renewed negative emotions. Cognitive interventions might attempt to help Barbara recognize society's contributions to her unrealistic expectations, and learn to use positive (downward) comparisons. A downward comparison would have Barbara compare herself to others who are worse off than she is. In this vein, she realizes that "it can always be worse" and that "there are others who have it worse off than I do."

A CRITICAL THINKING AND QUESTIONING PAUSE

Based on what you know of Barbara and the various alternative therapies that have been discussed, which approach do you think she and Dr. Davidson should choose? After you have made your decision, try to come up with at least three reasons that you have decided upon this strategy.

Barbara provides a good example of the opportunity for integrating treatments from more than one perspective. One aspect of her disorder is a lack of energy, including an inability to concentrate; a second involves negative thoughts and concerns; and a third is a lapse in effectiveness of her behavioral coping. Although they are somewhat interrelated, these three dimensions suggest different, but complementary, treatment interventions. Dr. Norton evaluated Barbara and gave her a prescription for antidepressant medication, and Dr. Davidson recommended that Barbara also receive psychotherapy that uses a combination of interpersonal and cognitive techniques.

Barbara's assets as a therapy client include being psychologically minded and having a stable environment. Interpersonal Therapy helped Barbara make the transition to a life without William. With Interpersonal Therapy, Dr. Davidson focused on communication and other relationship skills. When Barbara talked with her children, for example, this therapy stressed that she honestly express how she was feeling and what she was thinking. This approach also helped Barbara to reestablish some of the relationships she had slowly all but severed over the months since William's death. Rather than focus on past relationships (such as her relationship with her mother) as a psychodynamic approach would, this approach focused on Barbara's relationships in the here and now (such as with her children, Marcus, and her coworkers). This form of therapy also helped her identify new interpersonal resources, including substitutes for missing or needed supports (e.g., assistance with household repairs, weekend companionship).

Using Cognitive Therapy, Dr. Davidson gave considerable attention to Barbara's thoughts about work and to helping her develop coping skills relevant to work. He provided Barbara with a rationale regarding how thoughts can directly affect moods and had her help him identify examples of when her negative thoughts about widowhood or her job have led to negative moods and how more optimistic thoughts can improve her mood. After just two sessions, they had compiled a list of Barbara's negative thoughts.

One by one, Barbara articulated these thoughts and Dr. Davidson taught her how to challenge them. For example, when she said, "I'm not capable of performing adequately at work under the new system," the two of them worked together to generate more adaptive thoughts, such as "I remember how difficult it was to learn my job when I first started, or changed positions, or got a new boss, and yet each time, I adjusted before long, and did fine." In terms of widowhood she said, "It makes me unhappy to spend so much time alone," for which the corrective responses included "I have children who care very much for me, and friends like Marcus who I can get to know even better. As work becomes less stressful, I'm finding that even my coworkers are not as distant and unfriendly as I once thought."

As therapy progressed, Dr. Davidson was careful to monitor Barbara for signs that she was getting worse. Despite her "clean" status concerning these issues at intake, he took the opportunity from time to time to reassess her suicide potential and her use of alcohol. Although her treatment focused on reducing acute symptoms, it is important to understand that because depression can be episodic (recur over time), Dr. Davidson helped Barbara generalize the gains she achieved within therapy.

As she adapted and her life began returning to normal, Dr. Davidson made sure that she attributed these positive developments primarily to herself and to the skills and resources she had learned to use. After 3 months, she was feeling well enough to stop her therapy with him, although they continued to talk once a month by phone for another 3 months. At least part of Barbara's recovery was due to fluoxetine, and Dr. Norton had her continue taking it for several months after her therapy with Dr. Davidson ended, to reduce the likelihood of relapse. Once past the time when relapse is most likely to occur, he had Barbara taper off her use of the medication. Most clients have limited financial resources. As such, one-on-one professional therapy, regardless of the techniques used, is usually relatively short term. Major Depressive Disorder is often episodic, meaning that while eventual recovery from an initial episode is likely, the risk of reoccurrence is also high. To reduce the risk of relapse, Barbara's therapist has had her use an online Cognitive-Behavioral Therapy program that leads her through quizzes and exercises along with monthly "check-in" and "coaching" from her therapist to help her stick with the program (Hedman, Ljótsson, & Lindefors, 2012).

A word from Barbara:

> My husband died a year and a half ago, but I think I'm mending from
> that relationship and I think I'm mending from it well. I have good

self-esteem, I'm still hurting from that relationship, but I'm putting closure on that relationship. The reason I mention it is because in other losses I've had, previously, like my mother's death, I handled them differently and it took longer for the closure. I didn't have the level of self-esteem at that time that I do now.

There were times when I met someone that my husband's death was so much a part of my life that when I described myself and what I did, I would always add, "I have a husband who died." Now that isn't one of the introductory paragraphs when I meet someone new. I have a relationship with people. I don't find it . . . I find it comes into the conversation sometimes, and sometimes it doesn't, but when I refocused my life, I think I look at it differently.

Barbara's improvement with respect to acute symptoms in response to the combination of antidepressant medication and cognitive-interpersonal therapy was significant. After taking Prozac and undergoing weekly psychotherapy, Barbara can now focus and function in her daily life. Ironically, she is glad that she got sick enough to get diagnosed and get better.

The long-term maintenance of coping is important, and yet continuing in individual therapy is expensive and perhaps not necessary. Groups are relevant, especially when members share a circumstance such as bereavement, because the more successful members can help others by sharing information and alternative strategies for many of the common challenges. Where relevant, the group can focus on medication issues as well as social or work-related problems. Barbara was hesitant at first, but agreed to join a self-help group for widows, using her experience as an insurance claims processor to help others.

A Final Look at Barbara

Marcus pulls the car to the curb and squeezes Barbara's hand as a gesture of support. Barbara watches through the window as members of her widows' group shuffle through the rain and into the Mental Health America building. Barbara smiles but feelings of apprehension are betrayed in her eyes.

"I don't know if I can do this, Marcus," she says.

"Sure you can, Barb," Marcus offers in return. "You know these women asked you to come and talk about insurance because you have a lot to offer. They helped you to adjust to life after William's death and now it is your turn to give them some help. After all, you spent all of those hours at work learning the new laws and the new systems; it would be a shame to only use that knowledge with strangers calling the office over the phone. These are women you are starting to call friends—and friends use what they know to help their friends."

Barbara steels herself against the cold that she knew would accompany the outside rain. She clutches the leather briefcase Marcus had given her against her raincoat, pushes open the car door and runs to the door. With a final little wave to Marcus, she enters the Mental Health America door and prepares to share what she knows about insurance and life after the death of a spouse with about 35 other widows. As she disappears into the building, Marcus stares at where she had stood waving and breathes a sigh of relief. It seems to him that Barbara is truly on the mend.

6

THE CASE OF SALLY W

Bipolar Disorder

Introduction

"Just listen to me," the scraggly haired woman exclaimed. "I can make you a fortune. This plan cannot miss." She grabbed a man by the arm as he walked out of LuLu White's Mahogany Hall on Bourbon Street in New Orleans. "I've got a great idea for making money," she told him. The man was startled by her behavior and even more by her appearance, with her face painted in shimmering green-and-gold eye shadow and her neck surrounded by more than a dozen sparkly necklaces.

"Get away from me, you nut," the man bellowed as he moved hurriedly away from her.

This scene continued for several minutes until one of the waitresses from the music hall noticed. Dixieland Jazz music wafted through the air when the waitress opened the door to see what was causing all of the commotion. The odd-acting woman tried to grab her by the arm, asking, "Do you like to make money?" The waitress pulled herself away, headed back into LuLu's and called the police.

The police arrived to find the young woman, Sally, wandering through the French Quarter in New Orleans. She seemed barely coherent as she talked in animated tones about a money-making scheme she had developed. She walked right up to sightseeing tourists and other strangers she encountered and asked for help in getting envelopes and rubber stamps with certain dates on them because she believed that she had a business plan that would make billions. Just moments after the police arrive, Sally went from being animated and excited to lethargic and significantly less responsive. She collapsed in the back of the police cruiser, with tears streaming down her face.

The Diagnostic Interview

The police took her to Central Lockup at the Orleans Parish Prison. The next day, she was transferred to Charity Hospital by the sheriff on a coroner's order for protective custody. At Charity Hospital, she was seen by Dr. Rodriguez, a psychiatrist, who conducted the intake interview. Within her first hour there, Sally was alternately excitable, irritable, and upset. She talked excitedly of her many business ideas, suddenly began pacing around the small interview room, and then became agitated when Dr. Rodriguez suggested she sit back down.

When he asked her why the police brought her to the hospital, her eyes teared up. She sat down hard in the chair and began to sob. Dr. Rodriguez coaxed out of Sally the story of the last 7 weeks, including suddenly leaving home, her excitement at arriving in New Orleans, and the many ups and downs that she experienced over the 7-week period. He noted in particular that Sally reported sleeping very little and eating only sporadically.

Dr. Rodriguez conducted a mental status exam as described in the cases of Ricky and Barbara. As with Barbara, the psychiatrist was particularly interested in Sally's risk of suicide and other violent tendencies, and her current and lifetime history of substance use. Given her behavior as noted by the police, he asked Sally about her business plan, and asked open-ended questions that revealed a variety of other examples of risky behavior, including financial excesses, sexual promiscuity, and general recklessness. Her symptoms strongly suggested some form of bipolar mood disorder, but Dr. Rodriguez needed to distinguish this disorder from substance abuse and various personality disorders (e.g., Hilty, Brady, & Hales, 1999).

Dr. Rodriguez decided that Sally's behavior indicated both mania and depression, and it was important that she had described the past several days of this kind of pattern as typical for her. Further assessment entailed both current symptoms and other details, and also past history and features of the disorder over time. Dr. Rodriguez concluded, based on her present symptoms and history over the preceding weeks, that Sally's disturbance met the criteria for Bipolar I disorder (most recent episode mixed), which is severe but without psychotic features. In particular, he was struck by her rapidly alternating moods and occasional suicidal thinking, her impaired social functioning, and her apparent need for hospitalization. He was also confident that her symptoms were not directly attributable to a general medical condition, intoxication with a substance, or reaction to a treatment for mood disorder, such as antidepressant medication, ECT, or light therapy.

Given Sally's instability, the possibility she would do something self-destructive was a serious concern. Suicide risk is lower during the manic phase of Bipolar Disorder than the depressive phase, but is still above average. Suicide risk increases if, as in Sally's case, the individual experiences rapid shifts from one mood to another. The presence of substance abuse increases the risk here, and Sally acknowledged having used alcohol to excess in the past. Dr. Rodriguez understood that use of substances can reflect efforts at self-medication and can mislead the clinician by masking the underlying Bipolar Disorder. He also asked for a complete account of prescription and nonprescription medications Sally had taken.

Satisfied that he had enough evidence for a tentative diagnosis, Dr. Rodriguez turned his attention to Sally's ability to care for herself, whether she was pregnant or might become pregnant (see the Medications section later in this chapter), and her readily available support system and other resources (family, friends, finances, living situation, work situation). His immediate consideration was whether Sally should be hospitalized. Persons in the throes of a manic episode usually benefit from a calm, stable environment.

Sally's labile moods, risky conduct, and poor judgment were such that Dr. Rodriguez doubted she was presently in a position to care for herself. He wanted to be sure Sally did not abuse substances and considered there to be some risk of intentional or unintentional self-harm. Dr. Rodriguez realized that 72 hours was probably not going to be long enough to get Sally's situation turned around. The way Sally was strenuously objecting to remaining in the hospital caused him to fear that she would not be willing to stay after the 72-hour order had run out. At that point, he would have to struggle with a decision about the possibility of getting an involuntary commitment.

A CRITICAL THINKING AND QUESTIONING PAUSE

Based on what you have read about this case so far, do you think Dr. Rodriguez should try to have Sally hospitalized against her will? What are the reasons why you believe he should? What are arguments against doing so? Try to generate at least three reasons for and three reasons against hospitalizing her against her will. Once you have generated your list, which side do you find most convincing and why?

Sally's History

Bipolar Disorder has a more variable course over time than most other mental disorders. Dr. Rodriguez was also interested in how effective Sally's "normal" functioning (e.g., social, work-related) was between episodes and what previous treatments she had received. He was interested in finding out how many manic episodes Sally has had, how long they lasted on average, and how much time typically elapsed between episodes. He also wanted information about Sally's family history of mental illness, in particular mood disorders (most particularly manic and other bipolar illnesses). She consented to having medical records from her previous hospitalizations faxed to him. From these he obtained the following history.

Sally was 27 years of age and was trained as a recreation therapist. From birth until the age of 15, Sally was a quiet child but had lots of friends and fit in very well in school. She took gymnastics lessons, horseback riding, ballet lessons, was on sports teams, and was active in Brownies and Girl Scouts. At about the age of 15, she was sick with a respiratory tract infection for about a week. When Sally returned to school, she was unable to think clearly at school and had no energy or ability to tackle her homework. She could not even start dealing with material, and seemed to have lost some of her ability to think. She developed what she referred to as a "short fuse" and lost much of her ability to cope with stress and the added work of making up what she had missed. She began making a series of "bad choices," such as skipping school and taking off in the afternoon. Her parents took her to a child psychologist, thinking that something might be wrong. The psychologist concluded that there was nothing wrong with Sally other than a rebellious cycle that some teenage children go through. He did suggest that they learn more effective parenting skills.

The following year, Sally had more problems with school and her grades were worse than ever. Her parents thought that perhaps she was having an off year and things would get better when she went on to high school, but in the spring of that year, her behavior became quite bizarre. One morning at about 4:00 a.m. her mother discovered Sally coming in from outside the house. She told a very bizarre story about seeing a camel run through the neighbor's yard. She went outside to get closer to it. Her mother was concerned about this behavior and kept Sally home from school that day. Sally, however, kept trying to leave, and finally disappeared entirely at about 2:00 in the afternoon. Her family called the police, then drove all over looking for her. At about 6:00 that night, the police called to say that they had picked her up after she wandered into someone's house. Sally spent that night in the local hospital. The psychiatrist did not have a firm diagnosis for Sally, but mentioned the possibilities of problems with family dynamics.

Although Sally continued to be very depressed the following year, over the summer she improved a little, found a part-time job, and did a little dating. Within just a few days of starting school, her bizarre behavior recurred. She started picking up small items that did not belong to her, such as watches and rings. She came home with them and then lost them all as she wandered about the neighborhood. After several days of this, her parents contacted their doctor and had her admitted to the Children's Hospital psychiatric unit. She stayed there for 3 weeks, at which point the psychiatrist said he didn't want to label her as having a mental illness, but put her on Lithium.

Taking Lithium, Sally went back to school for her senior year, and by the time she graduated had made plans to attend college and study recreational therapy. She had observed recreational therapists while in various psychiatric hospitals, so she took the appropriate tests and applied and was accepted at the state university. Sally got along very well there, but her parents suspected that she was drinking too much at times. She certainly was acting immature, but did not have a recurrence of the earlier bizarre behavior. Her grades were only average, but she did well enough to graduate and was accepted for an internship in recreational therapy.

Toward the end of her senior year, Sally reported that her psychiatrist had told her that when the stress of college was over, she could stop taking Lithium. He was concerned about long-term health risks since Sally began Lithium treatment at a relatively young age. As her internship ended, Sally decided on her own to stop taking the Lithium. The hospital where she did the internship hired Sally for a full-time job. She did well at first, but within a year, the cycle resumed with another bout of bizarre behavior. She lost her job, which made her very depressed.

Given that keeping an individual with Bipolar Disorder taking her medication is a primary concern during the treatment process, we should consider why Sally would stop taking her medication when it had apparently helped her so much. Prior to taking Lithium, Sally had always described herself as, "energetic, creative, high-strung, and up on life." With the medication, however, Sally felt her "highs" were diminished and she was less creative. Writing poetry had always been an outlet for her, but she found herself unable to "create" while taking Lithium. In addition, Sally was truly feeling better. Her moods were more stable, people were responding more positively to her, and even the psychiatrist said that she appeared to be "much improved." ("Maybe I am better now and don't need the medication anymore," she thought.) Finally, Sally had to acknowledge that the long-term prospects of being on the medication frightened her. Although the side effects she had experienced so far were mild in comparison to the symptoms of the disorder, she couldn't help but wonder if the side effects and risks to her health would get worse the longer she took the medication. All in all, these issues seemed to Sally to add up to pretty convincing reasons to stop taking Lithium.

The summer after stopping the Lithium treatment, Sally got a job in the horse stable at the local state park. While working there, she met and fell in love with a young man who also worked with the horses. Sally was extremely happy, and by the end of the summer, they talked of getting married. Sally considered herself engaged. The job was only for the summer, and after returning home to live with her parents, Sally found a job there and moved to her own apartment. Before long, she became unhappy that her fiancé was not coming to visit her, and then she was unhappy with her job. A few months later, her fiancé broke off their relationship; soon after, Sally was let go from her job. She found another job, but soon began to show up at her parents' house every weekend, depressed, crying, and upset. Her mother spent many hours talking with her, trying to cheer her up. Sally was supposed to be taking Lithium, but her parents began to doubt she was doing this. They also began to suspect that she was abusing alcohol and perhaps also smoking marijuana.

Eventually Sally lost her most recent job and stopped taking care of her apartment. Her parents refused to let her move back with them because she would not take her medicine and was abusive to them. Sally would not attend therapy sessions, and at times, would leave town for days on end, such that her parents did not know where she was. She acquired a new boyfriend and left her apartment to move in with him, but he kicked her out within 2 weeks. She tried to live with a girlfriend but the girlfriend soon kicked her out as well. She told her parents that the only choice left was to do herself in. In desperation, they contacted the courts and filed a request stating that Sally was mentally incompetent. The psychiatrist cooperated with them and Sally was admitted to the psychiatric unit of a general hospital. However, when she saw the psychiatrist, Sally claimed that nothing was really wrong with her. The psychiatrist got a separate history from Sally's parents, and after he confronted Sally with the discrepancies between her story and theirs, Sally abruptly went AWOL from the hospital. The next her parents heard, she had been picked up in New Orleans.

An Interview with Dr. Chapman

I am really surprised that Sally gave you my name as someone you could talk to about her. I met her when she first came to New Orleans. I'm a psychiatrist and she made an appointment with me. I realized after we had talked for 10 or 15 minutes that she is bipolar, but she never said that to me. I also realized that I was not going to be able to keep her as a patient.

It is the first time it has happened to me in my five years of practice, but I could not ignore the strong attraction that I felt for her. At the end of the session, I suggested that I would refer her to a psychiatrist who would be more appropriate. I had my receptionist give her Steve Owens' office number, but I called Steve myself to ask if he could see Sally right away, because I realized how shaky things were for her right then. Steve owed me a favor, so I didn't hesitate to ask. As it turns out, Sally never went to see Steve, which explains how she ended up in lockup at Orleans Parish Prison. Many times the police do not know what else to do with someone in the state Sally must have been in. I guess it worked out for the best, though, because she ended up with Dr. Rodriguez. According to what I have heard, Rodriguez is one of the best when it comes to helping people with bipolar illness.

Wouldn't you guess, I saw Sally again that weekend in my favorite spot in the Quarter. A friend of mine since I was a kid plays there. Jones can play every wind instrument known to humankind and then some. Well, Sally was there by herself and we started talking and have been seeing each other since then. Never, since she left my office that first, day, has either of us mentioned her health or her illness.

That's one of the reasons that I am so surprised that she gave you my name. Come to think of it, she probably doesn't have that many friends here in New Orleans who know that she is ill. I know that Randy, one of the guys who plays with Jones, has schizophrenia. He wasn't doing well at all until he got a chance at Clozapine, and that has turned things around for him. I know he has kept an eye out for Sally and for a couple of days she stayed with Miss Lillian.

Lord, that woman is a saint!

Jones told me that Randy calls her home a "safe place" for people who are ill and just need a quiet place to be for a few days. She's not a professional. She doesn't give meds. She's just there for them. She'll feed them and remind them when it's time to take their meds if they need that. She doesn't see gender, color, age, poverty, or wealth. She just sees hurt and does her bit to make it better. Jones told me that Randy wouldn't have made it through the years before Clozapine without Miss Lillian and her "safe place."

To my knowledge, that's all the people in New Orleans who know anything about Sally's illness. I know that she is from Baton Rouge, but I'm not certain that there is anyone in her family she speaks to. From the little she told me, I'd put money on a hunch that her father and probably a grandmother, an aunt, and uncle have bipolar illness also. She didn't say that, but just listening to her on the rare occasions that she mentions her family at all, I got that picture. She told me once that both of her parents and her brother Alexander (Sandy) are all pathologists, but I don't know any more than that.

So, when you asked for people to talk to, I guess that explains why me. Well, I'm not sure how helpful I can be. There's no way I can be objective about Sally. I've never felt this way about anyone before, and it isn't an easy one to figure out.

Even when she's not doing well and off on one of those hare-brained money making schemes of hers, she has a way about her that I can't turn away from. She isn't a "knockout" at all. I've dated a lot of those, but Sally has a kind of haunting, subtle beauty. She's bright, but certainly not intellectual. Frankly, she's not "my type," or at least that's what I would have said before that day in my office.

"Creative" describes her without a doubt. She wrote a song, and the melody is haunting. Jones plays it all the time. She wrote words to it and sang it for me one night when there were only a few people there. Jones talked her into singing it while he played. It was just that one night that she sang it, for me at least. I think she and Jones had gone over it quite a bit, because they sure had it down pat. The words weren't as haunting as the music, but they were so revealing. Something like, "Touch me and hold on as we fly, fly past the moon and toward the sun. The sky goes on forever and I don't want to go alone." There was a middle part and then something like, "Touch me and hold on. Here we go deeper than the grave, beyond the river where we see Charon wink and wave. Hold on. Don't let me down. I cannot go alone."

Well, I'm holding on because I can't let go of her. I have no idea what will happen. I know she has sex with other men when she's on a high that is out of control. That scares me for both of us, but I can't let go of her.

It isn't rational. I know that. Before I met Sally, I would have predicted that the other factors—rich or poor background, religion or color differences—would have stopped me short. But those are trivial compared to this one. Every time she's had an episode it is a new choice for me to stay. I don't know where things will end.

Even though Sally never went to see Jones much after she sang the song that one night, he remembered her name. He heard the police had picked her up, and he called me. I found out she was in lockup. I guess it did not surprise me, although it should have been obvious that she needed hospitalization. A lot of times, people who should be taken to the hospital end up being taken to lockup because the police don't know what else to do. Once someone is in lockup, it is extremely difficult to get them transferred to Charity Hospital. Once in lockup, it takes someone from outside, like me, to advocate for them to be transferred to Charity. It is really pretty fortunate Steve heard about Sally being there. It was not too difficult for me, since I am a psychiatrist, to advocate for the transfer. The coroner signed the order within just a few minutes of my describing Sally's condition.

I love Sally. She gets away with things no one else can with me. Since that first night, she's called me Davey. Even my mother doesn't get away with that one. But Sally doesn't do it as a diminutive or to tease or wheedle. It's just her way. She is not at all manipulative, even when she is in the throes of the illness. In fact, in spite of the words in the song, she makes no efforts to hold me or ask for me to commit. It doesn't seem to matter to her. She lives for the moment, and that is enough. And she seems able to make the most of each moment, even during the lows. She values her freedom and seems to respect mine. The problem for me is letting go of her. I keep telling myself that loving someone isn't the same as being able to live with her, but that is easier to say than to act on by leaving or by pressing hard for something permanent. We'll see what Dr. Rodriguez can do. We'll see what time brings.

A Note From the Authors

This relationship that developed between Sally and Dr. Chapman was not included to in any way "shock" you. Instead, it was included to address the topic of professional issues. It was also included to remind you that the persons we are describing are persons with disorders; they are not defined by those disorders. Working to understand the problems a client might be confronting requires the clinician to work closely with the individual and get to know him or her very well. Because of the vulnerable position in which this puts the client, most states have adopted laws making it illegal for a clinician and client to be romantically involved.

For this reason, and for the good of Sally, Dr. Chapman clearly understood that his feelings for Sally made him a bad choice in terms of working with her. Thus, Dr. Chapman did the appropriate thing by attempting to put Sally in contact with another clinician. Once it is clear that Dr. Chapman would not be

Sally's clinician (and he clearly stated that the two of them did not discuss her illness), it was perfectly alright for the two of them as consenting adults to decide about having a relationship.

Sally is a beautiful, creative, expressive woman who has a disorder. She is not the disorder. David Chapman is a man who was drawn to the person that Sally is and is acutely aware of the difficulties that the disorder that she suffers bring to her and to him through the relationship. He is a human being who responded as a human being and made a decision immediately regarding the ethical and professional implications of a relationship with Sally. His response is one that is intelligent, responsible, and effective.

Treatment Considerations

Bipolar mood disorder is a chronic, cyclical illness. While the likelihood of recovery from a given episode is reasonably good, the probability of a recurrence is also high. Sally's history suggests that for her, as for many persons with bipolar illness, the intervals of time between major episodes are characterized by mood fluctuations and distress greater than that experienced by individuals without the illness.

Although at times Sally denies having a serious mental illness, it is likely that she will struggle with bipolar illness for the rest of her life, and that, without treatment, her suffering and problems are likely to be much worse. Dr. Rodriguez developed a treatment plan that was designed to reduce the number of episodes Sally experienced over time, and the severity of those episodes that did occur. He also tried to find ways of reducing the psychosocial problems associated with the current episode and any recurrence, and to improve Sally's coping and functioning between episodes.

Dr. Rodriguez's objectives were to develop and maintain a positive, collaborative working relationship with Sally; develop an arrangement where the two of them monitor her situation carefully for indications of new problems or other changes; provide education about Bipolar Disorder; maintain her cooperativeness with the treatment regimen; and work to manage related problems in living that she experienced. Since different strategies would be effective at different times, Dr. Rodriguez insisted that Sally make and keep regular appointments so that he would be available to help as events and her condition changed.

Patient Education

A key objective was for Sally to understand that bipolar illness is a lifelong, cyclical illness. She needed to learn to identify early signs and symptoms that mark the beginning of a new episode. For this purpose, Dr. Rodriguez made use of the "life chart" approach (Post, Roy-Byrne, & Uhde, 1988). This is a graphic representation of the life course of illness in patients with affective disorder. In this procedure, the severity of mood disorder episodes is plotted over time in conjunction with related information such as life events, medication regimens, and psychosocial interventions. Of particular importance are changes in sleep patterns or lifestyle activities (e.g., recreational pursuits) and, for Sally, substance use. For example, in some patients, insomnia can be a precursor of a manic episode.

The occurrence of insomnia in a patient like Sally could be troubling enough that Dr. Rodriguez would prescribe sleep aids. In some patients, the anniversaries of certain events, like the death of a loved one, can provoke excessive ruminating and other maladaptive coping responses. It is important that the patient help to maintain a collaborative effort in dealing with bipolar illness, and attention to information in the life chart reinforcing a sense of meaningful collaboration.

Medications

Sally needs direct medical intervention to help return her mood to something closer to what is normal for her. Since even the periods between full-blown episodes can be marked by significant mood fluctuations, a critical need of the person with Bipolar Disorder is mood stabilization. Given Sally's agitation and degree of disrupted functioning, and the consequent possibility she may not have cooperated with treatment, Dr. Rodriguez considered several ways of stabilizing her mood relatively quickly: He could prescribe neuroleptic or anti-anxiety medications, or he might use ECT. ECT is effective in reducing acute mania, but in the face of Sally's denial was unlikely to be acceptable to her. Dr. Rodriguez also decided against use of antipsychotics because of the strong side effects, and opted for a benzodiazepine for the sedative effect needed to establish cooperation.

The most common medication used for mood stabilization is Lithium. Because she previously responded positively to it, the likelihood that Lithium would help Sally was relatively good. However, the procedure entailed in using it is relatively demanding. Lithium's "therapeutic window" (that is, the range of doses that are both effective and low enough in toxicity to be tolerable) is relatively narrow, and the levels of the drug in Sally's blood would need to be monitored carefully. Valproate, another mood-stabilizing medication, may be more effective than Lithium for the kind of "mixed" or fluctuating mood type of Bipolar Disorder that Sally has. In addition, Valproate has a wider therapeutic window than Lithium and overall a lower risk of toxic overdose. If Sally did not respond to Lithium after several weeks, Dr. Rodriguez planned to try Valproate, or perhaps a combination of Lithium and Valproate. It may also be appropriate to reconsider using ECT.

As part of the preparations, Sally receives a physical exam, including blood tests and an evaluation of kidney, heart, and thyroid gland functioning. Lithium can increase the incidence of certain skin problems such as acne and psoriasis. Dr. Rodriguez had a pregnancy test done, and he explained to Sally that Lithium should not be taken by a woman who is pregnant or becomes pregnant, because it increases the risk of birth defects (especially in the first trimester of pregnancy). Given that Sally has at times had an active sex life, he strongly urged her to practice contraception and to inform him immediately of any change in her pregnancy status. Should she become pregnant, the treatment options would be reduced. ECT would become a stronger possibility, and the frequency of counseling sessions might need to be increased.

It was also important that Sally limit her use of other kinds of medications, since certain medications can interact with Lithium. Dr. Rodriguez reminded Sally to expect some side effects, including being thirsty, having a frequent need to go to the bathroom, internal discomfort (nausea, diarrhea), weight gain, and difficulty concentrating. However, he reassured her that troublesome side effects do not always occur—and if they do, there are likely to be ways to manage them by reducing the Lithium dose or taking the medication with meals or at bedtime.

Sally was young and healthy, and aside from the risk of unexpected pregnancy, she was a good candidate for Lithium. Dr. Rodriguez discontinued the benzodiazepine medication and prescribed a daily dose of Lithium, starting with a low dose to minimize side effects and with small increases over time. Each time the dose was increased, the Lithium level in her blood was checked. After 3 weeks, Sally's manic behaviors had lessened substantially. Because of her therapeutic response to Lithium, and her success in tolerating the side effects, Dr. Rodriguez decided that Sally should continue a daily dose of Lithium as a maintenance treatment intended to reduce the chances of another episode. If a new episode of either mania or depression does arise, there is some chance that having taken Lithium will reduce the intensity of the mood disruption that occurs.

Dr. Rodriguez's decision to continue Lithium indefinitely was not automatic, nor was it made lightly. Sally was fully involved in considering this option. She realized that her success in establishing a more stable lifestyle, and better coping, was due in part to the effects of Lithium. Even after it was made, the decision to continue Lithium was not considered final and was reevaluated at each of Sally's monthly sessions with Dr. Rodriguez. He cautioned Sally that it was possible she would experience further mood swings while on Lithium. Should this occur, it would not mean the Lithium was not working or that she would necessarily have another serious manic episode. He emphasized that no treatments for bipolar mood disorder are 100 percent effective, and again stressed the importance of Sally learning to identify signs that indicate a worsening in her mood disturbance. A return of full-blown mania or depression would not only cause significant problems for Sally, but would bring with it a renewed risk of substance abuse and suicide.

As promising as the maintenance regimen seemed to be, it was important for Sally to continue seeing Dr. Rodriguez because the side effects can become troublesome. In addition to immediate side effects described earlier, Lithium can have other adverse effects with prolonged use, including thyroid gland problems and kidney problems. These risks mandate the continued medical monitoring of her kidney and thyroid functioning. Sally has been prone to feelings of denial about her illness. As her life returned to normal and her functioning improved, there was some risk that she would stop taking the Lithium, as happened before. If this were to happen, the chances of a new episode within 6 months would be greater than 50 percent (Faedda, Tondo, Baldessarini, Suppes, & Tohen, 1993). It was important that Sally communicate to Dr. Rodriguez any thoughts she had about stopping Lithium. If she was convinced that it was necessary to stop the medication, and he agreed to this, the chances of a recurrence would be less if the Lithium was tapered gradually over time instead of stopped all at once.

Psychosocial Management

Until her current mixed-mood episode subsided, it would be unproductive to pursue any form of psychotherapy with Sally. The primary psychosocial intervention until this happened was to reduce the amount of external stimulation she received through brief hospitalization.

Sally's recognition of the seriousness and lifelong nature of her mood problems, including the stigma she may feel and the expectation that she adhere to a demanding treatment regimen, were significant blows to her self-esteem and expectations for the future. In addition, her recent and previous episodes of mood disturbance have created problems in living. Aside from the medical management of her Bipolar Disorder, there were important emotional, interpersonal, vocational, and other issues needing attention. The demanding treatments, and her tendency toward denial, suggested a significant risk that she may ignore important indicators regarding her health and be uncooperative with ongoing treatment. As a young adult with many of the normal aspirations for a healthy family and successful life, she needed to understand the impact of her illness and its treatment on these long-term expectations.

Support from family and significant others is sufficiently important that family therapy focused on helping the family understand and accept the illness and recognize indications of impending relapse is often recommended in conjunction with medication. Although Sally's family lives in Baton Rouge (some 65 miles from New Orleans), she preferred to remain living in New Orleans, so her treatment was oriented around that choice. Given the importance of psychosocial support and the risk that Sally would again lapse into denial, Dr. Rodriguez referred her to Brenda Johnson, PhD, a clinical psychologist who specialized in Cognitive-Behavioral Therapy. The purpose of this referral was to reduce Sally's denial, educate her regarding Bipolar Disorder, help her improve her coping skills, and help her maintain cooperativeness with treatment. This treatment would include establishing clear limits on some of Sally's tendencies, such as her attempts at self-medication via substance use, plus specific prescriptions for lifestyle modifications designed to help Sally maintain a regular pattern of daily exercise and other structured activities. (Should Sally enter a depressive phase in her mood fluctuations, some of the psychosocial interventions described in the case of Barbara M could be considered.)

Sally managed to make some friends in her 7 weeks of living in New Orleans, including Randy and Dr. Chapman—but both of these individuals brought some level of instability to Sally's case. Randy suffered from schizophrenia and his ability to serve as a support person for Sally was largely dependent upon his own level of functioning. Dr. Chapman was another story. His love relationship with Sally clearly influenced her treatment progress. When he and Sally were getting along well, Sally was clearly happy and very cooperative with her treatment regimen. When the two of them were fighting or had "broken up" again, Sally was uncooperative, bombastic, and very difficult to treat. Dr. Jordan must consider all of this, as Sally had no family living in New Orleans to serve as a support for her.

Sally was young and, aside from the mental illness, her health was relatively good. As a recreational therapist, she understood the importance of following a daily exercise program that would help structure her time, improve her degree of fitness, and help her get sufficient rest. Dr. Johnson helped Sally develop and maintain a regular schedule of daily activities. Although she had some reasonable prospects for getting a job in New Orleans and had her own apartment through the supported living program of the local mental health center, Sally sometimes thought she should pick up and move to someplace new to start all over. Dr. Johnson discouraged her from dwelling on this plan and urged her instead to rebuild and expand her current network of supportive relationships in New Orleans. Dr. Johnson also encouraged Sally to attend meetings of the local chapter of the Depression/Manic-Depression Association.

Bipolar Disorder Beckons to a Biologist's Interest

Of great interest to biologists about Bipolar Disorder (alternately called *manic depressive disorder*) is its tendency to "run in the family." Certainly we saw this in Sally's story as Dr. Chapman told what he has learned about the family she left behind in Baton Rouge. There have been many studies over the years that attempt to find direct evidence of the heritability of bipolar illness. The authors of a study in Finland that was reported in 2004 (Kieseppä et al.) described their participants as representative of a nationwide twin sample with the diagnosis of bipolar illness being determined by extensive face-to-face interviews. Much of the paper argued that their results support the heritability of bipolar illness.

There have been numerous attempts to link the occurrence of Bipolar Disorder with certain chromosomal abnormalities. Studies involving linkages on chromosomes 18 and 22q and others involving chromosomes 5, 11, and X indicated the need for more studies. Attempts to find a gene or genes that are linked with the disorder have had to narrow the focus to a reduced number of families. Thus, it appears that using multifamily studies to search more thoroughly will be necessary to finding an answer (Escamilla & Zavala, 2008). The complexity of this study was impressive, but we will focus only on one outcome here. Their results included a single family in which a genome search using 193 markers indicated linkage on chromosome 4p (Blackwood et al., 1996). This biologist mentions these many efforts to convey, at least in part, that genetic studies and determining their implications are very complex processes. It seems that even finding genetic linkages with a family or several families is of limited value in integrating or replicating those findings with larger numbers of families.

Looking at the medications used to treat bipolar illness helps us to understand some of the biological implications. Lithium is the time-honored medication of choice used to "level" the moods of a person who has Bipolar Disorder. A number of studies implicate abnormalities of the serotonin systems as a feature both of Bipolar Disorder and suicide. It is of particular interest that the use of Lithium drastically lowers the incidence of suicide, including that associated with bipolar illness. Although anticonvulsants have been used successfully to decrease the incidence of symptoms of the disorder, they do not share the same suicide prevention properties. Antidepressants are also used successfully in many cases to treat the symptoms of Bipolar Disorder successfully.

Another arena of interest for the biologist who looks at Bipolar Disorder is the role of the thyroid hormone (secreted by the thyroid glands) and thyroid stimulating hormone (secreted by the anterior pituitary to signal the thyroid gland to secrete hormone) in mood regulation. Astute clinicians have incorporated thyroid-regulating medications in the treatment of some persons with certain forms of bipolar illness. Recent studies that address basic physiological mechanisms involved point to possible mediation of cerebral blood flow patterns related to the levels of thyroid hormone or corresponding levels of thyroid-stimulating hormone or both. For more discussion on the potential role of thyroid functioning in mood disorder, you are referred to the case of Barbara M.

In a turn-of-the-century article by Manji and Lenox (2000), the authors summarize the issues that complicate our understanding of Bipolar Disorder. They describe challenges that include profound changes in mood; evidence of dysfunction of limbic-related areas of the brain such as the hypothalamus, hippocampus, and brain stem; evidence of progressive decline in overall function; and the fact that monoamine and neuropeptide pathways originate and project within these limbic-related regions. They also state that signal transduction pathways such as PKC (Protein Kinase C) are possibly related both to the manifestations of the disorder and represent targets for the action of treatments such as Lithium. These authors assert that it will require an experimental design that takes all of these challenges into account to provide scientific evidence to support our clinical understandings of this illness. Their assertion appears to be the ongoing challenge to understanding a most complex disorder.

7

THE CASE OF CARL V

Borderline Personality Disorder

Introduction

Carl stood on the overpass watching the traffic stream by underneath. He began swaying back and forth to the rhythm of the flowing vehicles. Tears streamed down his face as he whispered her name over and over again: "Cyndi . . . Cyndi . . . Cyndi." This scene continued for more than 30 minutes until a passing motorist noticed the swaying man on the concrete edge of the overpass. He pulled over to the side and called the State Police.

The officer who arrived first, Adam Granell, was specially trained to deal with such situations and calmly began talking to Carl. He learned that Carl became despondent after his girlfriend Cyndi broke up with him, "once and for all," only 2 hours earlier. Through sobs Carl explained that this was "the most meaningful and intense relationship I have ever had." Another half hour passed before Officer Granell succeeded in talking Carl down off of the overpass. He and his partner then drove Carl to the hospital emergency room. Officer Granell was not surprised to find that this was not Carl's first visit to the ER.

The Diagnostic Interview

During his intake interview with a psychiatry resident, Dr. Posner, Carl cried and wrung his hands as he described the preceding month. Cyndi broke off her relationship with him 4 weeks prior to that important night. At first, Carl seemed to understand and accept the end of the relationship—but then he began calling Cyndi and begging her to take him back. Cyndi had only recently found the strength to tell Carl it was over, so Carl's unwillingness to let their relationship end was particularly troublesome to her. On that night, in the face of Carl's last-ditch effort to make her reconsider, Cyndi had finally expressed herself in clear and uncertain terms. Carl recalled her words with precision: "If you were the last male to populate the earth, I still would not take you back."

Although the severity of these words hurt Cyndi too, she thought that being so rude would finally convince Carl that it was time to let things go. However, Carl was so upset he could feel nothing but her anger. After she stormed off, slamming the door behind her, he all but collapsed. As if suffering from "emotional hemophilia," Carl screamed and sobbed, unable to stem the flow of anger and sorrow that poured out. Before long, he had decided that it was finally time to end the mess that was his life.

This latest relationship breakup was one of many Carl has been through. Since adolescence, Carl has shown a destructive, self-defeating pattern in virtually all of his close relationships, involving a variety of different partners. At the moment, almost nothing about him was stable. His life goals and vocational aspirations, as well as types of friends, seemed to shift with the wind. He gambled, drove recklessly, and succumbed to risky temptations when it came to sex and use of substances. His education had frequent interruptions, and his vocational history was haphazard, with recurrent job losses. Carl recounted recent episodes in which he isolated himself for 20 or more hours per day in his room, spending virtually all of this time drinking, popping pills, and smoking marijuana.

Although the resident asked Carl the standard questions about prior psychiatric treatment, use of therapeutic medications, and family history of mental disorders, she soon realized, based on a large folder she was handed containing voluminous notes and forms, that the hospital had many previous encounters with Carl. She saw many different diagnoses listed in Carl's chart, the most recent of which immediately caught his eye: Borderline Personality Disorder (BPD). It certainly seems to fit, she mused—unstable interpersonal relationships, moods, and self-perceptions, as well as impulsivity, that began in adolescence or young adulthood and are evident in a variety of life contexts.

Leaving Carl in the care of ER staff, the resident retreated to a small office and quickly became absorbed in reading Carl's thick chart. Although most of the people diagnosed with BPD are female, she realized that, aside from this detail, Carl is almost a "classic" case of this disorder.

The process notes of countless previous therapists described how Carl vacillated between extremes in his appraisals of significant others. He was easily smitten by new romantic interests and was quick to disclose sensitive information about himself. However, he soon became very demanding of the other person, expecting similar levels of intimate emotional disclosure from her. When she did not reciprocate, or tried to back away, Carl was easily disillusioned, thought he was in danger of being abandoned, and reversed his appraisal of the woman as someone who cannot be counted on.

Carl could be sweet and considerate one day, argumentative and sarcastic the next. When challenged, he could react with explosive anger about which he later felt shame and guilt. He had great difficulty being alone, but had trouble maintaining close relationships for more than a few weeks. Relationship problems came to dominate his life to the point where it was hard to understand Carl as a person separate from whatever his most intense current relationship happened to be.

Carl did not show evidence of paranoid thinking, as some persons with BPD do. Carl's suspicious preoccupation that he will be abandoned is not the same as paranoid thinking. In many ways, this fear of rejection was supported by the many relationship rejections he experienced. Although it is true that the relationship difficulties that lead to rejection are a manifestation of his illness, this does not make the fear any less real to him.

Whether Carl is a classic example of BPD or not, there is nothing simple about people like him. More often than not, BPD co-occurs with one or more other mental disorders that may be pronounced enough to be diagnosed in their own right. The most common kind of disorder would be major depression or another mood disorder. Also possible are anxiety disorders, substance use disorders, and PTSD. Adding to the complexity, there are several other personality disorders that may be present along with BPD.

Carl's History

Although Carl's parents lived together off and on for many years, they never married. As a child Carl was physically victimized by his father, who appears to have had antisocial personality disorder. His mother did nothing to stop or prevent the abuse, perhaps because she also showed signs of mental illness, especially depression, and Carl's father was abusive to her as well.

Carl vacillated between strong dependence on one or the other of his parents and intense ambivalence about that parent. This pattern of vacillation between dependence and ambivalence or even hostility affected most of his adult relationships as well. He showed significant interpersonal difficulties with peers and authority figures beginning in adolescence. Many of his relationship problems amounted to self-fulfilling prophecies, in that the more demanding Carl became, the more the other person tried to back away from him. He showed the same kind of pattern with respect to jobs: Each time he started a new job, he was filled with hope and interest. As problems and stresses cropped up, however, he became ambivalent about the job and failed to deal with the problems effectively, causing him to lose or quit the job.

The concept of self-fulfilling prophecy is an important aspect of this illness. Carl is unlikely to have successful relationships because his fears of rejection cause him to behave in ways toward his relationship partners that cause them to back away. Carl then interprets this backing away as a sign of rejection. Carl's certainty, then, that he is being abandoned, causes him to become even more demanding, which initiates a further backing away by the relationship partner. This does not need to happen too many times before the relationship is destroyed.

Treatment Considerations

Carl left the hospital emergency room with an appointment to see a therapist at the medical school's outpatient clinic. Carl had no insurance and a limited ability to pay for therapy, so his therapist was Dr. Posner, a young psychiatry resident. Because having more than one treatment provider may encourage "splitting" in someone with BPD, Dr. Posner was his only therapist.

Splitting is an example of the kind of black-or-white, all-or-nothing thinking that also characterizes Major Depressive Disorder. In Carl's case, he will first idealize someone, but then quickly devalue the person as soon as he perceives the person is rejecting him. In addition, Carl vacillates internally between considering himself a good person who has been mistreated by others, which nurtures feelings of anger and resentment, versus seeing himself as a bad person whose life has no value, in which case he becomes self-destructive or even suicidal. When it comes to therapy, if Carl has more than one therapist, he will be inclined to pit one against the other, such that one is "all good" and the other is "all bad." When with the latter individual, of course, Carl might attempt to work the process in reverse.

Carl responded quickly to attention and support from the hospital staff. In fact, he was pleased with the chance to "start over" with a new therapist, and was initially eager to make progress. He noted that his earlier experiences in therapy always started out in a promising way, but eventually failed due to the questionable competence of the therapist (another example of splitting). For her part, Dr. Posner looked forward to the challenge of working with Carl. She was aware of the pessimism most therapists have about doing therapy with persons whose diagnosis is BPD. Nevertheless, she found Carl an interesting and challenging individual and believed his previous therapists may have had insufficient hope and too many negative expectations for Carl.

A CRITICAL THINKING AND QUESTIONING PAUSE

Should Carl's therapist be someone who is still in training and has relatively little experience? What might be the advantages of having someone who is still in training? What would be the disadvantages? Should his therapist be a female who is younger than him? Given that it is best for Carl to have only one treatment provider, what suggestions do you have for minimizing the disadvantages to having a provider who is in training and for maximizing the advantages?

Dr. Posner's first step is to determine as carefully as possible whether Carl also has any comorbid mood or anxiety disorders, because these may be more treatable (e.g., using medication) than is BPD. Carl's history does not support a diagnosis of major depression but does indicate dysthymia, a milder but very chronic form of mood disorder.

Medications, including antidepressants, are often prescribed for persons with BPD, but no medication has consistently been shown to be effective. Tricyclic antidepressants have not been shown to be helpful for persons with BPD, and could be lethal if taken in overdose. MAOI antidepressants impose dietary restrictions and are also lethal in overdose. Given the presence of dysthymia, Dr. Posner writes Carl a prescription for Prozac, an SSRI. Use of this medication is not expected to eliminate the BPD symptoms, but improvement in his dysthymic symptoms will give Carl a better basis for working on his many other problems.

Most people with BPD need highly structured treatment that is focused primarily on their core symptoms. With Carl, the most difficult problem Dr. Posner could likely face was his deliberate self-harm and self-destructiveness, such as suicide attempts. Self-punishment is the way Carl tries to manage his negative feelings, and in his case is most likely to occur in association with intoxication (Gunderson, 2011).

Interpersonal problems and issues are central to the experience of someone with BPD, so a relationship-based treatment such as psychotherapy would seem to be an appropriate choice. BPD is theoretically interesting from a psychoanalytic perspective. In Carl's case, the childhood victimization by his father and unavailability of his mother would be important to focus on in therapy. Psychodynamic Therapy has attracted interest because of the specific theoretical relevance of psychodynamic treatment to BPD. However, this option is lengthy and expensive, and Carl's treatment history suggests that committing to the intense demands of this treatment will be difficult for him.

The approach Dr. Posner took was a cognitive-behavioral approach called *Dialectical Behavior Therapy* (Linehan, 1993). This approach focuses on problem-solving skills and other adaptive responses. It assumes that the adult symptoms of BPD reflect both long-standing emotional "fragility" (e.g., heightened sensitivity and reactivity to emotional stimuli), such that emotions can easily become "disregulated," and also experiences during childhood and adolescence that are consistently "invalidating." Emotional disregulation means that all emotions—love, hate, fear, depression—are experienced too intensely; it is as though the person is somehow "allergic" to stressful events or to intimacy. Invalidating child and adolescent experiences are ones that reject or make inconsequential the experiences and needs of the developing individual. Usually, this invalidation comes from significant others whom the young person typically would depend on for validation of his or her own importance.

The Dialectical Behavior Therapy that Carl undertook was based on efforts to accept and validate him in an attempt to compensate for and challenge his efforts to be self-invalidating. If Carl suggested, for example, "Cyndi left me because she hates me," Dr. Posner insisted that Carl counter that assertion with an opposing viewpoint: "Cyndi left me because she loves me." These viewpoints, of course, could not both be accurate. Carl needed to reconcile (or synthesize) these extreme viewpoints. He might decide, for example, that "Cyndi left me because she cares deeply for me but cannot deal with all of my difficulties."

Dr. Posner worked with Carl to help him develop problem-solving strategies that moved him away from self-invalidating responses to those problems. The goal was not to get him to stop accepting all responsibility for problems, but to more accurately accept only the responsibility that was truly his to accept.

According to a paper by Kiehn and Swales (1995) that Dr. Posner read, she would have to accept a number of working assumptions if Dialectical Behavior Therapy was to be effective. These assumptions include: (a) Carl wants to change and is trying his best to do so, (b) his behavior is understandable given the invalidating background and current tendencies to continue that self-invalidation, (c) harder work will still be required from him if therapeutic progress is to be made, and (d) if things do not improve, it is not Carl who has failed but rather the treatment that has failed. Point "d" is included as a reminder that failed attempts should not be utilized to further invalidate the client.

Along with these assumptions, Dr. Posner knew that Carl needed to make an agreement promising that he would: (a) work in therapy for an agreed–upon time period (Linehan suggests one year), (b) focus on suicidal or parasuicidal thoughts and/or behaviors, (c) vow to work on eliminating thoughts and behaviors that interfere with therapy, and (d) attend skills training (Kiehn & Swales, 1995). He also agreed that as long as he was in therapy with Dr. Posner, he would fill out a diary card every day, checking off specific skills he worked on that day and any problem behaviors he engaged in (e.g., substance use, suicidal thinking). He understood that Dr. Posner would begin every session with him by scrutinizing that week's entries on the card and confronting him about each problem he reported. These are demanding expectations, and Carl was apprehensive about them—but at the same time, he understood that life had become hell for him, and that (to use Linehan's metaphor) Dialectical Behavior Therapy just might provide the ladder he needed to climb out.

Therapy usually begins with a pretreatment stage in which assessments and other introductory steps in the treatment process are taken. Given that the assessments were already completed, Dr. Posner was ready to develop the additional stages of treatment. Her goals were that Carl acquire skills to regulate his emotions, tolerate distress, and manage better his more self-destructive behaviors (e.g., suicidal thinking). Based on what she has learned about Dialectical Behavior Therapy, she suggested a three–stage treatment plan to Carl.

Stage one treatment focused on his suicidal behaviors and other behaviors and thoughts that may interfere with the success of therapy. Carl was taught problem-solving skills and the dialectical process of countering arguments with opposing arguments and then synthesizing a moderate solution between the two extreme viewpoints. Dr. Posner also focused on making mindfulness skills part of Carl's daily practice. Using these skills, Carl learned to avoid reacting so intensely to outside stress by breaking away instead to a state of calm internal awareness and acceptance of the immediate moment in time.

Stage two dealt with the problems associated with posttraumatic reactions to the stressors of Carl's life. It is quite common for individuals with BPD to be dually diagnosed with PTSD. This is primarily due to the high incidence of physical, sexual, and psychological abuse in the childhoods of these individuals. Even if Carl was not diagnosed with PTSD, he could very well exhibit some of the symptomatology.

Stage three focused on helping Carl to be more self-validating, and using self-esteem enhancement strategies. Discussing his suicidal reaction to Cyndi's breaking up with him, for example, Dr. Posner rationalized his reaction up to a point, noting that "Everybody who's really upset has trouble thinking clearly at that moment—it's normal!" In addition, Dr. Posner required Carl to set individual treatment goals for himself.

After a month of therapy, Carl began to express an interest in Dr. Posner's personal life. He asked if he could call her after hours in the event he needed to talk to her. She explained politely that there was an "on-call" phone number he should use in the case of an emergency. Carl learned that Dr. Posner worked out at the nearby YMCA. He joined the Y and managed to time his workouts to coincide with hers. She was uncomfortable about bumping into him there, but decided that inadvertent contact with her clients was bound to happen from time to time, and that Carl always behaved appropriately during these encounters.

Although Dr. Posner was attempting to keep her relationship with Carl at strictly a business level, Carl's tendency to "go all out" in a relationship caused him to strive for more. This, of course, related back to his intense fear of rejection. Carl believed that the more special things Dr. Posner did for him, the less likely she was to reject or abandon him. Dr. Posner usually walks the mile and a half home from the Y to her apartment. One evening, it was raining very hard and Carl offered Dr. Posner a ride home in his car. Dr. Posner thanked him graciously for his thoughtful offer but declined, saying she likes to use the walk home to cool down from her workout.

A CRITICAL THINKING AND QUESTIONING PAUSE

Should Dr. Posner have accepted a ride from Carl? How does this question relate to the concept of "splitting" suggested earlier? If Dr. Posner had accepted a ride from Carl, how might that have changed the nature of the therapeutic relationship? Could Carl have been attempting to manipulate Dr. Posner into having a "special" relationship with him? If so, what potential impact could this have had on the therapeutic process?

As the weeks passed, Carl behaved more erratically and his emotions were more uneven. Where during early sessions Carl confided to Dr. Posner that she was the first therapist who really understood him, and cited examples of mistakes by previous treatment providers, after some perceived rebuffs from Dr. Posner, he became stiff and guarded in therapy and began criticizing her behind her back. For example, he became very upset when Dr. Posner interrupted a session to handle a crisis involving another patient. In Carl's self-centered world, this action demonstrated that she thought Carl was a "bad" client.

As time passed, Carl was less and less motivated to work on his interpersonal skill deficits and career progress. Dr. Posner was tense as well. When he voiced some anger with her over canceling a session with him so she could attend a professional conference, she responded in kind, insisting, "That's ridiculous! You cannot possibly be angry just because I canceled one session in three months!" Ruminating on this exchange later, she realized how her loss of composure probably upset Carl and invalidated his feelings. Dr. Posner was starting to feel very inadequate and began dreading her sessions with Carl. She dutifully reported these feelings during the regular supervision she received from an experienced psychiatrist (a normal part of residency training). Her supervisor listened intently and encouraged her to learn from the dread and the other feelings she experienced during and between her therapy sessions with Carl.

Dr. Posner's biggest concern was that Carl was not getting better. In fact, he seemed to be getting worse. He phoned her at her office almost every day, and during these highly charged conversations could abruptly pour forth a stream of suicidal thoughts. She began to dread these calls. Her supervisor had Dr. Posner set some limits on the phone calls. It was a bit like walking a tightrope, since Dr. Posner could not acquiesce to Carl's intrusive behavior but also did not want to impose too much "distance" in their therapy relationship, or her effectiveness in helping Carl would diminish. She pointed out firmly that "your suicidal threats are harming what we do in here. It is critical that you understand that you are responsible for your life and your health."

Following the instruction of her supervisor, Dr. Posner carefully added detailed, written notes to the chart she maintained on her treatment of Carl. She quoted each of Carl's suicidal statements and her responses to them verbatim. She added comments assessing the seriousness of suicide risk indicated in each contact with Carl, and also recorded her supervisor's analysis and suggestions. These steps were taken because of the serious risk Carl posed to himself, and the need to monitor this risk continuously and to document the facts in the clinical record. With a good record, Dr. Posner can compare recent suicidal indications with those he displayed earlier, and such details will also help future therapists who might see Carl. Also, in the event Carl does attempt or complete suicide, it would be important to have a complete account of his therapist's prior handling of this issue. Some studies suggest that up to 75 percent of persons with BPD may attempt suicide, with success rates possible around 10 percent (Stone, Hurt, & Stone, 1987).

The situation deteriorated until Carl made a dramatic self-mutilation gesture. Carl came to therapy one day with multiple cuts on both of his forearms. Dr. Posner suspected that they are self-inflicted and Carl admitted they are. Carl justified his behavior by suggesting that it was the only thing he could think of to do to bring all of the negative emotions in his head into focus. Carl was relatively calm during the therapy session and agreed to begin attending a group session that Dr. Watkins, a colleague of Dr. Posner, was holding. It was during these group sessions that Carl met Rachel and things began to get better for him. For Carl, of course, "getting better" still means plenty of ups and downs. We will let Rachel help us finish this chapter by explaining what having BPD has been like for her.

An Interview With Rachel

Maybe the best way to explain my connection with Carl is to tell my whole story. It's the only way I can think of to make his and my relationship make sense. Carl and I are lovers but we're also more than that. In order to understand why our relationship works, I think you need to know where I am coming from.

At the age of 5, I was forced to perform oral sex on a cousin. Then, at the age of 9, I was forced to have sex with my half brother. I had really low self-esteem after that and I used school as a way to escape. At age 13, I got really depressed and escaping with school wasn't working anymore. I can remember at the age of 5 sitting on a swing set wishing I was dead. At 13, I was thinking suicidal things again. I couldn't talk to my parents. I would tell some teachers that I had crushes on about how I was feeling but none of them did anything about it.

My senior year I got really "manic." I got into religious fanaticism—rebuked everything that I thought was evil. I rebuked a lot because I thought everything and everyone was evil. I started going to church and the pastor told me I should go to a certain college. When I told him that I could not afford to go there, he told me that if I went there and believed that God would take care of me, the money would rain down from heaven. So I went but the money did not rain down from heaven. I had a lot of problems that year and the school contacted my parents and told them that I could finish out the year but only if I commuted. The school did not want to be liable for me if I was living in the dorms.

That summer after leaving college, I was devastated because the pastor who had told me to go to that school had run off with his secretary. I began to drink heavily and whenever I drank, I drank like an alcoholic. It was at this point that I became suicidal again. I also became very promiscuous. I was promiscuous with security guards, police officers, the UPS delivery man, the Pepsi man, the Sprite man, and the snack machine man. I had a thing for men in uniforms—any uniform. I was also drinking all the time. It was at this point that the psychiatrist I had been seeing diagnosed me with Bipolar Disorder, along with Borderline Personality Disorder, and put me on Lithium.

The BPD caused me to be on an emotional roller coaster. I would not call them mood swings; they were different than that. It was like an emotional rush but it was not well defined. With BPD, the emotion could be anger, excitement, confusion, sadness, or several of these might occur together. I had trouble identifying what I was feeling. But I can sit down with my crayons and a piece of paper and color my feelings. I can just reach for my crayons and know what color I am feeling. When I color, it covers the whole page and leaves no white. I don't feel white very often. White would be like a fish out of water. It isn't me. When I look at what I've colored, I can then label the emotions I am feeling. With the Bipolar Disorder, my mood swings were severe and extreme. The emotions were pure. With bipolar, I had two moods. It was either the hell pit of depression or ecstatic mania. I have trouble describing it but these emotions are cleaner. It's not that they are less troublesome, they are simply less confused emotions that are intense.

After being diagnosed as Bipolar along with BPD, I started to have real trouble with boundaries. I also became sexually dysfunctional. I was going to AA meetings and being promiscuous with all of the AA members. One of these guys told me he was going to take me to town and buy me a pretty ring. I said okay. He took me to a jewelry store, handed me a ring, and asked me if I liked it. I said I did and he said we would get married. I didn't say no, I could not say no because I could not establish boundaries. So I married this guy 17 years older than me who I did not know. During the marriage, I was self-medicating my emotional turmoil by drinking. I was also diagnosed with posttraumatic stress disorder.

All through the marriage, I was seeing a psychiatrist. Eventually he said that I was falling in love with him and that he could not treat me anymore. He referred me to a psychologist. I was treated by him for six years and got no improvement. At times, I loved this psychologist, and then I hated him. I had these strong feelings for him but I got no improvement. Around this time, I went home from an AA meeting and my husband was drunk. That wasn't unusual, he was always drunk when I came home from AA meetings and usually, I would just pick the bottle up and get drunk too. This time he was out of beer and told me to get him some and he came at me and started strangling me. I told him I would get him his beer. I did get him his beer and the next day, I left him.

Right about this same time, my insurance money ran out and the psychologist suddenly decided that I was better. So, I had just left my husband and needed this psychologist but he was saying I was better because I could not pay him. I did think I could get a handle on the drinking. I thought that once I left my husband, I could stay sober. I was drunk in three days. I started isolating in my apartment, I wasn't bathing or taking care of myself and eventually entered alcohol rehabilitation.

At rehab, I met a guy and we would take walks around the grounds. One day while we were walking, I asked him if he would burn me. I thought that the burning would relieve my emotional turmoil. This guy taught me that I could burn myself and it would release the physical tension. When having the crazies,

I could sit very calmly and burn myself. Some people think Borderlines self-mutilate to get attention. It isn't true. Self-mutilation is a release, not attention seeking. The pain was wonderful because it relieved the turmoil. I had finally found something better than alcohol.

Someone recommended a certain pastor to me and I talked to him. He invited me to his church and told me that I could call him anytime and he would help me. I didn't have a psychologist anymore so I accepted. But I wanted to test him. I got really good at testing people. "Will he come running like he says he will?" I was thinking. So I made a noose and called him at two in the morning and told him that I was going to kill myself. And he did come running. I tested him a few more times and he always came running, just like he said he would. He worked with me and taught the Bible to me and I started to get better. We started going fishing and eventually it turned into a sexual thing. He asked me to go to Tennessee so I sold my car for $500.00 and went with him. After we got there, he abandoned me and went back to his wife.

I was sent to the state hospital, and a 90-day commitment turned into nine months because I was dead set on killing myself. I had this obsession with dying. My diagnosis was changed from Bipolar to Schizoaffective Disorder. It is overwhelming to think that I have a mood disorder, a personality disorder, and I am an alcoholic. I am on 1200 mg of Lithium, 40 mg of Paxil, and 3 mg of Risperidol. I get depressed and suicidal without the Paxil. Without the Paxil, I isolate, sleep a lot, write morbid poems, and think morbid thoughts. I start to think that everyone is dying. I think things like I should die in the woods so my body can feed the animals and I will live on that way.

When I am manic, I have a false sense of happiness. But when I'm on the medication that keeps me from being manic (Lithium), I miss the good manic qualities like being creative. I remember seeing a fake fish swimming in a fish bowl in a psychiatrist's office. It was a toy fish that just swam back and forth. I felt like that fish. My life was like that fish in the bowl—constrained. But instead of a fishbowl, my life is constrained by mental illness. Mentally ill people are people with dreams and goals and they have struggled. I think they are heroes. I think I am a hero.

This is where my relationship with Carl comes in. When I met Carl, I had had so many dysfunctional relationships with functional people that I thought, "Why not? It can't be any worse than any of those relationships." Hell, this is the most functional relationship I've ever had. Carl and I give each other permission to say NO. I used to be a "yes" woman in relationships and that would become overwhelming. Carl and I always do "feeling checks," like, "Are you okay?" or "Do you need some space?" When he says "no" when I ask him to do something, I am happy and so relieved because he is being honest with me. Carl and I are learning to notice things and then let them go.

Carl and I want to help. We want to make a difference. I have a problem with the Borderline diagnosis because everything I do is defined through that label.

I heard people at the hospital ask, "What's her diagnosis?" When someone told them, "Borderline," they went, "Oh no!" I like having a label for the disorder so I know what it is. But I don't want people to see me as a label. We are getting to the point that we are proud of who we are. We see ourselves as separate from the illness and that is important for others to understand. We are people first, and we have a disorder second.

Should a Biologist Comment on BPD?

Interest in considering a biological basis for personality disorders, including BPD, did not begin to develop until the 1980s. In the decades since then, the numbers of biological studies that focus on BPD has increased as scientists have learned more about other brain-based disorders that are called "mental illnesses."

For instance, in a 1991 paper, Winchel and Stanley discussed the possibility of attributing the practice of self-mutilation by persons who are vulnerable for various reasons to the release of a number of biochemical agents, including endorphins. Endorphins are natural opiate-like substances produced by the brain and released in response to injury. Cutting or burning oneself would stimulate a release of these chemicals that might bring some relief of other symptoms associated with conditions and disorders such as BPD.

As we have learned more about neurotransmitters, the behavioral symptoms of persons with BPD point to the possibilities of neurotransmitter systems gone awry (Lieb, Zanarini, Schmahl, Linehan, & Bohus, 2004; Silk, 2000; Winchel & Stanley, 1991). Persons who have a diagnosis of BPD frequently have symptoms that indicate cognitive difficulties. Such a situation might implicate dopamine systems. Impulsivity and aggression can be symptoms that persons with BPD experience. Such symptoms are often associated with serotonin regulation problems. Mood instability is frequently exhibited and may be related to difficulties with acetylcholine levels, and super-sensitivity to the environment could be associated with ineffective norepinephrine regulation.

It is of considerable interest to biologists that recent metabolic scanning studies indicate possible brain related differences between persons with BPD and persons serving as matched controls (NC). Of special interest is a 2003 paper by Donegan and colleagues. These researchers cited articles by others who had used various technologies and patients who responded to several symptoms of BPD for their studies. Based on those results, Donegan and his colleagues designed their study, in which they reported that female and matched control subjects with BPD viewed pictures of a subject exhibiting a range of facial expressions from neutral through happy, sad, and fearful. Functional magnetic resonance imaging (fMRI) was used to capture possible differences in brain activity between the two groups. Among other results reported in the paper was that planned comparisons of the BPD and NC groups indicated that BPD patients showed significantly greater levels of left amygdala activation to three of the four images in BPD patients over the NC group. It was only the happy face that showed no significantly different response. The authors proposed that because of their careful design and their ability to identify such precise outcomes, their study provided a sound foundation for further research.

As one final point that emphasizes the importance of considering the biological aspects of these disorders, our attention is drawn to recent work on gender differences in the occurrence of this disorder (e.g., Nowinski, 2014; Sansone & Sansone, 2011). For example, Nowinski (2014) suggests previous views about gender differences in the prevalence of BPD (women significantly outnumber men in terms of diagnosis) may have much more to do with the expression of BPD than the occurrence itself. In other words, the expression of BPD might "look" quite different in men and women and hence be more likely to be diagnosed in women and less likely in men. Men who have BPD, for example, are often more aggressive, controlling, demanding, and open to the use of alcohol and illegal drugs than women with BPD. For these reasons, they are more likely to be jailed and seen as persons with addictions rather than individuals with BPD. From the biologist's perspective, however, this does not change how we understand the underlying etiology of the disorder. The biological underpinnings of BPD are very likely to be the same in women and men, whereas the expression of that biology may differ and result in differential diagnosis.

Certainly with time and more research, there will be major advances in understanding this disorder and developing more effective treatment for those who suffer.

8

THE CASE OF MARGARET H

Obsessive-Compulsive Disorder

Introduction

"Damn it, Margaret!" Bill screamed. "We need to leave, now! If you make us late for this wedding, we're going to have one helluva big fight." Margaret seemed unaware of what Bill was saying. As he frantically paced by the door, she was completely focused on emptying trash containers, locking doors and windows, checking that all household appliances were off and secure, and making sure to wash her hands between each task. This had become a common pattern. Bill had been with Margaret long enough to know that if he rushed her out of the house before she had her "rituals" done, she would get so distraught that he would have to turn the car around and drive her back home. Still, it was incredibly frustrating. When Margaret was finally finished with her predeparture rituals, Bill was relieved. He still worried they would not be on time to his sister's wedding, in which he was supposed to assist, but at least now they could get on the road.

Unfortunately, because of road construction and several awful traffic tie-ups, they arrived very late, missing the actual wedding ceremony entirely. After posing with others for some pictures, Bill exploded in anger at Margaret, precipitating a major shouting match that people who were still at the church overheard. In frustration, they skipped the wedding reception, canceled their hotel room for that night, and immediately returned home. On the tense drive back, Bill insisted that he and Margaret make an appointment to see Dr. Jordan, a clinical psychologist their family physician had recommended.

A few days later, Margaret sat reluctantly in front of Dr. Jordan, who began by interviewing Margaret and Bill together. Margaret was reluctant to say very much in reviewing the events leading up to the argument at the church. Dr. Jordan did learn they were delayed in leaving home by Margaret's need to complete a number of time-consuming tasks. Even though the wedding was in a city only 2 hours away, and they planned to return the next day, Margaret had written out a long list of household jobs that had to be completed before she would be comfortable leaving home. Some of these tasks, such as vacuuming the entire downstairs part of the house and laundering all the bed sheets and bath towels they had used that day, seemed unimportant to Bill. Margaret fell behind in her preparations to leave because of interruptions and her desire to complete all the tasks according to her preferences. She admitted, "I knew it was getting late but I couldn't leave until I was ready. There are things I simply have to do before I leave town overnight. It wasn't my fault there was a terrible traffic jam on the way out of town." Turning very defensive, she added, "The next time we have to leave town, I just won't go."

The Diagnostic Interview

Dr. Jordan asked questions about Margaret's motivation to perform these household cleaning rituals to make sure these behaviors were not simply a dutiful response on Margaret's part to some culturally prescribed rituals regarding food preparation or cleanliness. Satisfied that they were not, Dr. Jordan asked how much time these activities required and what Margaret was thinking before, during, and after performing the rituals. Dr. Jordan also asked Margaret whether she had ever had any unusual thoughts, such as beliefs that she has special powers or is subject to external influences that control her behavior, and whether Margaret had heard voices or had visions other people claimed not to see.

As the interview progressed, it became clearer that one of Margaret's primary symptoms was intense anxiety about germs and contamination. The anxiety led to a number of avoidance rituals, chief among which was washing her hands. Margaret's handwashing was "ritualistic" in the sense that a carefully prescribed series of procedures must be followed before it was "safe" to return to what she was doing previously. Furthermore, Margaret disliked being interrupted by the telephone or by a request from one of her children while in the midst of one of these rituals.

Although Margaret was clearly upset about the focus on handwashing and the way she organized the family's out-of-town trips, and so was reluctant to give further details about her symptoms, Bill was not. From him, Dr. Jordan learned that Margaret's handwashing ritual was virtually mandatory after almost any activity where she touched something—her car, a doorknob, the vacuum cleaner, and, of course, any food or laundry item; the ritual itself involved copious amounts of disinfectant soap, vigorous rubbing, and careful drying of her hands and arms using many disposable paper towels. Although each handwashing episode might take only one or two minutes, the frequency of episodes was such that Margaret typically spent more than an hour a day in front of the sink washing her hands.

Dr. Jordan also discovered that numbers were quite important to Margaret. If she touched something that she felt was particularly dirty, she might need to wash her hands with a circular motion a certain number of times. The dirtier the object, the more times she "needed" to complete the circular washing motion. Bill recounts one particular time when Margaret picked up what she thought was a discarded paper towel. When she picked it up and discovered that it was a used tissue, she felt compelled to wash her hands and would not stop until she had counted 50 circular washing motions.

Other Rituals and Worries

Another very time-consuming part of every day was taken up by Margaret's laundering of clothes, towels, and other household items, which followed a careful and rigid protocol. First, all items needed to be thoroughly shaken outdoors behind the house, to rid them of crumbs, lint, hair, and other germ-carrying elements. All items were then presoaked in a tub with strong, bleach-containing detergent dissolved in hot or warm water, and only after soaking for an hour or more were small groups of similar items put in a full-cycle wash and rinse. Each family member's clothing or linen was washed separately from those of other family members. If an item fell on the floor or brushed against the door or the toilet, it had to be put through the entire procedure again, beginning with vigorous shaking outdoors. After they were washed, all laundry items must be machine-dried, since Margaret believed that hanging items outdoors on a clothesline would expose them to airborne contaminants that would require that they be laundered all over again. In following these procedures, it could take Margaret an entire morning to do two small loads of laundry.

Bill described several other difficulties that suggest Margaret suffered from excessive anxiety. During the day while their children were at school, she often worried for no reason about their safety. When Bill left town on business, Margaret worried that he might have an accident or even be killed. At times, it seemed to Bill that Margaret was a hypochondriac. For example, there were occasions where Margaret acted as though ordinary complaints like temporary abdominal pains were potentially serious problems like a heart attack or cancer. Finally, when she was driving, Margaret was sometimes seized with a concern that she has carelessly hurt someone—a pedestrian or bicyclist—or has run over something that may have damaged the underside of her car. When parking her car, she feels it must be perfectly aligned within the space and as close to the curb as possible. This usually required her to take extra time repeatedly backing in and out of the space. After she exited the car Margaret could not walk away without further examination of her car's condition and her parking job. Sometimes Margaret's tight parking resulted in minor problems like scraping tires on the curb, which caused Margaret to become very upset.

The Initial Diagnosis

Dr. Jordan diagnosed Margaret as having obsessive-compulsive disorder (OCD). Several criteria must be satisfied to diagnose OCD using the DSM-5. The first is the presence of *obsessions* (unwelcome ideas that intrude into consciousness and are recognized by the individual as inappropriate) or *compulsions* (ritual behaviors that Margaret feels driven to perform in order to neutralize the obsessions), or both. For Margaret, the obsessions most often concern germs and contamination or harm that could befall loved ones. Her compulsions revolve around cleaning and counting rituals that she performs in an effort to prevent harm to herself or others. By performing the rituals (and usually, performing each a certain number of times), Margaret feels that she can "fend off" the harm that would befall her or a loved one if the ritual were not performed or performed incorrectly.

To qualify for a primary diagnosis of OCD, the obsessions or compulsions must be recurrent, disruptive, and a source of distress to the individual. For example, they may be time-consuming to the point of taking up to an hour a day or longer. Other requirements are that the individual has at some point recognized that the thoughts and rituals are excessive, and that the disturbances are not attributable to the effects of a substance (medication or abusable drug) or to a general medical condition. In diagnosing OCD, the clinician also indicates whether there is poor insight or not. At the time of her interview with Dr. Jordan, Margaret recognized that her obsessive-compulsive thoughts and behaviors were inappropriate and self-defeating, and Dr. Jordan concluded that she did not have poor insight or any delusional beliefs.

During a second intake interview Dr. Jordan conducted with Margaret alone, Margaret complains of fatigue, irritability, difficulty in concentrating, and occasional feelings of worthlessness. As a routine part of the intake procedures, Dr. Jordan asked questions designed to evaluate other disorders that may occur along with OCD, such as depression, panic disorder, and substance abuse. She asked Margaret to have her family physician conduct a physical exam to help evaluate the possibility that Margaret's symptoms are related to a general medical condition (e.g., thyroid dysfunction) or to a medication she might be taking.

A CRITICAL THINKING AND QUESTIONING PAUSE

At one time or another, nearly all of us have had persistent, intrusive thoughts (such as being unable to get an annoying musical tune out of our minds), or perhaps engaged in excessive checking of locks or keys or important papers. What makes Margaret's symptoms different enough to warrant a psychiatric diagnosis? Try to delineate at least three reasons from the information already provided about the nature of Margaret's symptoms.

It is important to note that while Margaret's intrusive thoughts bear some relationship to reality (that is, germs can contaminate clothing, and accidents can befall family members), they entailed scenarios that were so improbable that the amount of time and energy Margaret devoted to worrying about them was excessive. Neither Margaret nor anyone else in her family has ever acquired an infection from having unclean hands or from inadequate laundering on her part. Furthermore, Margaret does not drive carelessly and has never even come close to hitting a pedestrian. Thus, although the concerns Margaret had were not delusional in the sense of completely departing from reality, they were clearly excessive and inappropriate.

Also significant is that her rituals did not bring Margaret any pleasure, but only temporary relief from her obsessions and the anxiety that they triggered. At times in her adult life she has recognized the excessively time-consuming nature of her rituals, but in the past whenever she resisted performing them, her anxiety level rose significantly. This anxiety would continue to rise to the point that Margaret felt absolutely compelled to engage in the rituals. Nothing would relieve the anxiety until the rituals were performed. When Margaret would finally give in and undertake one of her counting rituals or busy herself with cleaning, the relief from anxiety would quickly follow. The more intense the anxiety, of course, the more times each ritual would need to be performed.

With obsessions, it is important to note that the content is not only inappropriate in the view of others, but is also recognized as such by the OCD sufferer herself. In other words, Margaret was very bothered by these thoughts and the necessity of "undoing" them through her various rituals, wished they did not exist, and tried to resist them. It was also clear in Margaret's mind that she herself was the source of the thoughts and impulses, making this experience different than that of a person with schizophrenia who may be convinced that external voices are implanting thoughts or demanding the compulsive responses. Margaret's reality testing was intact, her speech was coherent, and she did not experience hallucinations or delusions.

Other Possible Diagnoses?

Although she showed indications of mild depression (e.g., fatigue, irritability, obsessive worrying, difficulty concentrating, occasional sleep disturbances, and feelings of worthlessness), Margaret's symptoms were not severe enough for a diagnosis of major depression. In addition, these symptoms often persisted only briefly (i.e., for a few minutes at a time) rather than continuously for 2 weeks or more (as required by the DSM-5 for a diagnosis of major depression). Margaret's symptoms were not persistent enough (that is, present more days than not for at least 2 years) to diagnose dysthymia. Similarly, her intermittent hypochondria (excessive worrying over minor health complaints) seems secondary to the anxiety associated with her obsessions and compulsions.

What about another anxiety disorder other than OCD? For example, was Margaret's clearly irrational fear and avoidance of unseen germs sufficient for a diagnosis of a specific phobia? By themselves, her carefully scripted avoidance behaviors resembled phobic responses, but in Margaret's case, her phobic avoidance was clearly a secondary reaction to strong, disruptive obsessions and compulsions rather than a distinct phobia.

Finally, there is also an obsessive-compulsive personality disorder that includes rigid, stereotypic behavior patterns, such as elaborate cleaning routines. However, most of the time, individuals with this condition are not so overtly anxious as Margaret and do not see their rigid preferences and rituals as "alien" or repugnant. For these individuals, their compulsiveness is better understood as a pervasive lifestyle pattern emphasizing orderliness, inflexibility, control, and placing work responsibilities above pleasure.

One other point is worth noting: There may be a public perception, fed to some extent by media influences, that gambling, sexual activities, and drug use can be "compulsive" in nature. Excesses in these areas are not the same as OCD, since in the former conditions, the individual is driven towards performing the behaviors for their pleasurable consequences and experiences anticipatory excitement beforehand (instead of, as in OCD, discomfort and resistance to performing the response). Also, when it comes to gambling, sex, or substance abuse, any anxiety present is most likely related to the real risks that may be involved (losing the money gambled, feeling guilty about a sexual indiscretion, and so on).

Margaret's History

As part of some history-taking during the second intake session, Dr. Jordan learned that Margaret's parents did not get along while she was growing up, and eventually they divorced. Margaret was anxious during her parents' many arguments in her presence, and later, as their marriage fell apart, Margaret worried about being abandoned by one or both parents. To cope with these distractions and worries, she developed counting rituals. These began normally enough, as when she concentrated hard on counting the seconds between a flash of lightning and the subsequent clap of thunder during storms.

As the fighting of her parents intensified, so did Margaret's fears that she would be abandoned. The more her anxiety level rose, the more intensely she relied on her rituals. For example, if her parents were having a loud argument, Margaret might intensely count the flowers in the wallpaper pattern, trying to block out the sound of her parents' argument with the loudness of her own counting. If she lost count or missed a flower as she scanned the wall and counted from right to left, she would become increasingly anxious and feel compelled to begin the counting ritual over.

When her parents finished arguing, Margaret would feel "dirty" and "ashamed." She somehow felt that the arguments were her fault and this compelled her to scrub herself to "wash away" the shame. Similar to the counting rituals, her compulsion to clean was intensified by the level of hostility displayed by her parents when arguing. If the argument consisted primarily of her father yelling, for example, Margaret felt less need for cleansing than if both parents were yelling at each other. Still, however, Margaret's anxiety and resulting compulsive rituals were evident primarily when her parents were fighting. In most other situations and around most other people, Margaret was relatively anxiety free.

At the time she met Bill, Margaret's most serious symptoms had not yet developed. In fact, Bill appreciated some of Margaret's fussiness about keeping things clean and orderly, since it meant there was less need for him to attend to those matters. Margaret's most disruptive symptoms became evident to Bill when she was in her late 20s. Their first child, Steven, had serious respiratory problems as an infant and was hospitalized several times. His breathing problems alarmed Margaret greatly, and each time Steven returned home from the hospital, Margaret sat in his room for the first two or three nights listening to him breathe and worrying about him. On one of these occasions, as she was thinking how fragile and vulnerable Steven was, Margaret was seized by the thought that it would be easy to suffocate him with a pillow in only a minute or two. She was horrified by herself, seeing little or no difference between having the thought she could suffocate Steven and actually committing such an act. To her dismay, such thoughts about harming Steven persisted long after that. Margaret found that once she had such thoughts, the most effective way to push them out of her mind was to focus intently on cleaning or some similar household chore.

Although Steven's breathing problems improved as he grew older, Margaret continued to be very worried about him and became rather overprotective. In particular, she was concerned that dirt and other contaminants in the home environment were responsible for his breathing difficulties and the frequent infections he came down with. Failing to keep his room spotlessly clean would mean that she was the cause of his illness. By the time he entered school, the doctors were optimistic that Steven's susceptibility to ear and respiratory infections would eventually disappear. Margaret had another child by this time and was determined that this child, Brian, would be exposed to the absolute minimum amount of dirt or germs. She developed very elaborate cleaning rituals to guard against germs and contamination, and also became quite anxious if she spotted any bugs such as ants or spiders in the house. To further minimize problems related to germs or dirt, Margaret forbade her children any pets other than goldfish, and insisted that the goldfish bowl be emptied and scrubbed with a strong household cleanser every other day.

These elaborate rituals and precautions did not eliminate Margaret's worries, and as time passed, the only option she saw was to increase and intensify her compulsive behaviors. Margaret's anxiety and the resulting compulsive rituals became worse when she was under stress, as when her husband was out of town for several days on business, or when a problem developed in the house such as a broken pipe or appliance.

Until her children were born, Margaret worked outside the home. By the time they were in school and she was in a position to return to work, her obsessions and compulsions had become serious enough to hamper her mental efficiency and productivity. She often had difficulty concentrating, and if interrupted, could not easily return to the task at hand. It was also much easier for Margaret to work by herself (be self-employed), since she could organize the work the way she wanted and would not have to explain if she became distracted or preoccupied and had to stop. Yet in her housework and other activities, many projects were only partially finished. Spending the vast majority of her time at home had the added advantage that Margaret could avoid contact with foreign objects (doorknobs at public restrooms, money that strangers hand her, and so on).

During the day, Margaret often had the television on, and she came to be strongly affected by shows that purport to document the threats posed by environmental toxins, viruses, and other illness-producing germs. From one of these shows, Margaret also learned that in rare instances, an electrical storm can damage household appliances. Because storms can begin quickly or happen when no one is home, Margaret insisted that all electrical appliances be unplugged when not in use. Although, in and of itself, this demand is not that unusual, the intense anxiety that accompanied Margaret's concern about unplugging the appliances is beyond normal.

Margaret needed to be in control of details in her immediate surroundings. She spent a significant amount of time checking things. She also requested (and eventually might demand) assurances from her family members that they have followed the steps she prescribed, such as washing their hands as soon as they enter the house from outside, regardless of what they have been doing. Before and after meals, and at other regular intervals (e.g., when they left for school or returned from a friend's house), Margaret scrutinized her children for dirt, stains, or lint on their clothing—and if she found anything, there was consternation and immediately a cleaning operation needed to commence. The boys resented these incidents because they interrupted their activities and sometimes made them late. Margaret herself had to work very hard to complete all preparations to go out or to receive visitors, with one consequence being that if at all possible, she avoided morning appointments. When her husband or children attempted to hurry Margaret along, she found such intrusions distracting enough that they sometimes interrupted her to the point where she becomes frustrated and angry.

Margaret's relationship with Bill came to lack spontaneity and warmth. She rarely felt relaxed enough and free of worries to the point where she could enjoy herself. She found entertaining guests very taxing because of the many exacting preparations required. She became easily upset if the guests were close friends or family members who commented innocently on her compulsive antics while they were there. In recent years, entertaining became very infrequent. Even her children were unable to have friends over to spend the night. In response to complaints from her family about this, Margaret said that she would like to move out of the city to a brand-new house, which she believed would be easier to keep clean than her present house.

Trips out of town were very stressful for Margaret because she feared exposing herself and her family to hotels and eating establishments of uncertain cleanliness. The preparations required for family trips meant that either the time of departure was midday or later, or Margaret needed to work most of the preceding night to get everything ready. As a result, she did not enjoy traveling. The one exception was the annual summer vacation the family took to a cottage at the seashore, because the trip was arranged well in advance and the 3 weeks spent there give Margaret enough time to clean everything in the cottage when they arrive and still enjoy most of the remaining time.

Margaret initially found that following her rituals was reassuring and provided temporary relief from anxiety, but—given the number of them and their elaborateness—they became burdensome and were taking a toll. Margaret felt weighted down by the demands of these rituals and was less and less able to complete routine tasks (like laundry and food preparation) in a timely manner. She felt tired much of the time and became irritated when her husband or children made unexpected requests or complained that Margaret was not ready or did not complete an errand or chore on time.

A CRITICAL THINKING AND QUESTIONING PAUSE

Before discussing Dr. Jordan's recommendations for treatment, consider what you might recommend. What are the major challenges with which Margaret must cope? What are the main reasons for the elaborate rituals that Margaret feels compelled to follow? If you want the rituals to become less frequent, what other coping strategies would you recommend to Margaret? These are just a few of the questions that Dr. Jordan must confront as she begins to develop a treatment plan for Margaret.

Treatment Considerations

Dr. Jordan was a psychologist and limited her direct treatment services to psychotherapy, so she recommended that Margaret consult with her family physician about the possibility of trying an antianxiety medication. As in the treatment of depression, the newer SSRI medications have become more common as treatments for OCD. They are especially worth trying if the individual with OCD also experiences dysphoric (mildly depressed) moods or does not respond to other treatments (such as those described in this section). Compared with older antidepressants, SSRIs are helpful for many persons with OCD and have fewer risks and side effects.

Dr. Jordan also took time to describe several psychological interventions that people with OCD have found helpful. Because it can be very difficult to gain control over obsessions and compulsions, Dr. Jordan and Margaret discussed her motivation for working hard to make significant changes in her compulsive behaviors. They also discussed alternative arrangements for therapy (length, cost, format, the frequency of sessions, whether Margaret's husband would participate, and so on).

In the psychodynamic perspective, the obsessive thoughts that people like Margaret experience are associated with a much greater amount of anxiety than is warranted by any environmental or situational conditions that are present. The anxiety is seen as internally generated and irrational rather than connected in any causal way to specific external conditions. Margaret has sufficiently good reality testing and awareness of her symptoms that she might benefit from an approach designed to improve her understanding of what causes the obsessions.

The psychodynamic perspective assumes that many people have ambivalent feelings toward important others in their lives, and that reminders of this ambivalence can trigger anxiety. Normally, however, most people have sufficient control over such thoughts that they do not become intrusive. In addition, the psychodynamic perspective assumes that these strong cognitive controls (referred to in psychodynamic terms as having a "strong ego") are lacking in persons who are vulnerable to OCD (in other words, people with OCD have "weak egos"). In Margaret's case, her thoughts of hurting Steven when he was small and vulnerable (and her overprotectiveness of him after that), and more recently her obsessions with dirt and compulsive cleaning, would be explained as resulting from ambivalent feelings.

For Margaret, cleaning expresses a defense mechanism called *reaction formation* in that Margaret feels unworthy and angry at herself for being neglected by her parents and believes she can compensate for this emotionally charged problem by being "clean." Psychodynamic Therapy would focus on Margaret's childhood relationships with her parents, including her perceptions of their punitiveness, demandingness, and inflexibility, and also her fears that they would abandon her.

Dr. Jordan was concerned that psychodynamic psychotherapy would take too long to be of help to Margaret, and that—given the daily stresses the family faces—Margaret and Bill would become impatient at what may be very slow progress at best. With Margaret's consent, Dr. Jordan opted to use Behavior Therapy, an approach that is more direct and less time-consuming. This approach also enabled Bill to participate actively in the treatment.

Dr. Jordan explained to Margaret that because she has been feeling anxious about germs and contamination for at least several years, and has strong compulsive habits built up in response to the thoughts and fears, it would take effort on her part and considerable practice to modify those habits. However, Dr. Jordan encouraged Margaret to be optimistic about improving her ability to manage these problems eventually.

The Behavior Therapy program Dr. Jordan prescribed had several components. The first was relaxation training. Because the pattern of compulsive rituals was developed by Margaret in an attempt to cope with the anxiety resulting from her fear of germs and contamination, she needs to be taught more effective methods for coping with that anxiety. Relaxation techniques such as controlled breathing could aid Margaret in dealing with situations more realistically. If Margaret could do a more effective job in "fending off" the anxiety she feels about germs and contamination, the doctor believed, she would have less "need" to engage in her compulsive rituals.

Margaret also kept a journal of her obsessive episodes and compulsive impulses, and noted intervals of time when she was relatively free of these symptoms (which tended to occur when Margaret was busy doing things that she enjoyed or that demanded all of her attention). For each episode, Margaret described in writing the time and place of the episode, what she was doing, the thoughts she had, and her responses to the thoughts—whether she was able to resist the compulsion or, if not, what she ended up doing. The purpose of the journal was to help Dr. Jordan confirm what were the higher- and lower-risk times and places for Margaret's symptoms, and establish a baseline frequency and intensity of symptoms against which progress might later be measured. This baseline could also be used to establish treatment goals. If, for example, Margaret was suffering nine episodes a day and did not resist the compulsive rituals any of those times, a first treatment goal might be to resist the compulsive ritual at least once each day.

The primary component of Behavior Therapy for OCD is in vivo (direct) exposure and response prevention. Exposure can be in the form of "flooding"—direct or imagined exposure to anxiety-provoking stimuli for a significant length of time. Flooding makes the client very anxious, but for a nonpsychotic individual in a safe setting like the therapist's office, this experience carries little or no risk. Instead, the client learns that intense anxiety is something he or she can tolerate. If the individual knows that intense anxiety can be tolerated, he or she might also be convinced that there is less "need" to engage in the compulsive rituals to fend off such anxiety. The purpose of flooding, then, is to counter the client's "fear of fear."

Dr. Jordan opted for in vivo exposure and modeled for Margaret direct contact with contaminants in a graded series of steps. In other words, Margaret was exposed to contact with objects that were increasingly more contaminated. "In vivo exposure" means exposure to the actual feared object rather than asking the client to imagine such exposure. For contamination obsessions, in vivo exposure is not difficult to arrange and may have more lasting effects than procedures that use imagination only. For an example, Margaret might first be required to pick up a clean tissue off the floor and made to throw it in the trash, then be required to wait 2 minutes before she could wash her hands. Margaret would be reminded to use her relaxation training if she started to experience anxiety about the required action. As a second step, Margaret might be required to touch the office doorknob and wait 3 minutes before washing her hands. Again, she would be reminded to utilize her relaxation training. A third step might involve picking up a discarded soft drink cup from the ground and putting it in the trash. For each successive step, the actual level of germs and contamination will be higher and Margaret will be required to wait longer time intervals before washing her hands. Eventually, Margaret will be required to engage in exposures without engaging in a subsequent cleaning ritual of any kind.

Margaret also agreed to observe "laundry-free" holidays. To make this work, she and her family wore their clothes more often in between launderings. Margaret continued to keep her journal, noting successes and times she gave in to the compulsive rituals. "Homework" between her once-per-week therapy sessions included gradual, stepwise reduction in handwashing frequency and number of paper towels used, and in general, the promotion of Margaret's self-management of risky situations. Margaret was asked to keep a journal. One goal of the journal was to assist her in documenting situations that placed her at risk in that they were most likely to cause her to experience obsessive thoughts. Such situations were also ones in which she was least likely to be able to resist engaging in a compulsive ritual. She was also encouraged to delegate more and more housework to other family members. Social skills (such as delegating tasks) were important to focus on, so that external stresses in Margaret's life did not build up without being dealt with.

Some sessions included Margaret's husband, Bill, so he could understand the procedures and what Margaret was going through. He would also be better able to help Margaret with homework assignments she carried out between sessions. These homework assignments included an increase in activities involving others and taking place outside the home. You will recall that Margaret was staying home more and more because eating at restaurants and going to other external places exposed her to a wide array of contaminating situations and objects.

Group therapy or an ongoing support group, or both of these combined, might have been helpful for Margaret, but she was reticent to disclose her problems to strangers. Dr. Jordan simply left the door open for a possible referral when and if Margaret declared an interest in a group experience. Although group sessions are certainly not for every client, they can be a very effective method for illustrating to the client that there are others dealing with the same issues. Others in the group who are being successful are also good role models for those just beginning treatment or having lower degrees of success. To note Margaret's progress in treatment, we will soon turn our attention to a current interview with her husband Bill. Before moving on to this interview, however, let us hear about OCD from a biologist's vantage point.

A Biological Perspective on OCD

Among the changes that we observe in the DSM-5 from previous *Diagnostic and Statistical Manuals* is that OCD has been moved from the category of Anxiety Disorders to a category titled "Obsessive Compulsive and Related Disorders."

OCD and the other disorders in this classification have a common symptom in that persons with these diagnoses all exhibit certain repetitive behaviors; however, those behaviors and their response to treatment may vary widely.

Although diagnoses for such brain-based disorders as OCD are based on symptoms of behavior, cognitive psychologists and biologists attribute these symptoms to brain structural and functional characteristics. In fact, researchers are able to use imaging techniques to demonstrate brain differences in persons who are diagnosed as having OCD from those who are not. Unfortunately, current imaging technology is not yet precise enough to be used as a clinical diagnostic tool.

Persons with OCD have been shown to use both bilateral inferior striatal activation and medial temporal lobe activation in responding to tasks (Shepherd, 2013). When the stimulus called for persons with OCD to recruit corticostriatal systems, they appeared to access regions of the brain normally associated with conscious rather than implicit information processing. Thus a biologist might consider Margaret's inability to be on time as a logical consequence of the possibility that it takes her longer to process information that would allow a person without the disorder to simply put himself or herself on "automatic pilot." If Margaret has to consciously process information and make conscious decisions that others would make implicitly (without much thought or effort), it will take her longer to make decisions. Margaret has to think about what she does and possibly rethink what she does to be sure she "got it right."

Another possibility to consider is that Margaret's inability to focus on the task at hand (such as completing those actions that will allow her to be on time rather than be late) is related to her inability to know that other distracting tasks are completed. There is a word for this lack: *yedasentience*. It is a word that refers to the subjective feeling of knowing something. A deficit of yedasentience has been proposed as a symptom of OCD. There is research evidence to support the notion that the symptoms of OCD can be achieved by blocking the signal that gives a person this feeling of having "enough" (e.g., Woody et al., 2005). Early imaging studies relied on PET, which involves injecting a radioactive material into the persons being tested. Because safety considerations exclude persons under the age of 18, researchers were unable to study children, who represent a large portion of the population with an OCD diagnosis. The increased availability of imaging techniques that are safer, especially for children, has made it possible to assess the brain structures and functions that help us understand the correlation of symptoms of this disorder with the underlying biology. Newer imaging technology has led researchers to confirm greater involvement of such brain structures as the globus pallidus, the anterior cingulate cortex (ACC), and the intratelencephalic (IT) and pyramidal tract (PT) type neurons, as well as the balance among them (Szeszko et al., 2004).

A very recent case study examined behavioral activation (BA) as the treatment choice for a woman who suffered the symptoms of chronic comorbid OCD and Major Depressive Disorder. In Cognitive-Behavioral Therapy, the patient is guided or coached into focusing primarily on the cognitive components of his or her situation. BA, used in persons with depression and one or more comorbid diagnoses, focuses primarily on the "doing" aspects. Although the patient with OCD in the case study was aware of the mood disorder and the difficulties of managing the symptoms of OCD, she was guided to keep working on completing the task at hand. It is not a "quick cure," but after 21 months of treatment that included compulsive checking behaviors, the woman no longer had symptoms at the clinical level and the initial use of multiple medications for mood stabilization and anxiety was reduced to a single antidepressant (Arco, 2015).

An Interview With Margaret's Husband, Bill

Progress over the last few months has been slow but mostly successful. Margaret works very hard between sessions and generally follows the homework regimen that Dr. Jordan has prescribed. I am glad that I decided to attend some of the sessions with Margaret. Before going to these sessions and hearing how anxious Margaret has been over the last several years, I really did not understand how much she has suffered. It is a real eye-opener to hear your spouse talk about how your own idiosyncrasies, like my need to be everywhere we go early, cause anxiety for the spouse. Whenever the boys and I would make jokes about Margaret's "rituals," we were belittling the coping mechanisms she had developed to deal with the anxiety she was feeling when her obsessive fear of germs and contamination would pop up. I guess I just never realized how complicated her issues were.

I have tried to work with the boys, too, so they can understand what Margaret is dealing with. We have had monthly laundry-free holidays. These involve choosing a week during which no laundry will be done. The boys and I may wear the same pair of jeans twice or three times that week. In addition, when laundry is done after one of these weeks, either the boys or I will do it. Margaret is slowly getting used to wearing clothes that may not have been laundered following her elaborate cleaning rituals. I know she worries intensely for the first few days after one of us does the laundry. When none of us come down with some sort of infection, though, she seems to relax. Each month, I sense less anxiety from her under such circumstances.

Therapy sessions have been very difficult for Margaret but I can easily understand why. These sessions require her to confront the things that she fears with increasing levels. This has been difficult. Again, though, I am proud of her progress. Just the other day, Dr. Jordan had Margaret hold a soiled towel for 15 minutes during a session. The whole time that she was holding the towel, Dr. Jordan was discussing things with her and requiring her to answer. This forced Margaret to resist the urge to cleanse and the answering of questions allowed her to stay focused and not have to engage in a relaxation technique. When the session was over, Margaret was beaming. When she was allowed to wash her hands at the end of the session, she did so without any elaborate rituals. It was quite a step forward.

The only thing that really concerns me is the possibility of a setback. A lot of Margaret's obsessive thinking seems to stem from concerns she has that the boys or I will get sick if she does not sterilize everything. I am worried that on one of our laundry-free holidays, the boys or I will then do the laundry and, for whatever reason, one of us will get sick. I am sure that Margaret will blame the illness on the fact that the laundry was not done properly and all of her progress might be for nothing. Dr. Jordan assures me that such a setback can be avoided if Margaret can come to realistically assess where our illnesses come from and the role she actually plays in our health. It still worries me. Don't worry, though, I am not obsessing!

Before we started therapy with Margaret, I never really understood why engaging in the elaborate rituals helped her. In fact, they took up so much time and they were so complicated, they seemed to do more harm than good. I understand now that Margaret was creating her own methods for confronting and resolving the anxiety she was feeling and the obsessive thoughts that would accompany that anxiety. In that context, the rituals make some sense. The more intrusive the obsessive thoughts she was having, the more elaborate and intense the rituals would be. That is why she would sometimes engage in the rituals so many times. Repetition seemed to make her feel a little better. The more intense the anxiety and the obsessive thoughts, the higher the number of times she would repeat some aspect of a cleaning ritual. If one of the boys got sick, she might have to sterilize the towels five times before completing the laundry cycle, whereas usually, she might only sterilize them twice.

I don't want you to get the wrong impression about these rituals, though. Engaging in the rituals never made Margaret feel "good." They simply allowed her to cope with some of the anxiety. Margaret once described it like a painkiller turning a sharp, cutting pain into a dull, constant pain. Although the rituals did not eliminate the anxiety, they made it more tolerable for her. It sure has helped me to understand just how heroic she has been all these years. As a result, our own relationship is getting better again. You cannot put a price on that.

9

THE CASE OF JACOB T
Autism Spectrum Disorder

Introduction

"Get your clothes back on," the teacher demanded. It was the third time she had substituted for this second-grade class and it was the third time that Jacob had left the room without asking and returned wearing nothing but his underwear and socks. "Why me?" she asked no one in particular. Jacob did not respond to the teacher's request. Instead, he just stood in the center of the room with a blank expression on his face. The other children were laughing but Jacob did not seem to notice. Exasperated, the substitute teacher went to the principal's office to call the boy's mother.

Jacob T, age 7, was referred by his second-grade teacher to the school psychologist, Dr. Gray, for a variety of serious behavior problems. These problems have existed for as long as Jacob has been in school, and his current classroom teacher has concluded that Jacob's misbehavior, though infrequent, is intentional and requires professional attention and intervention. In her mind, his is a classic case of "oppositional" behavior, meaning that he is willfully disobedient and defiant of authority. The teacher suspects that at the very least, Jacob has attention deficit hyperactivity disorder (ADHD), if not the more serious problem of conduct disorder.

The teacher's written referral to the school psychologist noted a variety of problem behaviors in the school setting. For example, Jacob would sometimes leave the classroom abruptly, ignoring the teacher's reprimand to return to his seat. He was especially likely to do this when the regular teacher was replaced by a substitute. On four occasions while at school, Jacob has taken off his outer clothing, leaving him wearing only his underwear and socks. Once this happened with the regular teacher and three times with a substitute. Each time this happened, he ignored either teacher's admonishment to put his clothes back on.

Given the uproars of laughter from the other children in response to some of Jacob's actions, the teacher was convinced that Jacob did this to make her look foolish and to get attention from the other children. On numerous occasions (including the clothing removal episodes), it was necessary to take him to the infirmary until his mother could be summoned to calm Jacob down or bring a different set of clothes to school because Jacob refused to put the original clothes back on. With his mother present, Jacob put on the change of clothes and returned to the class without further incident. The fact that Jacob cooperated with the mother and put the new clothes on further reinforced in the mind of the teacher that the original episode was deliberate.

A CRITICAL THINKING AND QUESTIONING PAUSE

Think back to the critical thinking model we outlined earlier in this text. What error does the teacher appear to be making by assuming that Jacob's "problem" behaviors are directed toward her? The subtitle of this casebook also provides you with a solid hint. That's right! The teacher is looking only at the behavior and assuming that the behaviors are the problem. In fact, however, Jacob's behaviors are more likely to be symptoms of a more severe underlying problem. What critical piece of information does the teacher apparently not take into account when assuming that the clothing removal is designed to make her look foolish?

Reread the paragraph just before this pause. When are these episodes most likely to happen? Yes, when the teacher is a substitute. Perhaps the clothing removal is an expression by Jacob of his displeasure over the change in teachers. It comes as no surprise that Jacob would respond more positively to the efforts by his mother to get him to put his clothes back on than a teacher who is also a stranger. This displeasure with change can be an important part of Jacob's illness and can be an important thing to consider during treatment. We will, of course, revisit this "need for sameness" as we discuss the details of Jacob's case.

On most days, Jacob was diligent in working with materials at his seat, especially when they involved drawings or pictures. He was also attentive during school activities that involved music. At other times, something as simple as a ringing school bell or sudden public address announcement would upset Jacob greatly. He appeared to have a very short attention span during organized group activities like gym class. Most of the time when another child approached him, Jacob moved a good distance away. His gym teacher has given up trying to interest Jacob in the cooperative games that take place in that class.

In the school cafeteria, Jacob sat alone, did not interact with other children (or anyone else), and when finished eating, often simply got up and walked back to the classroom on his own, before lunch period is over. After trying to stop him several times to no avail, his teacher began permitting this since all Jacob did while the others remain at lunch was sit at his desk drawing or reading.

Jacob's disinterest in being with other people was particularly evident during a recent field trip to a farm. Leaving the classroom to board a bus that would take the students to the farm, Jacob broke off from the others and went instead to a different bus, which happened to be the one he normally rode to school. Jacob cried and resisted strenuously when he was taken by the hand and led firmly to the bus that was to be used for the field trip. Think back to the critical thinking pause just a few paragraphs ago. Could Jacob's reaction be another example of a resistance to change?

Once at the farm, the teacher was surprised by his reaction. On the basis of Jacob's thorough effort to learn and demonstrate accuracy in identifying different farm animals depicted in pictures, she expected him to enjoy watching and petting live animals. However, he refused to approach any animals during the visit and spent almost the entire time playing with the pump handle at a well. When it came time to leave, he again resisted getting on the bus and returning to school.

Jacob's problems at school finally came to a head when, with no warning, he deliberately broke a classroom window and immediately began arranging the shards of glass into a pattern, as though they were pieces of a jigsaw puzzle. This incident was the last straw for his teacher, and the next day her referral report was sitting on the school psychologist's desk.

The Diagnostic Interview

Jacob's mother came to school and accompanied him to Dr. Gray's office. When prompted by his mother, Jacob shook hands in a perfunctory manner, looking away and saying nothing in response to her greeting. Dr. Gray noted that, physically, there did not appear to be anything wrong with Jacob. He was of average weight and height for his chronological age. However, she also noticed that once seated, Jacob seemed oblivious to the presence of his mother and the psychologist a few feet away, and was content to draw numbers, letters of the alphabet, and simple geometric figures on a pad of paper. Dr. Gray began by describing what she knows of Jacob's difficulties from reading the teacher's written report.

After hearing the psychologist's summary of Jacob's behavior problems at school, Mrs. T expresses some surprise at the extent of his problems but acknowledges that Jacob, her youngest, has been by far the most challenging of her four children to parent. Although her pregnancy and birth with him were normal, and he experienced only the typical run of illnesses during infancy, she noted that from the beginning he was not "cuddly" as her first three children had been.

He almost never looked directly at her, and he squirmed vigorously when she held him close during feeding. When he became upset, Jacob rarely cried and did not respond to hugs when it seemed that he might need to be comforted. If anything, receiving hugs seemed to make him more upset; he would flail his arms about and scream until put back in his crib. Until she learned to play his favorite music at bath time, Jacob often resisted his mother's efforts to bathe him. Mealtimes were also a frequent problem because, for a long time, he insisted on drinking from the same plastic cup and refused fluids when they were offered in anything else (another example of a need for sameness and of resistance to change).

As a toddler, Jacob continued to ignore his mother's efforts to interact with him. He actively resisted sitting on his mother's lap and looking at the pages of a book while she read to him, which was something all three of his older siblings had seemed to enjoy. He was also very slow to learn to use any recognizable language. Most of his verbalizations took the form of grunts, or every once in a while, a sudden burst of raucous laughter. Jacob did not begin to speak recognizable words until he was nearly 4 years old, and even now his speech is not nearly as fluent as that of most 7 year olds.

By the time Jacob was 3, he had begun to spend lengthy amounts of time in a variety of perseverative (that is, tediously repetitive) activities, such as rolling a ball back and forth, turning light switches on and off, and later flushing the toilet many times in succession. He also learned to reflect light coming in the window of his room using a small mirror and would become engrossed in moving the patch of light around the room for an hour or more at a time. Most of his enjoyment came from playing in this fashion with various inanimate objects. He would stack blocks on top of one another or line up small toy figures in solitary play that would often last an entire afternoon. Once when placed on the seat of his sister's tricycle, Jacob squirmed to get down, but later after someone else had turned it upside down on the ground, he amused himself by spinning the wheels with his hand.

In contrast to his marked interest in certain inanimate objects, Jacob was rather indifferent towards people. He paid no attention whenever anyone came or left the house, whether a family member, adult stranger, or prospective playmate. He seemed happiest when left alone and became upset if interrupted while engaged in one of his perseverative activities. However, if the interruption ceased, Jacob would resume what he had been doing and seemed to forget the interruption entirely. Although these peculiarities made Jacob different than his siblings, his mother noted that given the time her other three children required of her, she often felt relieved that Jacob made relatively few demands on her attention.

Other peculiarities were not so easy to tolerate. On one hand, Jacob learned to like throwing things on the floor, especially if they bounced or made a noise. On the other, loud noises that he did not anticipate—such as a vacuum cleaner, barking dog, or loud traffic—usually upset him. He nearly spoiled the only birthday party he was ever invited to by his intense reaction to the noises generated by party horns and popping balloons.

From his parents' standpoint, he was also very stubborn. For example, their efforts to toilet train Jacob were almost completely ineffective until he reached 5 years of age. At one point, his mother became concerned enough by these and other problems to describe them to his pediatrician. The pediatrician thought Jacob was probably just developing more slowly than the other children, or might be showing signs of mental retardation. Just one day prior to his fifth birthday, however, Jacob took off his diaper without saying anything, put on a pair of the underwear his mother had kept in his dresser drawer, and never used a diaper again.

In terms of more positive features, Jacob showed an intense interest in drawing, coloring, and working with jigsaw puzzles. His mother once found him putting a jigsaw puzzle together with the picture side face down, and was surprised when he completed it successfully in about the same amount of time it would have taken him to do it face up. He also demonstrated an unusually good memory for pictures and names, quickly learning the names of all US presidents in a picture book.

In gathering this information, Dr. Gray's interview with Jacob's mother lasted almost 2 hours, yet during all this time, Jacob had not become restless or bored. Dr. Gray decided to see if Jacob would talk to her. As she moved her chair over to where he was busy drawing and began speaking directly to him, Jacob abruptly turned his chair 90 degrees away from Dr. Gray so that he was looking off to the side. As Dr. Gray gently prodded him to converse, Jacob began to respond in a perfunctory manner and showed no change in facial expressions.

Increasingly long pauses separated her questions and his answers, and Dr. Gray eventually noticed that Jacob was looking steadily at a chart on the wall of her office that included pictures illustrating various units of measurement. She invited him to move closer to the chart and, after a few moments, began asking him about it. Jacob was able to respond very knowledgeably to simple questions about metric measurements (meters, liters, kilograms) displayed on the chart. As the questions continued, however, Jacob started showing signs of concern whether his answers are correct. He became confused when Dr. Gray pronounced "liter" in a way that rhymed with "meter" and abruptly turned away.

A CRITICAL THINKING AND QUESTIONING PAUSE

What diagnoses should Dr. Gray be considering at this point? Although you already know this is a case about autism, such a diagnosis would not be immediately apparent, especially in this case. Autism usually involves some fairly extensive speech challenges that do not appear to be evident in Jacob's case. Jacob's ability to learn rapidly from the chart on Dr. Gray's wall and to answer questions about that information suggests that his intelligence is at least of a modest level. But nothing that Dr. Gray has uncovered by interviewing the mother corresponds with the teacher's thoughts about oppositional defiant disorder, conduct disorder, or even ADHD. In order to reach conclusions about the nature of Jacob's behaviors, Dr. Gray still needs to gather more information and may need to consult with other specialists before making her decision.

Gathering the Data

Dr. Gray escorted Jacob to a play area and invited him to draw while she continued interviewing his mother. Accurately diagnosing a mental disorder in a child requires a careful, detailed history. Dr. Gray asked Mrs. T to summarize Jacob's significant childhood illnesses (especially fevers and infections) and also questioned her about certain other aspects of his behavior. For instance, Dr. Gray asked for examples of when Jacob's play has shown elements of imagination or creative fantasy. Mrs. T recognized the significance of this question since she could not come up with any examples. She could not recall any instances of Jacob role playing, or even attempting to play with a toy in a fashion other than that for which it was designed (such as using a broom handle and pretending it is a horse to ride).

Noting the episodes of disrobing at school, Dr. Gray asked whether Jacob ever seemed overly sensitive to touch. Mrs. T agrees that he did and noted that Jacob liked to keep doors and windows closed, that drafts of wind (e.g., sitting by an open window while riding in the car) bother him greatly. She also mentioned that he hated to be bundled up in cold weather. Dr. Gray then asked about Jacob's tolerance for change in his environment. You will recall several problematic behavior episodes at school as Jacob responded negatively to changes in schedule or buses.

Jacob's mother explained that he has little tolerance for change and offers a striking example. Once Jacob became upset when his father walked into the room and picked him up to give him a hug. Jacob made loud grunt-like vocalizations and would not calm down until his father put Jacob down, pulled his glasses from his shirt pocket and put them back on. Apparently his father had removed his glasses to clean them before walking into the room. Even this minor change in Jacob's environment was distressing to him.

After over two and a half hours, the interview ended and Jacob and his mother left. Reflecting on what she has learned, Dr. Gray noted that Jacob's problems were evident at a very early age and showed themselves as failures to demonstrate the normal developmental sequence or progression through which most children proceed. This led her to suspect some form of developmental disorder. The specific diagnosis she was leaning towards was Autism Spectrum

Disorder. Autism is not a single, homogeneous disorder but rather a collection of syndromes involving a constellation of symptoms that can vary in severity. Confirming a diagnosis of Autism Spectrum Disorder usually requires input from other specialists, such as a pediatrician, a professional (often a psychologist) who specializes in developmental and learning disorders, and a speech/language specialist.

Dr. Gray arranged for consultation with these other professionals. Jacob received a speech and hearing evaluation from the school's speech therapist, who used the Peabody Picture Vocabulary Test to assess his verbal comprehension. In a later session, Dr. Gray administered the Wechsler Intelligence Scale for Children. Jacob's overall IQ score was 88, which is in the low normal range. However, his performance IQ was significantly higher than his verbal IQ, suggesting that therapy to strengthen his language skills needed to be included as part of his treatment. Given his functional deficits, if his IQ had been below 70, it might be appropriate to diagnose him with Intellectual Disability (previously called Mental Retardation) as well as Autism Spectrum Disorder. To evaluate Jacob's overall functioning systematically, Dr. Gray also conducted separate structured interviews with Mrs. T and with Jacob's teacher, using the Vineland Adaptive Behavior Scales. Regarding the severity of Jacob's disorder, Dr. Gray tentatively gave him the least severe rating (Level 1—"Requiring support"), and added that intellectual impairment is absent, since his IQ is in the low normal range.

The Assessment Model

Jacob had difficulty staying connected to the social world. Although his behaviors gave the appearance of withdrawing or disconnecting from the social world, it is probably more accurate to state that he never fully connected to it in the first place. Persons suffering from Autism Spectrum Disorder may stare vacantly, ignore other people in their social environment, and may exhibit stereotyped (repetitive) movements, such as rocking back and forth.

One of the key problems Jacob displayed is impairment in one-to-one interaction. He also showed restricted, repetitive patterns of behavior and interests. Although his drawings of letters and other concrete images were often much better than those of his peers, his efforts in this regard were perseverative and showed little spontaneity or creativity. Jacob has not drawn objects he cannot see, thereby showing little use of his imagination. He also showed little to no use of imagination or fantasy when he plays. Again, his play appears to be perseverative and not designed for "fun."

It is very typical of persons with autism to show delayed use of language. Jacob's parents took note of his obvious slowness at demonstrating language in comparison with his older siblings. In contrast to most children, Jacob never learned to point to objects in the environment, although he was able to take his mother's hand, lead her to an object he wanted, and push her hand in the direction of the object (a toy, glass of water, etc.). Jacob tended to react to physical restraint by vigorously pushing the other person's hand or arm away, but he never learned simply to ask that it be removed. His first functional use of language was simply to respond silently (but appropriately) to simple, concrete instructions. Later, when he himself began to speak in a rudimentary way, the rhythms and cadence of Jacob's voice were somewhat rigid and artificial.

By the time he entered kindergarten, it was clear that Jacob could understand language and communicate his needs in a basic fashion, but the words he used tended to have very literal meanings for Jacob. For example, to Jacob putting something "down" always meant putting it on the floor. By age 6, Jacob's speech was more functional (such that he was more effective in communicating his wants), and adequate rote learning skills enabled him to acquire basic school-related information, such as letters of the alphabet and the names of colors. However, Jacob still exhibited social difficulties, including disinterest in others and a strong preference for rigid routines.

Jacob's gym teacher assumed that his disinterest in participatory social activities and sports involving other children reflected a short attention span. That assessment, plus Jacob's disregard of codes of conduct at school, led his teacher to suspect ADHD. A child with ADHD is distractible, impulsive, and may be learning disabled, all of which seem to apply on occasion to Jacob's behavior at school. However, a child with ADHD is easily angered, and the anger persists. Jacob, by contrast, does not get angry very often and will cease being angry almost immediately after whatever aroused him is removed. In autism, there is often one or more unusual interests or special preoccupations (such as music or drawing), a characteristic that tends not to be found in children with ADHD.

Asperger's disorder is another syndrome that entails repetitive patterns of behavior and impaired social functioning. Although it resembles autism with respect to the individual's social aloofness and peculiar interests, and in DSM-5 is one of the diagnoses falling under Autism Spectrum Disorder, Asperger's disorder entails normal language development and average or better intellectual functioning.

Treatment Considerations

Because autism is a "spectrum" disorder (which means that it seems to cover a group of different symptom patterns and may have more than one cause), no single treatment is effective in all cases. With Jacob, as with most other individuals who have autism, there are multiple symptoms and a variety of different interventions that are used simultaneously. The most important of these are behavior modification (with a once-per-week session attended by his parents to help them keep up with the program and maintain use of the procedures at home), and speech/language therapy.

Although antidepressant medications are sometimes used to reduce aggressiveness, and amphetamines are sometimes prescribed for symptoms of hyperactivity,

Jacob's aggressiveness and attention deficits were relatively mild and not disruptive enough to interfere with treatment. Also, antipsychotic medications like respiradone are sometimes used with persons who have autism, but Jacob's symptoms were not that severe, and side effects of these medications can be very serious, especially with someone as young as he is.

In contrast to an earlier era when a child like Jacob might have been placed in a residential program away from home, or at least have been required to attend a special training school, the intervention plan for Jacob entailed as much inclusion in normal classroom settings as possible, with any special help sessions (e.g., speech therapy) provided as needed there at school. His parents' needs and preferences were also taken into account. Such a complex and multifaceted plan required close collaboration among several different professionals and also Jacob's parents.

Jacob's problem was not that he was naturally resistant or recalcitrant in the face of adult expectations, but that in contrast to most children, he simply did not recognize how certain social and situational cues call for specific responses on his part. His more dramatic symptoms (isolating himself, having a tantrum) are usefully understood as his attempts to avoid becoming overwhelmed by a confusing or threatening situation.

The treatment program was person-centered, meaning that the emphasis was not on compliance with rigid procedures and goals (which often might not make any sense to Jacob) but on building from the strengths he has instead of focusing on eliminating his symptoms (or emphasizing his "weaknesses"). For example, those working with him tried to capitalize on Jacob's skills with numbers, measurements, spatial reasoning (as in pictures and puzzles), and music, and after Jacob learned to use a computer, his assignments and expectations for completing them were sent to him via email.

Relationship issues were also important to treatment. Jacob's teacher tried to maximize her face-to-face interaction with him, and was encouraged to maintain steady eye contact, speak slowly, and give Jacob plenty of time to respond. Important directions to him were put in writing. Changes in procedures, and in the staff conducting them, were accomplished gradually, and the program included an "integrator," Ms. Kellow, to help Jacob with one-to-one interaction whenever necessary.

Autism involves many sensory issues. For example, Jacob's problem with taking his clothes off might have been due to irritation or discomfort, and his mother attempted to resolve this by experimenting with different garments and fabrics to see what was most comfortable for him. At school his hypersensitivity to touch was addressed using what is called "Sensory Integration Therapy." Ms. Kellow uses a treatment known as "brushing" to desensitize Jacob to touch by brushing his body (with his clothes on) with a soft surgical brush several times during the school day.

Behavior modification was used to shape skills that Jacob could learn to apply in natural settings. As much as possible, interventions took place in the classroom and other relevant settings, and—if appropriate and effective—Jacob's classmates were involved. The content and process (e.g., intensity) of the behavior modification sessions were flexible. For example, sessions were brief, and incidental opportunities (like the few minutes between when lunch is over and class resumes) were put to good use. Ms. Kellow also used the Premack principle, wherein Jacob was given an opportunity to engage in preferred behaviors as a reinforcement for performing behaviors desired of him. Being allowed certain amounts of time to play with puzzles, for example, was a reward used as part of the behavior modification program to increase his participation in gym class.

It was useful for Jacob to understand future events and expectations as well as immediate "here and now" activities. Ms. Kellow used pictures and diagrams to help Jacob understand new classroom procedures and prepare for upcoming events, such as fire drills or field trips. Because transition times (e.g., arriving at school and going from the classroom to the gym or from the gym to the cafeteria) were some of the most difficult times of the day for him, Ms. Kellow used visual aids, as well as rehearsal, to prepare Jacob to transition from one activity or area to another. If he was having a bad day, he might also receive sensory integration (brushing) before moving on to a different part of the building to help him calm down and refocus. Ms. Kellow also helped prepare Jacob for any expected disruptions in the routine of school, such as when the class would be having a substitute teacher. She used a calendar to identify the given day in advance, and reminded Jacob what was going to be different on that day.

A speech pathologist helped Jacob learn to use language more effectively in social interactions. The speech/language component of therapy was intensive because learning to communicate effectively is an important predictor of better long-term adjustment for persons with autism. In other words, effective communication is a significant predictor of the degree of long-term progress in controlling symptoms.

Ms. Kellow and the language therapist did not worry about correct pronunciation or grammar, but strived primarily to establish an appreciation in Jacob of the functional value of communication. For example, if he couldn't articulate fully what he was trying to communicate, but can convey the information using gestures, then gestures were acceptable. A method known as PECS (which stands for Picture Exchange Communication System) was used, wherein Jacob took a picture of an item (activity) to his teacher or to Ms. Kellow, and in exchange, received what is on the picture.

Ms. Kellow tried to be precise: For example, instead of saying "your mother is coming to get you later," she explained that "your mother will come to get you at 4:00," and she showed him this time on the clock. She prepared "scripts" for social interaction with peers that she and Jacob then rehearsed. Regarding Jacob's problems in gym class, she obtained the gym teacher's consent to videotape some of the activities. She and Jacob reviewed the videos. Jacob became more interested when he learned that he would also be videotaped as he participated with classmates in the activities. He later enjoyed seeing himself as the tape was played back.

Jacob's mother adopted the school's procedures for discipline, to keep these consistent between home and school. For example, at home she had been handling tantrums using "time out" whenever he was disruptive. Jacob was required to stand in a far corner of the room, facing blank walls, and not move or make noises for 5 minutes. As the treatment team explains, however, punishment of a child with autism, even in the form of time out, is controversial. For example, punishing Jacob for removing his clothes (which could be directly related to his autism) might be something like punishing someone for having a seizure, if the sensation of the clothing is unbearable to him and he truly is just trying to escape an aversive situation. Jacob's mother decided to try sensory integration (brushing) instead of time out when he had tantrums.

Jacob's prognosis is much better than if he also had intellectual developmental disorder or more severe language deficits or both. Over the long term, he will likely do better if given support to develop those interests he seems to have a flair for (e.g., perhaps science). There is a reasonable likelihood that he will show gradual improvements in cognitive and even social functioning, although he is likely to retain at least subtle manifestations of autism for the rest of his life.

It is important to note that Dr. Gray was successful in diagnosing Jacob's illness because she "looked beyond the symptoms." Jacob's teacher had assumed that the behaviors were directed toward her when, in fact, the outbursts appear to be a reflection of Jacob's intense need for his environment to remain stable and predictable. Once stability was reestablished, the outburst would end. If the teacher had spent a little more time considering when Jacob engaged in such behaviors versus when he did not, she might have been more effective in aiding Jacob's success in the classroom. Teachers are, however, human like the rest of us. It is difficult in such situations not to assume that problem behaviors are personally directed. Once Dr. Gray took the time to develop a case history and interview the mother so extensively, the patterns of Jacob's behaviors and preferences became fairly apparent.

Returning to our critical thinking model, we note that Dr. Gray gathers information from multiple sources to move beyond simple knowledge (Jacob removed his clothes), questions what that behavior might mean (comprehension), generalizes that action to other situations (application), analyzes those situations to search for common components, reassembles the most meaningful information from that analysis (synthesis), and develops a diagnosis and treatment plan. The final step in the critical thinking process, of course, is evaluation. If Jacob responds favorably to treatment, such an evaluation would reinforce the accuracy of Dr. Gray's diagnosis.

Biologist Perspective on the Autism Spectrum

Discussing the biology of diagnoses comprising a syndrome of disorders that are classified along a spectrum is, indeed, a challenge! Regardless of what separates persons with a diagnosis of Autism Spectrum Disorder, the essential symptoms of the diagnosis are an inability to communicate effectively and an inability to interact well with others. The fact that traumatic injury to the amygdala elicited behaviors similar to those of persons with autism made that structure one of great interest. To determine whether more recent studies involving improved techniques support that traditional thinking, we examined the literature. We found a 2005 article by Schultz and another in 2012 by Kliemann, Dziobek, Hatri, Baudewig, and Heekeren that support a role for the amygdala in autism.

According to the National Institutes of Mental Health (NIMH), the characteristics of those whose diagnosis puts them on the autism apectrum are deficits in social communication and interactions. These typically present in the first 2 years of life and cause marked impairment in social, occupational, or other critical areas of current functioning. Because the amygdala is a part of the brain that has a role in the regulation of social behaviors, it was the primary focus of a 2002 review article on the pathophysiology of autism (see Sweeten, Posey, Shekhar, & McDougle, 2002). The authors were unable to find research involving imaging that could document deficits of the amygdala. There were limited studies, however, documenting other areas of the limbic system that showed some alteration in persons on the spectrum. The authors concluded that further research will be necessary to resolve inconsistencies in currently available data to corroborate supportive evidence that amygdala dysfunction is involved in the pathology of autism.

There have been several studies that are of interest to the biologist. A 2001 paper by Nelson reported on several studies that indicated possible implications of certain neuropeptides and neurotrophins, both in early development and later for persons on the spectrum. A 2006 study found that in a very highly restricted population, autism occurred more frequently among persons whose fathers were of advancing age (40 years of age or older) (Reichenberg et al., 2006). In addition, a 2014 article by Baron-Cohen et al. suggests that autism may affect males more than females because of the effects of steroid hormones on early fetal brain development. A male fetus secretes testosterone during fetal development whereas the female fetus does not.

Finally, one paradox of normal brain development during childhood and adolescence is that extensive pruning of synapses must occur so that the brain is not overloaded with stimulation as different areas begin to specialize. This pruning process may go awry in individuals with autism, leaving them with an oversupply of synapses in an area of the brain's temporal lobe involved in social behavior and communication. The excessive density of synapses makes individuals with autism overly sensitive to unexpected noises or changes in the environment, and also helps to explain the association of autism with epilepsy, since the overabundance of electrical signals being transmitted in the brain creates opportunities for epileptic seizures. All of these developments offer exciting possible directions for further research.

An Interview With Jacob's Teacher

Dealing with Jacob in the classroom has never been easy. I have to admit I got angry at him a lot of times. His behavior was just so hard to predict. It also was hard to deal with because I would see him respond so calmly to his mother's requests when we called her in. Many of the behaviors that I had assumed were intentional, though, appear to be a function of his autism and not deliberate attempts to irritate me. That has been a tough realization for me to deal with. I'd like to think I always give the students the benefit of the doubt, but with so many students needing so many different things, it can be tough sometimes, not to jump to conclusions.

I'm not saying things are really easier now. I simply understand better what is going on and have more flexible strategies for dealing with Jacob's idiosyncrasies. He really needs a predictable environment. A lot of school is like that—consistent and predictable. But some of it is not. I think back on our trip to the farm. I thought Jacob would love it. But I guess it was overwhelming for him. He could not understand why he was being forced to take a bus that "was not his bus."

Jacob still requires a lot of time. Most of the other students are pretty understanding about that but there still are some days where there is barely enough of me to go around. Usually, if Jacob starts to respond negatively to some situation, I can bring things back under control by reestablishing the predictability that Jacob seems to need. Some of the other children even help me with that. Kendra is a good example. She really seems to like Jacob and she also seems to understand him fairly well. She will explain to any new children that come into the classroom that Jacob prefers to be alone. One morning one of the new children rearranged the farm animal pictures on the felt board. Jacob started a very loud set of vocalizations and could not be soothed. Kendra picked up on the situation right away, calmly walked to the felt board, put the animals back the way they were, and explained to the new class member about Jacob's need for sameness. It was quite an amazing scenario to watch.

I have found other teachers come to me and ask for advice on how best to work Jacob into the classroom. I have to admit it was only a few months ago that I would have had nothing useful to say. I had no idea how best to ease Jacob into the classroom without completely allowing him to do whatever he wanted. I guess you could say we have learned to compromise. I expect Jacob to do his work and, in return, I try to maintain as much consistency in his environment as I can. It takes effort and patience on both of our parts but the episodes of outbursts in the classroom have diminished significantly as a result of our efforts.

10

THE CASE OF SARAH O

Bulimia Nervosa

Introduction

Sarah stood behind a tree, staring at the building. It had taken all of her courage to just get this far. Still, she could not convince herself to walk inside. Several times, she turned her back and almost walked away. But something kept her from running. She watched as other students walked back and forth on the sidewalk in front of the building and she was glad that she had hidden herself at the rear of the building. "Come on," she told herself, "you can do this. . . . No," she continued to suggest to herself, "you *need* to do this." Gathering every ounce of courage she could muster, Sarah moved toward the back door. She watched and waited. Finally, her chance came. One of the health center employees opened the back door to dump trash into the dumpster. Before the door could shut, Sarah slipped in unnoticed even by the employee who opened the door.

Sarah O is a 23-year-old college senior from an upper-middle-class background. Sarah went to the counseling center with complaints of depression, fatigue, disturbed sleep, and difficulty concentrating. Her therapist at the counseling center is Ms. Chu, a psychiatric nurse practitioner. Going to the counseling center was a difficult decision for Sarah to make and she was so embarrassed about going she entered through the shipment door at the back of the building.

Ms. Chu talked in a calm and even tone; she has found a calm voice to be a good method of beginning an assessment in a nonthreatening manner. She believed that the more comfortable she could make Sarah feel about the assessment process, the more Sarah would open up to her and respond to her questions.

As Ms. Chu assessed Sarah's condition, other aspects of Sarah's behavior became evident. While engaging in casual conversation during the examination, Sarah mentioned how much she liked to exercise. Ms. Chu asked Sarah a question about how often she exercises and Sarah's answer was surprising. According to Sarah, she exercises two or three times a day. She suggests that "at least I can control my weight." Sarah's choice of the word "control" piqued Ms. Chu's interest. Although it may have meant nothing, Ms. Chu tends to take her clients' word choices seriously. She decided to explore the issue of control further.

Ms. Chu showed good use of her critical thinking skills by actively listening to not only the meaning of what Sarah said but the particular words she chose to use. Notice that Sarah did not suggest she could use exercising to "maintain," "manage," "keep a handle on," or "reduce" her weight. Ms. Chu used logical inference processes (critical thinking) to select the most important aspects of what Sarah was saying and how she was saying it. This is a very important skill, especially during the assessment and interview process.

As part of her routine initial diagnostic interview, Ms. Chu asked Sarah if she has ever received treatment for eating problems or other disorders, or ever thought she might have a problem involving eating. Sarah suggested that she has a healthy appetite and mentioned her particular fondness for junk food but was otherwise evasive about answering the question. Ms. Chu noticed that Sarah did not directly answer the question, so she persisted with further questions about eating. The more uncomfortable Sarah became, the more deliberate and patient Ms. Chu was with her questioning. Before long, Sarah completely dissolved in tears of frustration and helplessness. Between sobs, she expressed her exasperation over a serious inability to control her preoccupation with her weight or her eating binges. She discussed how miserable she was and how medically and psychologically damaging her eating problems have become.

Sarah revealed that bingeing and purging had become a cycle for her more than 7 years prior to the meeting with Ms. Chu. Sarah said she realized she was becoming increasingly frustrated as her control over her eating weakened and weakened. It seemed the harder she tried to control the cycle, the more control it began to exert over her and her life. Several close friends and even Sarah's mother had begun to notice her unusual patterns and had been asking her questions about them.

Upon further coaxing from Ms. Chu, Sarah described what has become a fairly typical day for her: "I get up in the morning three hours before I have to be anywhere. I start out by eating breakfast and tell myself that I won't exercise. As I get dressed and plan my day, though, nagging thoughts about gaining weight keep occurring to me. Before long, I will be absolutely convinced that I will gain too much weight from having eaten that breakfast. Moments after thinking this, I hit the exercise machines. Exercising makes me feel good about myself and I stop worrying for a while about gaining weight. But exercising makes me hungry, too. If I eat another meal, though, I know I will have to deal with my worries about gaining weight. Sometimes I can control the concerns and have a pretty normal day. But good days have their price. I may suddenly have an overwhelming urge to eat and when I give in to that, I really give in. At one sitting,

I have actually eaten an entire bucket of fried chicken, a box of Twinkies, several pints of ice cream, a bag of peanut M&M's, and several diet drinks. While I am stuffing myself with food, I feel great. But, once I am done, the reality of what I have done hits me and I immediately start worrying about my weight again. I get really concerned and all I can think about is getting that junk food out of me. Those days are total hell."

Assessment

Sarah had been secretly hiding her disorder for more than 7 years. It is not obvious from looking at her that Sarah has bulimia. Unlike anorexia, where one would expect obvious physical signs, Sarah appeared to be of normal weight, and in between her episodes of bingeing and purging, she ate normally. Ms. Chu needed to verify the binge-purge cycle, which would not be easy since Sarah had considerable practice in hiding her aberrant eating behavior. Sarah had learned to use mouthwash after a purge to cover up any odor, and she could easily give the appearance of eating healthy amounts of food. As long as she could hide the binge-and-purge cycles, no one was the wiser. In addition, until recently, the episodes of bingeing and purging were somewhat isolated. But Sarah reported experiencing more stress in her life over the past year—and with an increase in her experiences of stress came an increase in the frequency of the binge-purge cycles.

Sarah demonstrated the most common pattern of symptomatology in bulimia, which involves the cycle of bingeing and purging. In an attempt to cope with stress and feelings of lack of control in her life, she engaged in bouts of overeating— usually involving huge amounts of junk food—and followed this with purges that are intended to compensate for all of the calories and fat consumed. Sarah's bingeing and purging occurred several times per week, a frequency that was more than sufficient to meet DSM-5 criteria for Bulimia Nervosa. In addition, she clearly displayed a lack of control over her eating during these episodes, and presented a self-evaluation that is excessively influenced by body shape and weight.

Ms. Chu posed a careful series of questions about Sarah's lifetime history of binge eating, self-induced vomiting, use of laxatives, food preferences, self-perceptions regarding her appearance, exercise habits, and understanding of factors that may be related to her binge-purge episodes. Ms. Chu was interested in understanding any potential relationships between events in Sarah's life and the tendency to binge and purge. It might be the case, for example, that Sarah was more likely to binge and purge after certain types of stressful events than others. If she was able to resist the binge-purge cycle in response to certain stressors, then Ms. Chu could illuminate that and show Sarah how she was effectively coping with some stressors and not others.

Ms. Chu also asked Sarah about other symptoms she may have experienced, such as anxiety, mood disturbances, use of substances, suicidal thoughts and behaviors, and impulse-control problems. She asked Sarah about her history of sexual activity (including unwanted sexual experiences). Ms. Chu inquired whether eating problems (including obesity), mood disturbances, or substance abuse have been problems for any other members of her family, and what Sarah perceived the attitudes of members of her family to be regarding eating, exercise, and appearance. Sarah was referred for physical and dental checkups. The physical exam included a test for electrolyte imbalances.

A CRITICAL THINKING AND QUESTIONING PAUSE

Why is Ms. Chu so concerned about documenting family perceptions about eating, exercise, and appearance? How could family perceptions be related to the perceptions that Sarah has for these same issues? Ms. Chu knows that many of our attitudes derive from the attitudes of family members. If Sarah's parents, for example, constantly questioned her about her weight, or mentioned to her that boys do not like "chubby" girls, this could establish in Sarah's mind that her body weight and appearance should be of great concern. In addition, though, such comments and questions can convince Sarah that her appearance, whatever it happens to be, is not "good enough."

Some sports, such as gymnastics and wrestling, also emphasize a particular body image that is difficult for some young people to attain. Have you ever known someone who was on the wrestling team, for example, who had to go on a crash diet to "come in at a certain weight" or had been asked by coaches to quickly put on weight to move to a new weight class? Without passing judgment on these sports, suffice it to say that this heavy emphasis on an ideal body weight places a lot of pressure on those individuals who want to be a part of that sport.

Sarah's parents may have inadvertently reinforced any weight loss that she did experience. Comments such as, "you look great," in response to a weight loss can be very reinforcing. In order to maintain this highly desired weight, then, Sarah may adopt some fairly unhealthy practices. Over time, these habits can become extremely difficult to break and Sarah may find herself involved in a vicious cycle that she knows is unhealthy. (Why else would she work so hard to hide her bingeing and purging if she did not realize that there was something "wrong" with it?) This is the state she is in when she first sees Ms. Chu.

Why would Ms. Chu refer Sarah for a dental checkup when her "problem" involves disordered eating? You may have heard that one of the warning signs of bulimia is damaged teeth. This comes from the frequent vomiting. Stomach acid eventually begins to destroy the enamel of the teeth, making teeth vulnerable to cavities and other problems.

Sarah's History

Sarah's mother recalled that Sarah was always somewhat "particular about her weight." She displayed some chubbiness as a youngster, and after her parents once kidded her about her big appetite, Sarah would often ask for reassurance that she was "not as fat as Jane," her best friend. As she moved from childhood to adolescence, Sarah's concerns about her body image escalated. She began to show some athletic prowess, and by the time she was a junior in high school, she had lost most of her "baby fat" and developed into a strong competitive swimmer. Her friend Jane was not athletic and had become noticeably overweight by the time they entered high school. Sarah and Jane began spending less time together, and Sarah agreed with her parents and her other friends that Jane was to blame for the fact her weight made her unattractive and unpopular.

This is a fairly typical case history for a young woman suffering from bulimia. Other life history factors sometimes related to bulimia include medical illnesses and surgeries as a child, deaths of significant loved ones or other forms of separations (divorce, etc.), and childhood sexual abuse. More often than not, these incidents are related to feelings that the world is "out of control" or unpredictable. Food can sometimes be perceived by the person as something that she or he can control. This perception that control can be gained through food may lead to the kind of patterns indicative of bulimia. Additionally, at least in Western society, images of physical attractiveness and self-worth are often associated with thinness.

Sarah's first binge episode came after a disappointing end to the swimming season during her sophomore year of high school. She had trained hard during the season and consciously restrained herself from eating to minimize her body fat. In spite of all this, Sarah did not improve on her top performances of the previous year and failed to qualify for the conference championships. Her swimming career seemingly over, she consoled herself alone later that night by eating an entire large box of chocolates. When she was finished, Sarah felt bloated and very guilty. As her anxiety and agitation increased, she decided to force herself to vomit, which she was able to do without much effort. Although rather disgusted by what she had done, Sarah was also somewhat intrigued that she had been able to consume such a heavy overdose of fattening food and then completely "undo" this act, apparently paying no price at all for what would have been a very serious transgression in her training regimen.

Over the next 2 months Sarah repeated the overeating and purging several more times, always in secret. She would eat little or nothing during most of the day, at most nibbling occasionally if food was around, but by afternoon would become increasingly preoccupied with thoughts of food and eating. For Sarah, feelings of fullness brought relief, not the taste of food or reducing hunger pangs. Her goal was to fill herself quickly, so food that was easy to swallow was what she preferred.

Sarah quit the swim team feeling her athletic career was finished almost before it got started. Without the swim team, school held little interest for Sarah and she withdrew from most contact with her friends, preferring to spend most evenings alone in her room at home. These times were not happy ones, however, and frequent arguments with her mother increased the temptation Sarah felt to overeat. Each day as school wound down, Sarah spent more and more time preoccupied with thoughts about eating.

Those evenings she spent away from home most often involved serving as a nanny for a local lawyer's children. On the way home, she would stop at a convenience store, spending most of the money she earned on junk food that she would wolf down in the car before entering her house. On evenings when she was at home, and no one in her family was paying much attention, Sarah would sometimes sneak large bowls of ice cream or potato chips from the kitchen and eat them in her room. Once she began eating, it was almost impossible for her to stop until the food was all gone. Only if someone knocked on the door and seemed about to enter would Sarah interrupt her eating. She always managed to purge what she had eaten by throwing up in the bathroom, and masked the noise she made by turning both faucets in the sink on full blast.

Over time, Sarah's mother became puzzled by Sarah's lack of spending money (in spite of frequent employment as a nanny) and by the occasional disappearance of significant amounts of food. The couple for whom Sarah worked commented to Sarah's mother that a whole half gallon of ice cream had disappeared from their freezer each of the last two times Sarah had taken care of the kids. Sarah's closest call came when she and her mother and brother went out one Sunday to an "all you can eat" smorgasbord restaurant. After quickly eating several plates of food, Sarah became visibly uncomfortable and suddenly excused herself to use the restroom. A few minutes later, her mother went to the rest room and was startled to discover that Sarah had been throwing up.

Upon further assessment, Ms. Chu discovered that Sarah's parents were divorced. Her mother divorced her father when Sarah was in ninth grade and her brother was in the sixth grade. Sarah explains that her father was an alcoholic and what her mother referred to as a "mean drunk." With coaxing, Sarah describes one of her father's drinking episodes. Her mother called all over town trying to discover which bar Sarah's dad was "holed up in." When she finally found him, he was furious that she had disturbed him in front of his friends. She told him to come home because it was Father's Day and Sarah and Billy wanted to give him his presents. Sarah suggested to Ms. Chu that it would have been better if her mother had just let her father drink and hadn't harped about it. "It only made things worse," Sarah reasoned.

Sarah continued to share the memory with Ms. Chu. As she listened to the details, Ms. Chu experienced a sense of déjà vú. The story sounded too familiar. She had heard similar memories recalled by many of the clients she worked with. Sarah's father did come home from the bar but not to celebrate the special day with the children. He had a point to prove. He was going to teach his wife not to call and embarrass him in front of his friends anymore. When he entered the house, he was obviously very intoxicated and extremely upset. Sarah remembered running to him and showing him the new lunch box she had gotten him for Father's Day. To Sarah's surprise, her father grabbed the lunch box from her and threw it out the front door. When it hit the sidewalk, it broke right in half.

Sarah burst into tears and ran to her room. Her mother tried to get her father to calm down by mentioning that she and the children had gotten him a new charcoal grill too, but Sarah's father was beyond reason. He demanded that Sarah come out of her room, grabbed Billy by the arm and went outside. Sarah and her mother followed. Fred had Billy pull the grill out into the driveway. Sarah, Billy, and their mother watched in uncertainty as Fred started the car. Sarah recalled to Ms. Chu simply feeling numb as her father took the car and backed it over the new grill. As if to add insult to injury, he pulled forward and ran over the twisted metal again, and backed over it one more time for good measure. When he seemed satisfied that he had made his point, he drove away and rejoined his friends at the bar.

Sarah revealed to Ms. Chu that much of her anxiety over feeling "out of control" started to skyrocket at that point in her life. Control became an important issue with her. She could not seem to control the chaotic nature of her family environment but she could control other things. She joined the swim team because she could lose herself in the regimen of training and the rigors of competition. Sarah also discovered that she was good at swimming. With each increase in her performance came a parallel boost in her feelings of self-control. As long as she could continue to perform better, it convinced her that she was in control.

Ms. Chu recognized Sarah's pattern of placing increasing demands for performance on herself. Ms. Chu also knew, as Sarah had discovered, it was a coping mechanism destined to fail. When Sarah's performance on the swim team her sophomore year was worse than her freshman year and not even good enough to qualify her for the conference championships, she felt out of control again. She quit the swim team to regain control, but losing the focus that had come from having such a well-defined sense of purpose caused her feelings of chaos and loss of control to skyrocket again.

Sarah managed to finish high school and move on to college, but her struggles with feelings of control and constant thoughts of eating continued to plague her. Whenever things in college seemed to be getting out of control, Sarah experienced an overwhelming urge to binge and purge. She reported to Ms. Chu that she has felt down and lethargic most of her college career—except when bingeing and purging. Sarah seemed disgusted with herself when she reported to Ms. Chu that during the binges and purges, she felt elated. Only after purging and realizing that the food has controlled her once again did she feel guilt and disgust.

Once again, Ms. Chu recognized the pattern. She suspected that Sarah is suffering from at least a mild depression related to her feelings of lack of control in life, among other things. If Sarah experienced an adrenaline rush while she was bingeing, that would provide a powerfully contrasting feeling to her typical depressed and lethargic mood. Research suggests diminished brain levels of serotonin in persons suffering with Bulimia Nervosa (Smith, Fairburn, & Cowen, 1999). It is believed that the tendency to overeat is an attempt to "self-medicate" and obtain needed serotonin. Although Sarah cannot verbalize why bingeing makes her feel better, in a biological sense, it may temporarily do so.

Treatment Considerations

For sufficient disclosure, it is important for the therapist to develop a trusting relationship with a client who has bulimia, since it often happens that important information does not emerge until treatment has been under way for some time. Clearly, the individual is disturbed by the pattern she or he is in and would prefer not to reveal the particulars of the pattern to the relatively unknown therapist.

Ms. Chu understood that a variety of contributing causes (neurological, hormonal, or psychological) have been proposed for bulimia, and that their relative importance in any given case is difficult to ascertain. Because Sarah was not reporting (or showing other evidence of) severe binge-purge behaviors (e.g., multiple daily episodes, continuous laxative abuse), and was not presently suicidal or actively abusing substances, Ms. Chu decided that hospitalization was not necessary. Ms. Chu explained to Sarah that treatment is likely to be lengthy and reminded her of the importance of involving a couple of friends she can trust to see her through it.

The first goal in treatment was to reduce the frequency and intensity of Sarah's binge-purge episodes. Overall, the treatment plan included nutritional counseling, meal planning, diary keeping, and Cognitive-Behavioral Therapy. Ms. Chu discussed with Sarah the use of antidepressant medications, which can help reduce binge eating even in persons with bulimia who are not depressed.

As mentioned earlier, reduced serotonin levels have been suggested as part of the pattern of bulimia (Smith et al., 1999). For this reason, and to reduce Sarah's feelings of depression, Ms. Chu prescribed Prozac. You will recall that Prozac is an SSRI. This causes serotonin to remain in the synapse between neurons longer, ultimately making serotonin available in the bloodstream longer.

Ms. Chu also held several sessions between Sarah and her mother to engage in family education. The goals with these sessions were to educate Sarah's mother about the nature of Sarah's illness and the role that family attitudes and comments may play in the development and treatment of the disorder. Although these sessions were painful for Sarah's mother, Ms. Chu believed she could play an important role in the success of Sarah's treatment. Family support can be a crucial predictor of the success of treatment programs for many illnesses, as we have already seen illustrated in other cases within this book.

Diary keeping was used to track Sarah's eating in general, not just binges and purges. Sarah made entries in the diary describing her thoughts and feelings during the day, especially those associated with temptations to binge. The therapy itself was not exclusively focused on eating; it also addressed other issues that made Sarah feel excessively anxious (or out of control). You will recall that Sarah was especially tempted to binge when she felt she could not control the world around her. These times were quite stressful for her.

Individual treatment sessions consisted of cognitive and behavioral procedures to help Sarah normalize her eating (that is, acquire a regular and flexible pattern of eating that includes a wider range of foods and avoids characterizing foods as "bad" or "good"), lessen her concerns over body shape and weight (e.g., challenging her automatic thoughts), separate her episodes of eating from her efforts at emotional self-regulation, and help her cope more effectively with situations that increase the risk of bingeing and purging. The focus with this approach was assessing the thought processes that may be leading to Sarah's anxiety and why she thought eating would make her "feel" better. In addition, this approach assumed that if Sarah had more accurate information about foods and how to constructively manage her intake of fat, she could avoid the fears and anxieties that lead to purges once a binge has taken place. In this way, cognitive-behavioral treatment also reduces the risk of relapse by helping patients develop the ability to identify and correct setbacks as they occur (see also Chapter 12). This treatment is structured and problem oriented, and consists of 16 to 20 sessions over 4 to 5 months.

The treatment process helped Sarah to become a more effective critical thinker. Sarah was taking the world and the things that happened to her very literally. If she could not perform better this year than last year, she externalized that and assumed it is the world that is out of control. Instead, Sarah needed to critically analyze the roles her own patterns of thoughts and behaviors were playing in her illness. Maybe the unhealthy style of eating resulted in Sarah being less strong than the previous year. Sarah needed to look beyond the obvious and search for more logical—albeit sometimes painful—answers.

Another component in the treatment plan involved decreasing the amount of time that Sarah spent alone and in private. This was pursued by increasing her participation in structured social activities and changing other aspects of her daily routine (having lunch dates with her mother and with friends that occur in public places, committing her evenings to social activities when previously she would have been home alone, and so on). It was important for Sarah to involve one or more of her close friends in her treatment. These individuals served as a support network for Sarah as she attempted to find healthier methods for maintaining feelings of control in her life.

As individual sessions led to a decline in the frequency of Sarah's binge-purge episodes, Ms. Chu had Sarah begin attending group sessions with other college-age women struggling with bulimia. These group sessions focused on support in recognizing and counteracting the occurrence of catastrophic feelings after eating just one high-fat serving of food (e.g., a single cookie or donut), and the "loss of control" that can result in someone prone to bingeing.

Although most individuals who receive the kinds of therapy techniques described here will improve, only a few of them are able to abstain completely from bingeing and purging. It also happens that mood disturbances and anorexic symptoms can develop over time in someone first diagnosed with bulimia. Although this is sad, in many ways this potential outcome also makes sense. For a person who is prone to bingeing but who wants desperately not to do so, the simplest way to avoid bingeing is to not eat at all. Sometimes Sarah would find herself unable to stop eating once she started. It is possible, then, that to avoid such loss of control, she may come to avoid eating altogether.

A long-term prognosis is hard to predict with eating disorders, as with many of the other disorders we have discussed. Although Sarah has struggled with bulimia for years, the fact that she has not displayed symptoms of substance abuse improves her long-term prognosis for recovery (Keel, Mitchell, Miller, Davis, & Crow, 1999).

A CRITICAL THINKING AND QUESTIONING PAUSE

There appears to be a close relationship between the experience of depression that can (and often does) accompany eating disorders like bulimia and anxiety. Although the person with bulimia may not be diagnosed with Generalized Anxiety, it has been suggested by some doctors that the symptoms can start out as depression and progress into anxiety. Although this may seem a bit confusing, it is worth critically exploring. Why would someone experiencing bulimia experience depression? A part of the answer could be the biological systems that are involved.

But the experience of depression can partly be explained by the person's feeling that he or she is losing control. Recall Sarah's feelings of being out of control when her swimming performance did not meet her expectations. How did she control these feelings? Right: She quit the swim team and she turned to food, which she felt she could control. Sarah's lethargy is a common symptom with depression. Yet Sarah is also experiencing many of the symptoms of anxiety. Perhaps this illustrates that transition for her between the despondent feelings of depression and anxiety symptoms in conjunction with her strong need to feel in control.

If these feelings are not rectified in some way, it is not difficult to imagine progressing from depressed feelings over a lack of control to feelings of anxiety because one has lost control. This is not to suggest that biology is not at play here. We simply wish to illustrate the potential continuum between the despondent feelings of depression and the more fear-laced feelings of anxiety. As one anonymous doctor stated, "treat the depression with antidepressants and you may be able to avoid the anxiety altogether."

Bulimia From a Biologist's Point of View

Although eating disorders such as anorexia nervosa and bulimia nervosa have been considered to be social disorders—with conversations focused on societal issues—recent findings have pointed to important biological implications related to these disorders. Although some of the findings overlap, these eating disorders are truly two different biological and behavioral phenomena. Sarah has bulimia rather than anorexia, so a biologist will focus primarily on bulimia. Certainly it is known that serotonin activity is closely related to food intake, impulsivity, and obsessive actions. All of these are possible symptoms of bulimia. It is not surprising to biologists, then, that medications that regulate the availability of serotonin in the synapse are frequently used to treat bulimia.

The medications that seem to be most successful when bulimia is treated pharmacologically are antidepressants that selectively inhibit serotonin transporters. It is interesting that many women who suffer from bulimia, like Sarah, report being depressed. Often they report that depression causes them to eat, and that eating leads them to become depressed. The relief from such depression appears to come by increasing the length of time that the neurotransmitter serotonin remains in the synapse. From a biological point of view, whether that outcome is achieved behaviorally through the bingeing and purging cycle or through pharmacological intervention with an antidepressant makes little difference. However, the physical and social consequences of bingeing and purging are considerable.

Although both anorexia and bulimia appear to rise from a blend of genetic, neurochemical, psychodevelopmental, and sociocultural components, there also appear to be differences in the neurotransmitter systems involved (Becker, Grinspoon, Klibanski, & Hertzog, 1999; Gorwood et al., 1998). Numerous brain sites have been implicated in appetite regulation. Among these are the anterior cingulate gyrus, the hypothalamus, the hippocampus, the Nucleus Accumbens, the insula, and the amygdala. Although there may be an apparent concern about body weight or image in both those with bulimia and those with anorexia, persons with bulimia have at least normal body weight and often seem able to assess their weight situation appropriately. However, those who suffer anorexia nervosa lose weight through avoiding food intake, through strenuous athletic activity, or both. In anorexia nervosa, there is a feedback mechanism that distorts the ability of the person to perceive that he or she is losing weight even when such loss occurs at an alarming rate. If there is no intervention, death occurs. The situation is made even more difficult by the fact that at this point, there is a lack of effective pharmacological interventions (Becker et al., 1999).

These earlier findings strongly supported the suspected role of diminished brain serotonin neurotransmission in the symptomology of bulimia; however, understanding the complexities of bulimia alone and comparing them with the complexities of anorexia required further research. With the increased availability and use of fMRI, there has been progress in unraveling some of those complexities of eating disorders through animal and human studies. This biologist will share some of the implications of those studies here.

Advances in imaging have brought our understanding forward more in enhancing how the brain structures and body signaling systems work or work together than implicating underlying mechanisms. Several recent articles implicate desensitization of the reward pathway in response to an excess of food and may possibly be comparable to substance abuse models (Bohon & Stice, 2011; Reynolds, Shott, & O'Reilly, 2011).

In a review article by Guido and Kaye (2012), the authors explore research studies that tie both structures and body signaling systems to bulimia and anorexia and mark them as similar but clearly different biologically. Some of these studies have touched on the stimulation of the emotional components of eating and the corresponding counterbalance of blunting those emotional responses. The authors state that imaging has led many scientists to offer research-supported hypotheses that well thought through neuroscience model based studies are needed to take us to our next level of understanding.

11

THE CASE OF LATISHA Q

Panic Disorder

Introduction

Driving home from work, Latisha suddenly became warm all over, felt her chest constrict as her breathing rate increased sharply, and developed a choking feeling in her throat as she struggled to get her breath. As sensations of nausea and dizziness crept over her, she began to shake uncontrollably. Several times before in her life, Latisha had gotten very warm, started breathing fast, and felt her heart racing. She had been frightened then, but all those times, she was okay after a few minutes. This time her heart was really pounding, harder than it ever had, and did not seem like it would stop. Latisha was more than frightened—she was absolutely terrified. Her heart felt as if it would pound through her skin at any minute. She was afraid it would explode.

Latisha wanted to stop the car and run somewhere to hide but, of course, she couldn't do that. Suddenly she remembered that there was a hospital near the exit, and decided that fate was being very kind to her: In all likelihood, she was having a heart attack. However, when the emergency room physician examined her, she could find nothing except a mild infection, for which she prescribed an antibiotic. Latisha was relieved that her heart was normal, but it troubled her greatly that she could make no sense of what had happened. She took it easy for a few days, and after that, felt she was fully recovered except for a persistent "gloomy" feeling.

When her next episode occurred, Latisha was lying in bed one night and experienced an even worse attack. All she could think of was that at least she wasn't stuck in her car someplace. Still, she wanted to run somewhere to hide, but there was no escape. Latisha could not figure it out. It was as if a stranger had jumped out of the bushes in her yard and yelled "Boo!" at the top of his voice.

Her sense of panic would be understandable if that had happened. But part of what made these episodes so frightening was that there was simply no event that seemed to trigger either of them. The attacks seemed to just descend on Latisha from out of nowhere.

After each of these attacks, Latisha called her mother. It helped for her mother to come and talk with her and offer support, but it did not make the problem go away. She also tried talking to her roommate about her experiences, but Latisha really did not know how to describe the attacks to someone else. In an attempt to calm Latisha, her roommate would say, "Don't be afraid—there's nothing to be afraid of." Although she was trying to be supportive, the roommate's attempts to reassure Latisha actually backfired. Latisha smiled weakly and told her roommate that she had hit the problem on the head—of course there wasn't anything to be afraid of. The most frustrating aspect of all of this for Latisha was the fact that she *was* afraid, felt afraid, and acted afraid even though there was actually absolutely no reason she could think of to be afraid.

Latisha's third panic attack was the worst by far. She had gone to Florida with some friends. She was struggling with a virus, a cough, and a sore throat, but went out in the sun during the day and stayed out late every night. She felt really tired and worn out, like her body had just really had too much. After leaving for home, with five people in a small car, Latisha had a major panic attack. She was so nervous that she thought she was going to have to tell the driver to pull off the Interstate and take her straight to the hospital, but still did not know how to describe what was happening so could not tell the others anything.

Although it was very frightening, Latisha somehow managed to stay calm enough that the others never knew anything was wrong. They made it back home, but Latisha felt so gloomy and depressed that she knew she would be unable to function very well at work in that condition. She called her mother and talked about it. With that help, she managed to return to work for about a week, but was very anxious and depressed the entire time.

Latisha's fourth attack occurred about a month later, while she was driving alone on an Interstate highway coming home from a friend's wedding. She became really nervous, felt really hot, and although the attack only lasted a couple of minutes, Latisha continued to feel anxious throughout the following week. She could tell that there was something wrong. Three weeks passed, and then while returning from a visit with her parents, Latisha realized that she just could not make it. She became too anxious to drive and had to stop in the middle of the trip. She telephoned her boyfriend, who came and got her. After still another severe attack 2 weeks later, Latisha had her boyfriend drive her home to her parents' house in the middle of the night. The next day she could hardly get out of bed. She was in really bad shape and seemed unable to function. She did not want to wake up in the mornings and did not want to get out of bed. This time it took more than a month to recover her prior level of functioning.

At this point, along with the panic attacks, the general anxiety, and depression, Latisha was having considerable trouble with obsessive and intrusive thoughts. She had trouble just getting through the day. In the middle of a meeting, for example, she would get very anxious and be afraid she was about to stand up and shout obscenities. It became too much for her to sit through meetings because the anxiety produced by those thoughts was so horrible. It was irrational, because she knew she did not want to get up and start yelling.

Latisha also began to fear that she was going to kill herself. This fear did not spring from a genuine wish to commit suicide and she later denied that she was ever really suicidal. It also was not a desire to get attention, but just seemed to be an irrational fear that she was going to do something out of control like that, something horrible, something that would completely devastate her life. The hardest part about that episode was those horrible irrational fears that Latisha could not get rid of.

What should Latisha do? By this point, it is quite obvious that Latisha is suffering from panic disorder. Although all of us may experience intense anxiety or fear at some point in our lives, the cause, or causes of that fear can usually be identified and we can predict when the fear will occur. Most people, for example, know that they will begin to feel anxious and fearful while standing in line to go on a roller coaster. But these same people also know that the fear will go away when the ride is over. Although there was no "obvious" cause for Latisha's panic attacks, the fear she was experiencing was quite real and quite profound. Could Latisha continue to compensate for these attacks by talking with her mother and staying in bed until she felt better?

After Latisha shared the feelings she had concerning hurting herself with her mother, her mother asked Latisha's permission to make an appointment with a psychiatrist and offered to go with her to the first appointment. Latisha did not really want to go to a psychiatrist because the symptoms seemed so real. She could not believe that they were "all in her head." But she knew that she had to do something, and she trusted her mother.

The Diagnostic Interview

Latisha arrived several minutes early for her appointment with Dr. Patel, a psychiatrist at the State University. Latisha was dressed neatly and wore stylish clothes. From all appearances, Latisha was an attractive, physically healthy 28-year-old woman with a previously solid work record.

Dr. Patel nodded her head as Latisha related what had been happening to her. Thinking back, Latisha explained that she has often felt ill at ease in certain situations, such as in heavy traffic or crowded elevators. However, the kind of disabling attacks she was currently experiencing have left her feeling frustrated and very demoralized. She wished she were a "stronger" person who could withstand the attacks without flinching. When she finished, Dr. Patel assured her that what was happening was "not in your mind." She explained to her that for some reason, her body was being tricked. The disorder she had, she said, is called *panic disorder*, and she had all of the classic symptoms.

Dr. Patel reviewed the DSM-5 criteria for a Panic Attack, which involves a clearly defined period of intense discomfort during which the individual experiences at least four of the 13 symptoms that are abrupt in onset and typically reach peak intensity in 10 minutes or less (American Psychiatric Association, 2013a; 2013b):

1. palpitations, pounding heart, or accelerated heart rate
2. sweating
3. trembling or shaking
4. sensations of shortness of breath or smothering
5. feeling of choking
6. chest pain or discomfort
7. nausea or abdominal distress
8. feeling dizzy, unsteady, lightheaded, or faint
9. chills or heat sensations
10. parethesias (numbness or tingling sensations)
11. derealization (feelings of unreality) or depersonalization (being detached from oneself)
12. fear of losing control or going crazy
13. fear of dying.

Dr. Patel asked Latisha whether her panic attacks could be anticipated at all, such that a panic attack was very likely to result whenever Latisha was in a given situation or circumstance, or if instead they are unexpected (i.e., are not associated with any specific cue or situation).

A CRITICAL THINKING AND QUESTIONING PAUSE

Given that Dr. Patel already believes that Latisha suffers from panic disorder, why is she interested in whether Latisha can anticipate the occurrence of an attack? Could there be another disorder that Dr. Patel can rule out if she discovers that these attacks are *not* associated with a specific cue or a particular situation?

Dr. Patel was struck by the great intensity of Latisha's panic attacks, leading her to tentatively discount obsessive-compulsive anxiety or phobic disorders. If panic attacks are clearly tied to a specific situation, the most appropriate diagnosis is probably a specific or social phobia. If the attacks occur completely unexpectedly, as in Latisha's case, the appropriate diagnosis is most likely to be panic disorder. Latisha's statement "I feel like I might die" was particularly indicative of a panic attack. Because many people experience panic attacks that occur on at least very rare occasions, a single one by itself does not constitute a diagnosable disorder. Latisha has experienced at least six major attacks over the preceding 12 months, which is more than frequent enough to indicate they are recurrent.

In addition to requiring that panic attacks be recurrent and unexpected, a diagnosis of panic disorder also requires that the individual be concerned about the consequences (e.g., worried about what they signify, afraid that she or he will die, and so on) for at least 1 month. Furthermore, panic attacks are so upsetting they are often followed by avoidance of associated situations. Latisha, for example, had stopped going on vacations because she feared she would have another attack while traveling.

A CRITICAL THINKING AND QUESTIONING PAUSE

Although Dr. Patel has asked Latisha many questions concerning the nature of the attacks, whether she can anticipate their occurrence, and if she has come to avoid associated situations, can you think of other questions she would want to ask? To address this question, skim again over the description given in the introduction to this case. Are there any symptoms or feelings Latisha experienced that Dr. Patel has not yet addressed?

Latisha had come to dread trips in cars in heavy traffic or on long, narrow bridges. Additionally, crowded airplanes, sporting events, crowded parking lots, or even trips to the mall could lead to dread. Dr. Patel therefore carefully considered a second diagnosis: agoraphobia. Agoraphobia amounts to an overwhelming fear of being in a situation from which escape would be difficult. Although not all persons with panic disorder become agoraphobic, many do. Dr. Patel decided that Latisha's dread of and reaction to these specific conditions were not severe enough to justify this additional diagnosis.

Dr. Patel also evaluated Latisha for major depression, which occurs in about half of persons who have panic disorder, and has important implications regarding treatment. For example, if major depression is also present, she believed that antidepressant medication should be started right away. It was also important to evaluate the possibility of other anxiety disorders and substance abuse. Alcohol withdrawal sometimes produces symptoms similar to panic attacks.

Because certain other problems (e.g., thyroid disorder, irregular heartbeat, as well as overuse of caffeine and certain nonprescription medications) produce symptoms that can mimic panic disorder, Dr. Patel refers Latisha for a complete medical evaluation. Noting the exhaustion and lethargy that Latisha reported following at least two of her attacks, she also has her evaluated by a neurologist regarding the possibility of a seizure disorder such as Temporal Lobe Epilepsy. In Latisha's case, fortunately, all test results were within normal limits.

Treatment Considerations

Treatment began with Dr. Patel educating Latisha about panic disorder. It is not unusual for persons with panic disorder to feel ashamed and demoralized, and it is helpful for them to understand the biological underpinnings of the disorder. The educational process included information about treatment alternatives, especially medications and cognitive-behavioral techniques.

Dr. Patel told Latisha that she could give her medicine to control her attacks. Medications that have shown success in reducing the number of panic episodes include tricyclic antidepressants such as imipramine (Tofranil), monoamine-oxidase inhibitors (MAOI) antidepressants such as phenelzine (Nardil), and alprazolam (Xanax), a benzodiazepine anti-anxiety medication. Dr. Patel assured Latisha that medications like these are helpful in at least 90 percent of people who have symptoms like hers, and she agreed to start taking medication right away. She explained that she would give her alprazolam for short-term control until the imipramine she prescribed would "kick in" in 3 to 4 weeks.

Medication was most likely to act physiologically in reducing Latisha's tendency to generate the dramatic arousal she experiences as part of a panic attack. Dr. Patel explained that although the medication would stop the attacks, it would not take away the fear of having another attack.

Although Latisha did not demonstrate behaviors consistent with a diagnosis of agoraphobia, she certainly had some of the tendencies. As part of her treatment, attention can be paid to her behavioral coping in terms of those tendencies.

In contrast to some other disorders, such as BPD, where the individual's motivation to change comes and goes over time, persons with panic disorder are seriously distressed about this problem and bring a great deal of motivation to treatment. Approaches that combine medication with behavioral, cognitive, or cognitive-behavioral procedures are usually more helpful than is a single approach alone. Dr. Patel explained all this to Latisha because she wanted her to understand her options.

Latisha starts taking both Valium and alprazolam, undergoes thorough physical and neurological exams, then starts taking imipramine. After a few weeks, the imipramine level has come up to the point in her blood that Latisha is able to taper off on the alprazolam. After pondering Dr. Patel's advice that it is helpful for people whose symptoms have been exhibited so frequently and over such an extended period of time as hers to work with a social worker whose expertise is helping people with "situational panic" and phobias, Latisha made an appointment with a social worker.

Latisha recounted her history to a social worker in private practice, Ms. Ralston. Although Latisha had friends as a child, she remembers feeling anxious around other people—her schoolmates, her friends, parents, and so on. As she grew older, Latisha often worried about what other people thought of her. In college, she worried about doing well. She worked hard, but thought that excessive anxiety may have hindered her performance on tests and oral presentations.

As an adult, Latisha placed high expectations on herself: Being the only person of color on her management team made her feel that she had to be "better than good." For important business meetings, and when she traveled, Latisha would arrive very early so that she could arrange a comfortable place for herself and cope by degrees with the arrival of others.

Ms. Ralston's assessment involved Latisha's thoughts about what might be triggering her attacks, as well as discussions about what coping strategies she has employed in the past to help her deal with anxiety. Ms. Ralston began using cognitive-behavioral intervention techniques in the very first session so that Latisha gained hope and started to believe that control of the panic attacks is possible.

Because panic attacks are usually associated with stressful life events, much of Ms. Ralston's discussion with Latisha focused on such events. She has Latisha use the "life chart" approach (see the case of Sally W) to plot the occurrence and severity of panic episodes over time in conjunction with related information such as life events (e.g., changes in relationships, or at work), significant illnesses, other medications, lifestyle changes, and substance use. Focusing on these issues helped Latisha maintain a sense of collaboration in her treatment with Ms. Ralston. Connections between life events and panic attacks helped Latisha and her therapist to develop a treatment strategy.

Cognitive-Behavioral Treatment

Ms. Ralston helped Latisha understand the rationale for undertaking psychological treatment even though the medication seems to be working very well. The thrust of this rationale is to highlight the importance of cognitions to the experience of panic attacks, in particular how people like Latisha interpret certain internal (interoceptive) sensations as immediate, serious threats to their well-being. Ms. Ralston uses Latisha's help to identify everyday examples of how cognitive interpretations influence her emotions. For example, Latisha sometimes found herself feeling anxious before making an important business presentation, not because making the presentation carries any real danger to her but because she was distracted by thoughts about what her audience thought of her, whether she would do her best, and so on. Furthermore, she often had these thoughts without really noticing them or remembering them afterwards.

When she experienced panic, the perception of bodily sensations (e.g., racing heart, difficulty breathing) triggered catastrophic thoughts about losing control and suffering a disastrous outcome (e.g., a heart attack), which understandably resulted in a rapid buildup of anxiety. The fact that each of her attacks seemed worse than the preceding one suggested that Latisha's cognitive interpretations of the events were playing an important role in how distressing they seemed to her.

The cognitive-behavioral treatment Ms. Ralston proposed was directed at arousal reduction, cognitive restructuring, and exposure (see Rapee & Barlow, 1988). Arousal reduction was addressed by having Latisha learn to breathe slowly and smoothly, so that she could do this in response to panic sensations. To shape slow, steady breathing, Latisha was taught to monitor each breath, counting "one" as she took in her first breath and saying the word "relax" as she breathed out, "two" on her next inspiration and "relax" as she breathed out, and so on, until she reached "ten" and "relax," at which point she started counting over at "one." Because breathing with her upper lungs and chest (rather than with her diaphragm) was likely to exacerbate her breathing problems, Latisha was taught to increase her diaphragmatic breathing by placing one of her hands on her chest and the other beneath that on her abdomen. She could tell if she was breathing appropriately, since diaphragmatic breathing produces greater movement in the lower hand.

Latisha received two sessions of training in breathing control and is instructed to practice for at least 10 minutes each time. Daily practice is important whether Latisha experiences a panic attack or not, because a coping skill must be ready to use as soon as it is needed. Ms. Ralston has Latisha pick regular times and places for her practice sessions, and asks her to evaluate each session with respect to its success on a scale from 1 (very unsuccessful) to 5 (very successful) and to report these evaluations to her. Latisha found that practicing while she was driving to and from work was useful, because there was time available then and because panic attacks have sometimes occurred in that situation. The technique of counting while she breathes is believed to work not only directly, by slowing and smoothing Latisha's rate of breathing, but also indirectly by providing a cognitive focus (the counting) that distracts Latisha's attention from the catastrophic thoughts she readily associates with panic sensations.

The cognitive dimension of coping was also addressed through "restructuring." In this process, Latisha received accurate and useful information about some differences in physiological arousal between anxiety attacks and genuine medical emergencies. For example, Latisha learned that chest pain experienced in connection with a heart attack would lessen very quickly if she were to stop what she is doing and rest, although in a panic attack, trying to relax does nothing to reduce the sensations of internal distress.

A second objective of restructuring was to raise Latisha's awareness of how catastrophic thinking—some of which occurs almost automatically—needs to be recognized consciously and replaced with a more objective analysis of her situation. She learned to identify high-risk thoughts and situations, and to find substitutes for her more anxiety-arousing interpretations. High-risk situations included those in which Latisha had only limited control over her possible responses. For example, she noted with interest that she had never had a panic attack after arriving at her travel destination, when alone in her office, and so on.

Once she recognized that panic-related thoughts were the products of her own interpretations of somatic distress, Latisha was able to evaluate them more adaptively by examining relevant evidence (e.g., asking herself, "Isn't this really the same thing that happened to me before? Didn't it turn out that I was not in danger then? Might I simply be feeling stressed about something at work, or a problem with my family?"). This process of cognitive restructuring is demanding and requires practice. However, Latisha is bright and motivated to work on overcoming her panic problems, making this technique very appropriate here.

The third and final component of Latisha's Cognitive-Behavioral Therapy has her practice coping as she is exposed by degrees to the interoceptive cues for panic attacks. Exposure entailed having Latisha experience internal panic states of gradually increasing intensity. The initial step was to create a hierarchy of internal sensations that was rank ordered from least anxiety arousing to most anxiety arousing. Latisha then confronted each level, using voluntary hyperventilation, stair climbing, holding her breath, and spinning in place to generate the interoceptive cues. In other words, Latisha engaged in actions that activate sensations similar to those that accompany an unpredicted panic attack.

Ms. Ralston also encouraged Latisha to use fairground rides, saunas, and other experiences that induce panic-related internal sensations for exposure practice. In addition, Ms. Ralston recommended that Latisha pursue an aerobic exercise program for lifestyle fitness and to "normalize" temporary states of high internal arousal. She was instructed to practice cognitive restructuring at these times as well.

Including Latisha's Boyfriend in Treatment and Maintenance

With Latisha's permission, Ms. Ralston discussed her case in depth with her boyfriend, Jim. Although Jim was quite supportive of Latisha when the panic attacks first started to happen, he became increasingly irritated, since such attacks would lead to middle-of-the-night phone calls and late-night drives to taxi Latisha to her mother's house. Ms. Ralston explained the nature of panic disorder to Jim, and explained in depth the treatment plan that Latisha was undergoing. Because Latisha was required to practice her breathing, cognitive restructuring, and coping in response to exposure to situations that mimic the internal sensations Latisha normally felt in response to the panic attacks, Jim must understand why she is doing the things she is doing.

Once Jim understood the nature of Latisha's treatment, he would be able to help her practice and to remind her to engage in the practices at the agreed-upon times. Jim decided to take Latisha to a nearby amusement park as part of the exposure process. There Latisha could go on roller coasters and other rides that have made her anxious. Jim understood that Latisha could then use her breathing and her cognitive restructuring techniques to work through the internal sensations that in the past might have induced catastrophic thinking, and ultimately, triggered a panic attack.

Panic Disorder: A Biological Perspective

One of the first hints that a disorder has biological implications is that there is a tendency for members of the same biological family to have the disorder. The incidence of panic disorder in the United States is high (estimated to be 2 percent or one in 50 Americans at some time in their lifetime). Thus, there are many opportunities for research on the disorder. Since early in the 20th century, many physicians have noted the familial tendency for this disorder. In fact, some noted in taking patient histories that greater than 20 percent of first-degree relatives of persons who have a diagnosis of panic disorder also suffer from panic disorder.

In 1983, Crowe and collaborators reported a study directly examining concordance rates or first-degree relatives of those with the diagnosis (rather than relying on patient interviews alone). These researchers found that first-degree relatives had a 41 percent morbidity rate compared with control values of 4 percent, and that increased alcoholism rates among male relatives was 15 percent compared with 4 percent among controls. Although studies on alcoholism tell us little about how to curb panic disorder, they do reinforce the need to understand the underlying genetics, which may influence outcome.

Twin studies are especially helpful in looking at genetic implications of such illnesses. It is assumed in such studies that the concordance for monozygotic twins (considered to be genetically identical) compared to dizygotic twins (considered to be genetically related in the same way as other siblings) reared in the same home (similar environment) might give a clue regarding the relative importance of genetics and environment in the incidence of panic disorder.

In 1983, Torgerson found concordance rates of 31 percent in monozygotic twins compared with 0 percent concordance in dizygotic twins. Further studies by several investigators have linked panic disorder with major depressive episodes in patients and also in relatives of patients.

These kinds of studies into hereditary correlation lead to several possible avenues for further study. The first approach would be to use genetic tools to identify etiologies. The second approach would be to look for anatomical and physiological links between panic disorder and major depression.

There are a number of studies that attempt to sort out the degree to which panic disorder is linked to significant life events and how much is apparently due to "pure" anatomic/physiologic differences. Some patients seem to have no history of significant problems in childhood or in adulthood prior to the beginning of the attacks. It seems that their condition arises from some kind of inappropriate triggering of the fear-panic mechanisms of the body. Recall Dr. Patel's comment to Latisha that her body plays tricks on her. For some patients, it seems to be entirely a matter of the body's playing tricks.

However, there are reports to implicate childhood experiences or significant life events for others. Some researchers suggest such childhood experiences or significant life events may lead to a "psychological vulnerability" that causes some people to interpret normal physical sensations in a catastrophic way. Once these sensations are interpreted as fatal (e.g., "I must be having a heart attack"), the sensations magnify and a panic cycle has been initiated (Clark, 1996).

Latisha (and others who suffer panic disorder as she does) responds to medications generally prescribed for depression. Recall the three kinds of medication discussed in Barbara M's story as we considered depression. When Latisha began treatment, the antidepressants of choice were tricyclic in nature. If Latisha were to present today for the first time, it is probable that the physician would prescribe a newer antidepressant that is selective for serotonin and effects an increased time for that neurotransmitter to remain in the synapse by preventing its reuptake (SSRI). Latisha continued with the tricyclic rather than change to a newer medication when it became available for panic disorder because she was doing so well on imipramine. Dr. Patel has explained to Latisha that if she is still taking an antidepressant when she becomes sexually active and could become pregnant, she will switch her to a SSRI such as Zoloft because studies suggest that SSRI medications are safer for the developing baby than other medications used to treat depression. This is not to say that there are no risks associated with drug treatment for depression during pregnancy. Perhaps the best summary of these findings can be found on Medscape.com:

> The evidence to date suggests that the safety of antidepressants may vary by trimester of exposure, class of antidepressant, specific agent, duration of use, and dose. Adverse effects can also be both short- and long-term. In general, authorities recommend use of the newer antidepressants, particularly the SSRIs, in pregnancy and lactation as first-line agents because more data are available about their safety than for many other classes of antidepressants.
>
> *(WebMD, 2015)*

For additional discussion of the potential side effects of these medications and research on making informed decisions about such use during pregnancy, see the following: ACOG, 2015; ACOG Committee on Practice Bulletins, 2008; Gonsalves and Schuermeyer, 2006; Raudzus and Misri, 2008.

About half of adults with an anxiety disorder had symptoms of some type of psychiatric illness by age 15, a NIMH-funded study shows. Researchers also found that some of the specific illnesses detected in youth were clues as to what kinds of anxiety disorders—there are several—the youth would have as adults. The results underscore the importance of early diagnosis and prevention of anxiety disorders, and suggest that different anxiety disorders may have different roots (Gregory et al., 2007).

The fact that the concordance for monozygotic twins was 31 percent and not higher leaves room for the biologist to look at other etiologic considerations.

Environment is fully within the consideration of biology. Many scientists view environment in terms of developmental and life-span issues, interpersonal dynamics, social influences, and cultural exposures and events. The biologist considers the effects of those influences, as well as other determinants such as microorganisms (including viruses and bacteria); physical trauma and abuse; and intake of food, drink, medications, and other drugs. The biologist considers not only the direct effects of such environmental factors, but also the conditioning effects.

Recall that Dr. Patel told Latisha that the medication would control the attack itself but would not prevent her fear of having another attack. Being in situations that have induced anxiety before or where attacks have occurred spontaneously, even though they are not usual "anxiety producers," can serve as triggers for attacks. Indeed, those factors are the basis for phobias, and especially for agoraphobia.

The classic experiment to remember is the conditioning of Pavlov's dogs. The stimulus that was repeatedly paired with food (which was used to induce salivation) was a sound (such as a buzzer or metronome) that announced the availability of food. Eventually, the food was not necessary for salivation to occur. The sound alone elicited the response. Such responses are "learned." Some people forget that both learned responses and reflex reactions are clearly rooted in biology.

We will close this section on a biological perspective on panic disorder by summarizing several theories of anxiety, fear, and panic disorder that are rooted in neuroanatomy and physiology. Remember that the intent of a biologist's comments are not intended to replace courses in neuroscience. They are intended to introduce you to biological links.

General Model for Anxiety

In *Brain, Mind and Behavior* (Bloom & Lazerson, 1988), a genetic/experience model for scanning the environment for threat and potential danger is introduced. Perception of a threat (which is often not conscious) leads to a vigilant state and body preparation for appropriate action. This pathway seems to be activated inappropriately and/or excessively in persons who suffer panic disorder. Structures affected in this pathway are found in the limbic system (hypothalamus, hippocampus, amygdala, and cingulum), other neuronal "nuclei" (thalamus, locus ceruleus, median raphe nuclei, and specific nuclei of the cerebellum), and structures that connect these entities. Using a combination of PET and MRI, Neumeister and colleagues (2004) were able to visualize serotonin, locate, and count serotonin receptors. They compared 16 patients with panic disorder with 15 persons determined to be normal controls. They determined that those with panic disorder had marked reduction in the anterior and posterior cingulate and in the raphe.

Septohippocampal Theory

There is evidence to support the idea that the septohippocampal system is responsible for integrating incoming and outgoing connections that regulate nonreward and punishment signals. Novel elements of the environment are particularly subject to this regulation. Its usual functions are to heighten arousal and inhibit motor output. Three neurotransmitters that are significantly involved in the incoming and/or outgoing connections are norepinephrine, acetylcholine, and serotonin. Other research has implicated the hippocampus, the parahippocampal gyrus, and areas of the amygdala involved in the generation of fear sensations with changes in left to right parahippocampal blood flow, blood volume, and oxygen metabolism in patients with panic disorder in the nonpanic state. Studies during panic have indicated increased temporal lobe blood flow and abnormal temporal activity. Continued studies using brain scanning techniques are being done to further elucidate these mechanisms.

Gamma-Aminobutyric Acid (GABA): Benzodiazapine Hypothesis

There is evidence to support the presence of Benzodiazapine (Bz) receptors that are linked to a receptor for Gamma-aminobutyric Acid (GABA). When Bz binds to the Bz receptor, it facilitates GABA action that results in increased cell permeability to chloride ion through the chloride ion channel. When there is increased chloride ion permeability there is hyperpolarization of the neuron and impulse activity decreases. Thus, the input to the Locus Ceruleus is decreased and possibly ascending activating systems that are implicated in the expression of fear are modulated. The neurotransmitters implicated in such systems are noradrenergic, serotonergic, and probably dopaminergic.

Lactate Theory/Hyperventilation Theories

There are several studies that implicate sodium lactate in panic disorder. The underlying biology behind this theory is that effort intolerance leads to increased oxygen consumption and greater serum lactate levels with vigorous exercise. (Lactic acid is a by-product of muscle metabolism during prolonged muscle activity after oxygen is no longer available.) Seventy-five percent of patients with panic disorder were found to react to 10 mg/kg of 0.5 molar sodium lactate by having a panic attack, compared to less than 5 percent of controls. It is interesting that patients with other diagnoses such as OCD, Major Depression, Social Phobia, or Bulimia Nervosa did not have the same response to sodium lactate infusion.

An extension of this hypothesis involves the conversion of lactate to bicarbonate and carbon dioxide. The increase in carbon dioxide in the brain stem triggers chemical receptors there that increase the rate of breathing. A finding by Gorman and colleagues (1988) was that patients with panic disorder were more sensitive to air with increased carbon dioxide levels than were controls. In fact, one theory explains that the tendency of people with panic disorder to chronically hyperventilate may be due to the fact that, by increasing the oxygen intake, they keep the carbon dioxide levels low.

Hyperventilation and tachycardia (increased heart rate) are the two consistent differences that infusion of lactate induce in patients with panic disorder as compared with controls. Most patients with panic disorder who are successfully treated with either imipramine or alprazolam and then retested do not experience the attacks.

A prominent derivative of this hypothesis proposes that panic attacks are a result of (or are associated with) abnormalities in respiratory function. Indeed, almost all patients with panic disorder complain of shortness of breath or of having trouble breathing during their attacks. Voluntary hyperventilation of room air has been shown to reproduce panic attacks in 30 to 50 percent of patients with panic disorder. Additionally, many of the stimuli that have been shown to induce panic (e.g., lactate, serotonin, epinephrine, carbon dioxide) share an ability to stimulate respiration or induce breathlessness or both of these effects.

It is interesting to note that panic attacks can be induced by lactate infusion only in humans or animals that are susceptible. Researchers noted that when rats that were susceptible were infused with the lactate, there was increased gene expression in those neurons that secreted a hormone called *orexin* (also called *hypocretin*). These neurons are located exclusively in a circuit that has origins in the hypothalamus. By injecting susceptible rats with an agent that kept the orexin genes from turning on, researchers could prevent the rats from developing anxiety behaviors. The authors also found that patients with panic disorder had excess levels of orexin, a key role for orexin in panic anxiety (Johnson et al., 2009).

Papp and Klein (1993) proposed that patients with panic disorder have an abnormally low threshold for sensing impending suffocation, and that panic results from the triggering of a "false suffocation alarm." So, when breathlessness is induced by whatever causes the panic (whether it is lactate, serotonin, etc.), they feel that they are suffocating and the false suffocation alarm is activated.

Theories that correlate possible links between biology and symptoms of panic disorder have been the focus of studies since the 1980s. More recent studies that have focused on panic responses in both humans and other animal species indicate possible linkages between some of the earlier, more "discrete" theories. These studies suggest the possible implication of several different neurotransmitter agents and potential neuroendocrine pathways (Dager et al., 1999; Saijdyk, Katner, & Shekhar, 1997; Shekhar & Keim, 1996, 1997; Shekhar, Keim, Simon, & McBride, 1996; Wiedemann et al., 1999). Such studies lead to possible speculation exploring the notion that the body does not put all of its alert to danger signals in one location. This speculation might at some point provide fruitful research opportunities for possible correlation with a disorder such as panic disorder.

A Few Final Words From Latisha

I have completed therapy with Ms. Ralston and am still taking the medicine that Dr. Patel prescribed. Since completing therapy, I have had no major panic episodes. I really believe that getting help has saved my life. I don't honestly know what would have happened to me if my mother had not convinced me to get help. Before all of this started happening, I was what I would call a normal person. Yet, every once in a while, my anxiety and depression would get so bad that I completely stopped functioning.

I don't think most people understand very much about the nature of the kind of problem I've had, but I think these problems are more common than people think. I also believe that an understanding of problems like mine is increasing among the psychiatric and psychological communities. It is important to disseminate information so that it reaches the common person. The treatment that I have received has literally, I think, saved my life and I'm scared to think what would have happened to me if I hadn't received it.

I think that for most people who have problems of anxiety and depression like mine, they would see several options. One is to continue living with the symptoms. Two is that the person might find some kind of illegal substance or just alcohol that would alleviate the symptoms. Three is suicide. I think that the first option for people with my problem is not really an option. It's just not possible. It gets harder and harder to live with the symptoms because you can't predict when the attacks will and will not happen. It really becomes debilitating. So, I think people are left with choices two and three, illegal drugs or suicide, and of course there's the choice of getting professional help. But I don't think most people realize that help is available and that it works. Most people, like myself initially, don't even know they have a problem that's treatable and they don't know how well the available treatments work. I really feel like some of the suicides and some of the substance abuse problems are probably caused by the kinds of problems I've had.

Don't get me wrong, though, the treatment has not been easy. I hate the fact that I have to take medication all of the time to feel "right." But the other option of risking another panic attack is worse. The cognitive restructuring and the exposure practice was excruciating sometimes. But I now recognize the role my own pattern of thinking played in magnifying my anxious feelings into full-blown panic attacks. Jim, of course, has been a big help. I don't know how some people get through something like this without someone close to rely on for help. I guess maybe some of them are the ones who don't make it. I'm glad I did.

12

THE CASE OF RICHARD B

Alcohol Use Disorder

Introduction

Two odors permeated the room. One was the smell of very strong coffee. The other was cigarette smoke. Richard looked around the room and was amazed by the assembly of people. Somehow the diversity of the group surprised him. He had half expected most of the patrons to be old, sad-looking, and pale. But this group represented the diversity of society. He watched swirls of smoke rise toward the ceiling and wondered if he really had the courage to be here. He sipped the too-strong coffee from his Styrofoam cup and thought for about the thousandth time how he had gotten to this point in his life. Somehow the last thought was relatively comforting. He had lived. Despite all that he had done, he was still alive and on the verge of surviving a battle that he had been waging for nearly two decades. Sweat broke out on his forehead as he moved toward the front of the room. He could feel the eyes watching him as he walked down the narrow aisle between the rows of chairs. He stepped to the microphone and prepared to say the words that until just a few months before he would never acknowledge: "Hi. My name is Richard, and I am an alcoholic."

Richard B just recently uttered these words for the first time after battling to hide his addiction problem for more than 20 years. Although it took being fired from his job, sued for divorce by his wife, and "written off as worthless" by his two college-age children to finally get Richard to utter those words, it is the first step of many that will need to be taken in order for him to recover. Many readers will have heard of 12-step programs such as Alcoholics Anonymous (AA). Although we have nothing negative to say about such programs, since this is a textbook that you are using within an abnormal psychology course, we will focus our discussion of the case and the treatment program employed on one that has a clinical psychology foundation.

To understand how Richard reached this point, let's return to the day several months ago when he was picked up by the police as he stumbled along a highway. He had been knocking on doors as he wandered down the road following a drinking binge of several hours. After one homeowner turned him away, he lingered in the yard long enough that this person called the police. When they arrived and began to question Richard, he could not remember his street address. He did remember his estranged wife's telephone number, however, and when they called her, she told them to take him to a hospital.

The Diagnostic Interview

In the emergency room of the hospital, Richard's vital signs were checked, but because he seemed too confused and groggy to be interviewed, the staff decided to put him in a bed for observation. He slept for nearly 7 hours. Richard finally regained consciousness, and after another hour, a resident physician, Dr. Ogden, began to interview him.

"What happened to you that caused the police to bring you here?" he asked. Richard described his most recent activities as best he can remember them. He was staying with a drinking companion in the rooming house where this friend lived. He and the friend drank heavily the night before. Richard woke up feeling very ill, and noticed that his friend was not there. He had a splitting headache, and decided to look for some aspirin. His hands were shaking so badly the aspirin tablets spilled out on the floor, and after scraping them up, it was hard for him to drink the glass of water he had poured without the water running down his chin. In desperation, he tried washing the aspirin down with the little whiskey that remained in a bottle, but within seconds of trying that, Richard became nauseous and experienced the "dry heaves."

He stumbled around the room and found a cigarette, but his shaking hands made it impossible to light it. Richard was now extremely anxious. He tried going back to sleep but an alarming sense of panic made it impossible to lie still. Instead, he stumbled out the door looking for his friend and for a place he could get more alcohol to drink. He does not remember what happened the rest of that day, what he had been doing when the police found him, or how he was brought to the ER.

A CRITICAL THINKING AND QUESTIONING PAUSE

Richard appears to be having a serious problem with alcohol. Given what has already been covered in this casebook, what questions do you believe the interviewer should ask Richard in order to assess the extent of the problem? By now, you may be remembering that we discussed prior history of alcohol and drug use in another case, the case of Barbara M. In particular, we described a technique that can be used to assess an individual's history of alcohol and drug use. This technique is called the CAGE questionnaire (as a reminder, the acronym CAGE standing for Cut down, Annoyed, Guilty, and Eye-opener).

In Richard's case, the interviewer may ask Richard what he drinks or ingests. Remember that the interviewer will probably ask, "What do you drink and how much?" rather than asking "if" Richard drinks. Hopefully this will make it easier for Richard to acknowledge that he does drink and how much he drinks. The interviewer will attempt to gain specific information from Richard in order to characterize specific quantities and frequencies of use, since different people's understanding of what "a little" or "a lot" means can vary a great deal. Richard may feel, for example, that his drinking is not "excessive" because it is no more than his friends are drinking. The interviewer should be diligent and aware of any hostility and unease coming from Richard in response to these questions.

Richard acknowledges regular drinking, and seems quite uncomfortable with any suggestion that the amount he drinks might be excessive. The interviewer may want to inquire further about Richard's own thoughts about his drinking patterns. He may ask, for example, if Richard has ever felt he should *cut down* on his drinking? Richard suggests that he has "Sometimes thought about that but have not given it much real consideration." In addition, it may be important to note if others have ever *annoyed* Richard by criticizing his drinking. This question clearly makes Richard uncomfortable. He suggests his wife and children have frequently and openly criticized his drinking. Richard seems to get upset just thinking about such criticism; this discomfort, of course, is noted by the interviewer.

Another line of inquiry may involve asking Richard if he has ever had bad feelings, or perhaps even felt *guilty*, about his drinking. Richard may also be asked if he has ever taken a drink first thing in the morning (the *eye-opener*) to steady his nerves or get rid of a hangover. Richard suggests that he has sometimes felt guilty about his drinking, but then he looks the interviewer straight in the eye and asks: "But what's so wrong with a man taking a few drinks? I work awful hard to give my family a good life. Don't I deserve a little pleasure, too?" The answers to these questions and Richard's behaviors in response to answering them are often used by clinicians to evaluate the likelihood that a person abuses alcohol (see Ewing, 1984).

As a reminder from our earlier discussion, the more "yes" answers the person makes to these questions, the greater the likelihood he or she has a problem with alcohol abuse. Richard answered "yes" to virtually all of the questions. He is clearly uncomfortable with any suggestion that his drinking is excessive or that he might have a problem with alcohol.

From this interview, Richard will be considered to have problems with alcohol. Although this was suspected all along, it is quite important that assumptions not be made. To minimize the potential for making assumptions, a good diagnostic assessment may include processes that may appear redundant on the surface. But if we know nothing about Richard's past, his thoughts about his drinking, whether it has ever interfered with his life, and other issues such as these, how can we truly assess the extent to which he has a "problem" with alcohol? By determining whether (a) this is not an isolated event for Richard, (b) Richard does not believe (on the surface) that his drinking is excessive, (c) that he has, nonetheless, sometimes, thought that he might have a problem with alcohol, and (d) that he sometimes drinks in the morning in order to feel "good enough" to go to work, we have a much more complete picture of the extent of Richard's problem.

Richard calculated that when the police found him, he had probably been drinking for several days in a row. Because Richard answered "yes" to many of the questions already asked, the interviewer inquired whether he has ever received treatment for an alcohol-related illness.

Richard stated that he has not received treatment in a substance-abuse facility, but one time he was hospitalized because he got drunk and vomited so forcefully that he tore his esophagus. At this point, it had taken the interviewer almost an hour to reconstruct some of Richard's history. It is important in any case to include a full medical examination as part of the diagnostic and assessment process. After the initial interview questions and the medical examination, the mental status exam was performed.

A mental status exam attempts to assess the person's functioning in areas assumed to be related to overall mental functioning. A very common version of the mental status exam is that recommended by Siassi (1984). An outline of this organization was presented in Table 2.2 in Chapter 2 of this text.

As a reminder, the topics include:

1. general appearance and behavior
2. speech and thought
3. consciousness
4. mood and affect
5. perception
6. obsessions and compulsions
7. orientation
8. memory
9. attention and concentration
10. fund of general information
11. intelligence
12. insight and judgment
13. higher intellectual functioning.

Questions might include, (a) "What is your name?" (testing orientation), (b) "What is the capital of the United States?" (testing the fund of general information), or (c) "Can you remember what you were doing five minutes ago?" (testing memory).

Richard started to complain that he was not feeling well—and the longer the session lasted, the worse he felt. Richard became more confused. His hands were trembling, and he was perspiring. He rubbed his hands in a rather worried, agitated way. His pulse was rapid—110 beats per minute. As the doctor continues talking, Richard began having trouble paying attention and his eyes intermittently darted away to small spots he noticed on the walls and floor. When the doctor asked about this, Richard explained that he thought the spots looked like bugs.

A CRITICAL THINKING AND QUESTIONING PAUSE

Based on the symptoms Richard exhibits while in the assessment environment, what seems to be happening to Richard? Focus on the fact that the longer the session lasts, the worse he comes to feel. In addition, consider the fact that the spots on the floor and walls were perceived by Richard as bugs. You have probably guessed by now that Richard appears to be experiencing withdrawal symptoms, in particular symptoms commonly referred to as *delirium tremens* (DTs). Experiencing physical withdrawal symptoms after a prolonged absence from ingesting an addictive substance is a very clear and incontrovertible signal that the person is, indeed, addicted to the substance in question.

The doctor decided to have Richard admitted to the hospital while he received detoxification for alcohol withdrawal. Although it is often possible to conduct detoxification in a less restrictive setting, Richard's withdrawal symptoms (DTs) were severe enough that continuous observation was necessary. He was given thiamine and the antianxiety medication Librium. Blood was drawn for laboratory testing, including testing for the presence of other abusable substances.

Three days later, after Richard had fully recovered from the episode of withdrawal, he was interviewed by Dr. Rose, a psychiatrist at the hospital, who determined that Richard came to the ER following a serious blackout episode. It also turned out that Richard was suffering from many physical ailments as a result of not taking proper care of himself. His diet had become increasingly liquid and he was consuming less and less regular food. In addition to the ravages that consuming that much alcohol has on the body and the liver, the fact that Richard was not eating healthy meals or exercising exacerbated his health problems.

The Assessment Model

Diagnosing abuse of a substance such as alcohol is complicated by the fact that moderate use of this substance is common in American society. Part of the diagnostic decision thus turns on drawing the dividing line between "alcohol use" and "alcohol use disorder." In addition, persons with alcohol problems vary in a number of important ways, and (as with Richard) their disorders affect many areas of their lives. Dr. Rose thus found it useful to do a comprehensive evaluation.

He asked Richard about his recent episodes of drinking prior to the current one, including how intoxicated he became and what symptoms of withdrawal occurred. He had Richard describe a typical drinking episode: how often he drinks, how much he drinks on a typical day when he is drinking, how intoxicated he becomes, and what other effects drinking has on him. Richard was carefully questioned about his use and abuse of other substances (since such complications are relatively common among persons who abuse alcohol) and about past experiences in receiving treatment for substance problems. He was also asked about any suicidal thoughts or attempts he ever had, and the most violent things he has ever done (whether drinking or not). Dr. Rose also asked questions designed to detect the presence of other mental disorders, such as depression.

In contrast to DSM-IV, DSM-5 interprets symptoms of abuse and dependence on a continuum, with no distinction to be made other than degree of severity. Richard has been unable to stop drinking despite multiple hospitalizations; his binge drinking can last for days; it has caused serious conflict with his wife and children, and created problems with his health. It also cost him his employment.

Richard's reports of the increasing amounts of alcohol he consumed on all recent drinking occasions, the discomfort he felt beginning several hours after he stopped drinking, and the relief that came with a resumption of drinking, are evidence of tolerance and withdrawal. The increasing amounts of time and energy he devoted to obtaining and consuming alcohol, in spite of the serious damage that drinking had done to his home life and work, also indicate dependence.

The DTs Richard experienced in the ER offers the final bit of evidence that his drinking reached the point of inducing physiological dependence on alcohol, making the appropriate diagnosis one of Alcohol Use Disorder, Severe (based on six or more specific symptoms).

Richard's History

Dr. Rose interviewed Janice, Richard's estranged wife, and also his mother. He learned that Richard's father grew up in an alcoholic home and was himself an alcoholic. Richard's older sister had some problems with drugs and alcohol when she was around 13 or 14. Richard and his mother knew that his older sister had been taking drugs and drinking. One night when his mother became upset because his sister had been out all night and was missing, the mother recalled Richard patting her on the shoulder and saying, "Mom, don't worry, I'll never do that. I'll never drink alcohol." Because Richard saw what drinking alcohol was doing to his sister, he vowed never to do that himself. But one night, Richard's mother was at a football game; Richard was there, too. As they left for home, his mother realized that Richard had been drinking. She was shocked and couldn't believe the drinking was happening again.

On several weekends after that, Richard's mother found empty beer and liquor bottles in the garage. She confronted him about his behavior, and he promised not to drink again, but invariably this promise was broken within a week or two. She tried to protect him when she knew he had been drinking by looking for him all over town and bringing him home so that he wouldn't get into trouble. Over the years, Richard's problems with alcohol escalated, and the family began to fall apart. His father dealt with Richard's problem by completely withdrawing from the family and from Richard's circumstances. It angered Richard's mother when her husband "went into denial" and pretended that everything was all right. The parents' marriage ended in divorce when Richard was 17.

Richard stayed with his father, and his drinking continued throughout the time he was in high school. After finishing high school, Richard entered the armed services. He completed his hitch, but had a few scrapes of difficulty surrounding drinking. After his return from the service, he was twice stopped by local police for driving under the influence of alcohol—but he lived in a small town and both times the policemen gave Richard a break because they knew him.

Richard attended classes at a two-year business school, and soon after he passed the test to sell real estate, he met Janice. The next year they married and moved to a larger town. The responsibilities of marriage and having a family helped Richard reduce his drinking to "normal" levels for a while. In fact, his initial good humor and talkativeness after having a few drinks helped him open up to Janice in a warm and intimate way that they both valued. Over the next several years, however, as children appeared, family life became more hectic, and work demands increased with the ups and downs of the real estate market, Richard's drinking returned to earlier levels.

As he explained to Dr. Rose, Richard enjoyed the sense of well-being he felt when under the influence of alcohol. The more stressful he thought the second half of the workday would be, the more drinks he would have for lunch in order to "prepare" for that stress. His well-lubricated business lunches would include three, four, five, or more drinks and last longer and longer into the afternoon. A downside to this strategy was that as Richard's degree of intoxication increased, he became boastful and argumentative, was unsteady on his feet, and showed poor judgment (e.g., bad-mouthing his boss, driving his car while still intoxicated). Although he would tell himself that the drinks were just to "take the edge off" and that they did not adversely affect his performance, his supervisor's evaluations of Richard's performance did not agree. In between drinking episodes, Richard came to spend more and more time thinking about his next drink. Worried about a sudden shortage of alcohol, he started to keep a bottle in his desk drawer at work.

Although Richard attempted to hide his addiction to alcohol from loved ones and employers, Janice noticed the change in him, since it became customary for Richard to have several drinks before leaving home for a party or dinner engagement, and then quite a few more during the event itself. She criticized him for this, which made Richard angry. Janice enlisted the help of Richard's mother in pressing the issue, but he ignored these warnings, insisting that his family and friends were overly concerned and that his drinking was not out of control. As Janice put it, "we went through this little game week after week after week."

Richard was not pleasant to be around when he was drinking. Given that there were increasingly fewer hours in the day when he was not drinking, the problems were increasing. Any mention that he might have a drinking problem would send him off in a rage. He would frequently return from such rages completely drunk and, therefore, even more difficult to deal with. Although Richard was not physically abusive as an alcoholic, he was verbally abusive and emotionally cold to his family.

Over the years, Richard's children slowly adapted to his unreliability and angry outbursts. On occasions when he admitted causing them pain, they felt sorry for him. As the family adjusted to Richard's inadequacies, they shut him off more and more from the responsible roles he had once played in their lives. The result of this combination of attributes caused his grown children to attend college in another state, and nearly all interactions between Richard and his children have ceased.

Before things progressed to the point that the children moved out of state, they and Janice had adapted amazingly well to Richard's problems. Janice would often make excuses for Richard and suggest that he did work awfully hard and deserved to "let his hair down" once in a while. Janice also compensated for Richard's unreliability with attending school functions. She made sure to attend every play and sporting event the children were a part of. Both children stopped asking Richard to attend events when he showed up at one of their basketball games completely intoxicated and had wet his pants.

Janice and the children became so good at adapting to Richard's behaviors and problems, and so good at compensating for him, that few others knew the extent of what they were confronting. Janice would call in sick to work for Richard when he was too hungover to get out of bed. She would often buy Richard's favorite whiskey as a present when she had something to ask him that she thought might make him upset. In essence, then, her behaviors and those of the children became intricately intertwined with Richard's alcohol abuse.

After years of erratic job performance, Richard was eventually fired by his employer. He promised Janice that he wouldn't drink anymore, but soon he was drinking again. As time passed, he gave up most of the earlier efforts he made to hide his drinking and spent his days in blue-collar drinking establishments where the alcohol was less expensive and the clientele more accepting of one another. Janice's ultimatum was that he seek help at a hospital in a city 20 miles away or move out of the home. After many weeks of arguing over this, Richard agreed, but that program turned out to provide little more than detoxification; after a cursory examination, the staff there discharged Richard with a clean bill of health. He promised Janice that he had learned his lesson, and that if she allowed him to return home, he would remain sober. However, three days later, he was drinking again.

By now Janice was starting to become afraid of Richard. She and his mother discussed what to do, and Janice decided that she would give him one more chance if he would check into the Veterans Hospital in the state capital for a month of inpatient treatment for alcoholism. He did so. The program was much more intensive than the detoxification treatment Richard had received before. This program included counseling sessions, group therapy, and total abstinence from alcohol. It was a difficult program for Richard to complete, but once admitted, he was obligated to complete the month. Janice was feeling fairly confident when Richard was released. Due to traffic, however, she arrived late to pick him up following his discharge and could not find him. Imagine how enraged she became when after much searching, she found him in a bar several blocks from the hospital, completely intoxicated.

Finally unable to tolerate his behavior, Janice told Richard she planned to divorce him and he had to move out. By the time she had the divorce papers drawn up, Richard was showing not only alcohol abuse but also most of the typical characteristics of the more severe diagnosis of alcohol dependence. He repeatedly drank to excess even though at some level he understood that in doing so, he risked serious problems. His inability to limit his drinking was accompanied by clear indications of dependence: a narrowing of his alcohol-related behaviors to drinking and little else, increased tolerance, repeated withdrawal symptoms, and relief or avoidance of withdrawal brought about by further drinking.

Treatment Considerations

Alcohol dependence involves much more than just excessive drinking and calls for comprehensive services. Treatment often includes a variety of procedures. The goals of Richard's treatment included restoring his overall social functioning as well as facilitating abstinence and avoiding relapse. Psychologically, there are reasons why Richard may be drinking too much. Biological perspectives assume that alcoholism is a result of a genetic predisposition that may be triggered when the person first begins to drink. But it is also important to consider the thoughts the person has about alcohol (a cognitive perspective that will address such things as what Richard thinks about his drinking and what he expects the alcohol to do for him) and the sociocultural aspects of alcohol consumption (such as whether Richard enjoys "being the life of the party," or society's image of the appropriateness of drinking).

Dr. Rose saw Richard as an outpatient. Before doing so, Dr. Rose assessed Richard's potential for initiating the process of recovery, which would assume a substantial amount of motivation on his part. If this assumption was tenable—that Richard was highly motivated to quit drinking—the other expectations for recovery could include an active and strenuous commitment to change, and long-term maintenance of the recovery process.

Dr. Rose stressed abstinence as the ideal outcome. However, he understood that alcohol dependence is a chronic, relapsing disorder; lengthening Richard's periods of sobriety between any slips he has, and taking precautions so that the consequences of drinking are less risky for him, can also represent progress for someone like Richard. He also understood that having Richard exercise an appropriate degree of choice or preference would be important, and assisted Richard's self-selection of treatment components by fully informing him of the available options. Richard opted for outpatient treatment because, with the encouragement of Dr. Rose, Janice agreed to let Richard live at home as long as he was sober and stayed in treatment.

Psychological treatment was relatively intensive, with two sessions per week of Cognitive-Behavioral Therapy, plus a minimum of three evenings per week that Richard was to attend AA meetings. Richard agreed to submit to unannounced Breathalyzer tests during his therapy visits. Participation in AA gave Richard needed support and regular reminders of the benefits of staying sober and the damaging consequences of drinking. AA meetings were especially valuable on weekends and over holidays, when loneliness could add to the temptations Richard felt to drink.

Dr. Rose considered having Richard take disulfiram (Antabuse). While it has no physiological effect on a person who abstains from drinking, disulfiram produces an extremely unpleasant physiological reaction in anyone who combines it with alcohol. Thus, taking disulfiram every day would provide a strong inducement to remain abstinent. Prolonging Richard's abstinence was useful because it would facilitate in vivo (direct) exposure to the high-risk situations he must learn to cope with in trying to achieve long-term sobriety for the first time in his adult life. Richard declined to use disulfiram, however, citing an experience he had at the VA hospital. There, a fellow patient drank while on disulfiram and experienced such a violent attack of nausea, vomiting, and breathing difficulties that he had to be rushed to the city hospital emergency room and placed in intensive care.

With Richard's consent, Dr. Rose instead prescribed naltrexone (ReVia), an opiate antagonist that has been found to reduce the reinforcing effects and increase the unpleasant sedative effects of alcohol. Naltrexone does this by blocking the effects of endogenous opioids that are released when alcohol is consumed.

Taking naltrexone has been found to reduce feelings of craving and also alcohol consumption in a subset of individuals who also received outpatient therapy with coping-skills training. A possible explanation is that reduced interference of craving in the individual's recovery effort gives the new coping skills a chance to work.

As the review of Richard's history amply demonstrated over the years, he received considerable pressure from his family, work colleagues, and treatment professionals to stop drinking, and yet he was unable to do that. Having a therapist who simply insisted that Richard immediately stop all drinking would thus be very unlikely to have a long-term effect. Instead, Dr. Rose used a less confrontational approach known as Motivational Enhancement Therapy (Miller & Rollnick, 1991) to leverage Richard's self-professed goals in helping him initiate the difficult first steps toward recovery. For example, rather than criticizing Richard's mistakes and expecting complete abstinence, Dr. Rose simply accepted that Richard was ambivalent about his drinking and was struggling to change. Second, an early focus of treatment was on developing and making salient to Richard one or more sharp discrepancies between his continued drinking and other important goals. Here Dr. Rose prodded gently rather than using "scare tactics." For example, Richard had certainly hit a personal "bottom" with the loss of his job and Janice's initiation of divorce proceedings. He felt intensely the humiliation, shame, and loss, as well as financial and legal problems arising from these events. Richard thought hard about how his life would be different if he sobered up for good and stayed away from alcohol. Granted, he would see some short-term drawbacks and difficulties with that path, but with the therapist's help, he recognized some benefits in the long run that he valued very highly.

The Motivational Enhancement Therapy sessions included advice, persuasion, feedback, goal setting, role playing, and brainstorming the choices Richard faced. Dr. Rose avoided arguing with Richard during therapy, no matter how wrong-headed Richard's thinking seemed to be. Confrontations were unproductive since Richard had considerable practice and skill in such verbal jousting from long years of battling his wife and other critics of his drinking. Provoking resistance on Richard's part was avoided (e.g., he might be uncooperative during sessions, or not show up at all); Dr. Rose supported Richard's sense of self-efficacy, his recognition that he has choices, and his need for hope.

Social support is important to recovery, and Janice reluctantly agreed to participate in treatment. Dr. Rose met with her separately to foster a collaborative alliance. She agreed to witness Richard's taking of naltrexone each day, and to help monitor Richard's coping with risky situations. Couples counseling for the two of them focused on communication skills. Early in their relationship, Richard used alcohol to open up to Janice in a positive way. She responded warmly and came to accept his heavy use of alcohol, even buying it for him on occasion. Richard's drinking thus became an integral part of their emotional relationship. Without alcohol, Richard would have to learn new ways of communicating his emotional needs, including assertiveness (where appropriate). For her part, Janice needed to develop skills for eliciting and supporting Richard's openness so that he no longer needed alcohol to communicate with her on an emotional level.

With Richard committed to recovery and Janice actively supporting him, more intensive cognitive-behavioral treatments were used to help Richard develop coping skills and self-efficacy, and to promote more adaptive attributions for stressful events and effective coping in response to them. The focus was on Richard's cognitive expectancies (e.g., that drinking will have positive effects, but also that he will be unable to exercise control if drinking occurs) and on the high-risk situations and thoughts that put Richard at risk for thinking about having a drink. These situations were conceptualized as the initial links in behavioral "chains" that culminate in taking a drink.

It was important to break these chains at one of their early links, since once Richard had had a drink, he stood little chance of stopping easily. Therapy worked on improving Richard's coping skills, both those that help him avoid or ward off cravings for alcohol, and those that promote a lifestyle free of alcohol and other risky substances. Specific procedures include self-monitoring (diary keeping) of the incidence of "urges" to drink, or other problem behaviors, to help Richard better anticipate problem situations, and helping Richard learn alternative coping skills for use in the high-risk situations that he identifies.

Once specific situational stresses and threats to his sobriety were identified, Richard and Dr. Rose constructed a hierarchy of these risky situations, a few of which are relatively easy to master. Over time, each situation in the hierarchy was confronted in sequence, using role playing, modeling (e.g., of drink-refusal skills), anger management skills, and so on, in response to the simulated situations. The goal was to begin with some successes, although in total, the hierarchy covers the full spectrum of risky situations.

Although Richard learned to identify behaviors he could substitute for drinking, and how to avoid times, places, and people associated with drinking, active coping in response to high-risk situations is a more powerful response than trying simply to avoid them. So, other therapy techniques include role playing a variety of skills, such as how to refuse a drink when offered one. To avoid awkwardness or misunderstandings with friends, Richard practiced ways to let them know in advance that he no longer drinks (e.g., for "health reasons"). More global intervention strategies designed to promote a lifestyle not centered on drugs included efforts to promote mental and physical wellness by reducing stress, maintaining good nutrition, avoiding caffeine and other drugs, exercising, and using relaxation techniques.

Richard was without a job, and before rushing out to look for a new one, Dr. Rose helped him try to understand the likely connections between his prior job and his drinking (e.g., lots of flexibility in his schedule) and what kinds of work schedules would assist his recovery. A further component of treatment is social/recreational counseling. As with Richard's prior work history, Dr. Rose had Richard identify the maladaptive aspects of his prior lifestyle (people and situations), and develop social and recreational opportunities that are conducive to sobriety. Richard worked on developing concrete, written plans to increase the likelihood he would discover interesting new activities (boredom in the absence of alcohol is a big problem in recovery). He worked to develop "positive addictions"—reading, movies, exercise, and increased involvement in spiritual or religious activities (including meditation or just free time for himself).

As Richard put his skills into practice and remained sober, therapy reached the final stage of dealing with "relapse prevention" (Marlatt & Gordon, 1985), which was designed specifically to counteract the feelings of failure and other negative self-perceptions that accompany temptations to drink, or an actual slip into resumed use. This therapy component assumed that the most significant aspect of taking a drink was not the pharmacological effect of the alcohol but rather Richard's cognitive and emotional reaction to his behavior, including the shattering of his view of himself as an abstainer, a personal attribution of failure, feelings of shame, guilt, and helplessness, and deep pessimism about his eventual recovery. Thus, the problem with a slip is not that it occurs, but that it is interpreted as a catastrophe.

Dr. Rose did not avoid the issue of relapse, but focused on it directly. Richard needed to recognize and accept that the risk of relapse was a normal part of recovery, and he also needed to rehearse (mentally) the experience of a slip and how to handle it. At first, Richard was skeptical about this focus and insisted that relapse happens quickly and uncontrollably. Cognitive-behavioral treatment sought to "reframe" his understanding of relapse in exactly the opposite terms: viewing relapse, instead, as the culmination of a chain of events that he had many chances to recognize before it was too late. For example, the most likely stimuli for relapse were the same risky situations that previously led Richard to drink, such as interpersonal frustration or anger, social pressure to resume drinking, and having to cope with negative emotional states like anxiety, boredom, and fear. Recall that early in Richard's relationship with Janice, he was more spontaneous and emotionally assertive when he was drinking than when he was sober, a fact that reinforced his drinking and masked his interpersonal frustration.

Richard came to understand that the process of relapse starts well before actual drinking resumes, and is marked by such signs as losing control of his judgment, behavior, emotions, attitudes, or otherwise moving away from the process of recovery (e.g., making "mini-decisions" to fantasize about drinking, enter certain settings, visit certain people, stop attending AA, reject others' efforts to help, keep alcohol in the house for "entertainment" purposes, and so on). In sum, Dr. Rose helped him understand that relapse prevention is a controlled choice he makes in lieu of other choices, and helped Richard identify the other choices (e.g., how to take "time out" for himself without alcohol).

What should Richard do if an actual slip occurs? This, again, is simply another very high-risk situation, and he should handle it as such. One step would be to use cognitive restructuring to attribute the slip, not to himself, but to the risky situation associated with the slip. A second step would be to apply self-control skills to avoid drinking, or to stop once he had started. Richard signed a contract with Dr. Rose stating that if he ever had a drink in front of him ready to consume, he agreed to observe a mandatory delay of 20 minutes before he started to drink, and if he did start drinking, to consume the drink at the slowest possible rate (taking at least 30 minutes to finish it), to observe a mandatory delay of 30 more minutes before ordering a second drink and, finally, to contact Dr. Rose and pay him a monetary fine if the second drink is actually consumed.

The purpose of Dr. Rose's therapy with Richard was the realistic goal of lengthening Richard's periods of sobriety, not achieving a once-and-for-all cure of his disorder. Given Richard's moderately good level of functioning during the early years of his marriage, he, Janice, and Dr. Rose are guardedly optimistic that his current efforts to recover would succeed.

The Biology of Addictions

The work of Nora D. Volkow, MD, Director of the National Institute on Drug Abuse (NIDA, 2015), and a research psychiatrist and scientist, has demonstrated that drug addiction is a disease of the human brain. Even more importantly, her work and that of other research scientists guide us in understanding why some people are more vulnerable to contracting one of these drug addictions. Let us explore how our understanding of the underlying biology put forth by Dr. Volkow and others apply to Richard, the focus of this case study.

Richard is addicted to alcohol. To the biologist, that means that he uses alcohol compulsively without consideration of the negative consequences of doing so. It means that his brain is different neurobiologically from the brain of a non-addicted person and that the difference is not necessarily one of quantity: The difference is qualitative in that the brain is changed in nature.

Although we may think that the longest journeys that have been made by humans are to the moon, in many ways the longest journeys from a biological point of view are inner journeys. These are ones that probe deeper and deeper into those secret places of the body that have been difficult to explore. One is the brain that has long been protected by the vault—the skull—that guards it from invasion. Another is the nerve cell (neuron), which defied deep probing until cellular and molecular techniques were developed and provided "biological keys" to unlock doors that previously served as barriers to discovery.

Regarding the brain, much attention has been given in recent years, to a part of the brain called the Mesolimbic System. Of particular interest in the area of addictions research are the Nucleus Accumbens and the Ventral Tegmental Area. There is evidence to support the idea that these structures are part of a common attention-getting pathway in the brain that results in a "spike" of dopamine release from the Nucleus Accumbens regardless of the addictive agent that stimulates it. This pathway has been considered a "common reward" pathway for the past few years until it was expanded to include the concepts of attention getting (e.g., Wickelgren, 1997). Rather than signaling pleasure as previously thought, the neurotransmitter dopamine may be released by brain neurons to highlight significant stimuli.

According to David Self (1997), "Dopamine released into the NAc (Nucleus Accumbens) acts on two major types of receptors, the D1 and D2 Dopamine receptors. Both of these receptors are coupled to the same intracellular messenger system, the Cyclic Adeosine Monophosphate (cAMP) second messenger system. Dl and D2 receptors have opposite effects on cAMP function. Dl receptors stimulate cAMP and D2 receptors inhibit cAMP" (pp. 4–5).

To make the connection between dopamine and the previous research on reward pathways, Self explains: "In these animal models of drug-seeking behavior, the experiments with the dopamine agonists and the PKA-acting drugs suggest that what enhances the cocaine reinforcement also acts to induce relapse. We believe that in NAc neurons containing Dl receptors, stimulation of cAMP may lead to a sense of satiety or satiation of the reward system. Thus the animal no longer craves reinforcement. Stimulation of neurons containing D2 receptors inhibits PKA activity leading to a sensation of craving. These two pathways may be operating in separate populations of neurons within the same brain region, the NAc" (p. 8).

Regarding the neuron, evidence points to the fact that there are basic physiological questions at the cellular level. Recent and continuing studies focus on the intricacies of intracellular adaptation. Membrane receptors, intracellular receptors, and intracellular proteins (especially intracellular enzymes and second messenger systems) continue to gain the attention of research scientists in efforts to satisfy the unrelenting curiosity for understanding and to provide a more solid basis of support for effective treatment modalities for those who suffer addictive disorders such as addiction to alcohol.

We know that no illness or disorder has a simple biological component. When we consider cancer, diabetes, heart disease, or addiction, we realize that there is a complex array of components that must be considered. Important physiological issues are genetics, age, sex/gender, circadian rhythms, and the presence of other disease conditions. Environmental issues (recall that environment is a part of the biological perspective) include physical characteristics of the environment such as toxins, allergens, industrial pollution, radioactive waste, stress, social interactions, conditioned stimuli, and educational influences. All of these different components—and surely others not mentioned here—join the addictive agent (drug) to influence the brain, which then processes these "inputs" and expresses them through behaviors that feed back into the brain. At the same time, the resulting behaviors influence the environment and the changed environment feeds back both on the behavior and the brain. The classical scheme for designating a Type A or Type B category for differentiating characteristics exhibited by persons who suffer alcoholism reflects similar thinking—this kind of feedback situation.

In addictions, all of these factors are critical. The environmental considerations are probably greater for addiction than for most other disorders. Conditioning is often an overwhelming component. Visual, auditory, and other sensory cues that link to previous habits associated with use and/or abuse can trigger a response that is too strong to ignore and may trigger a relapse.

All of this discussion leads to treatment from a biologist's viewpoint. What must happen is for the "changed brain" of addiction to be "changed back" or reversed in function. Ways to approach that are through pharmacological interventions or behavioral ones. If, indeed, those techniques are behavioral, they need to effect the same kinds of changes that medication would. In fact, recovery relies on simultaneous treatment through combined use of medicine and behavioral techniques.

Richard's Experience With Alcoholics Anonymous

It is probably impossible to calculate the number of persons dependent upon alcohol who have been helped by AA. How many of us are keenly aware of the phrase, "Hello, my name is _____ and I am an alcoholic?" But participation in this and other alcohol dependence programs is no guarantee of success. In the current case, Richard needed to come to grips with many realities before he could successfully control his drinking. First and foremost, he needed to acknowledge that drinking had become a problem. Second, Richard needed to consider all of the ways in which alcohol had an impact on his life. Third, Richard had to acknowledge he needed help and that he was currently less able to control his urge to drink than he needed to be.

At an early AA meeting, Richard was sitting toward the back of the room sipping coffee and trying to ignore the fact that such an environment is the very kind that activates the strongest urge in him to drink. Richard dislikes being around many people that he does not know. His typical coping strategy, then, would be to drink and "take the edge off his nerves" before confronting such a situation. As Richard looked around the room and held his Styrofoam cup of coffee, he wondered if he made the right choice. Clouds of smoke hover around the ceiling; Richard wondered ever so briefly why he never took up smoking. The thought struck him as amusing, but he stifled a chuckle as a speaker moved toward the podium and microphone.

"Hello," the speaker began, "my name is Julia and I am an alcoholic." Richard was not sure why, but the fact that the person who started the meeting is a woman strikes him as odd. Although intuitively Richard understood that alcohol dependence was not gender specific, he had an image in his mind that only men would be at such meetings. Julia related her story and Richard noted enough similarities between her comments and his own life that he began to feel uncomfortable.

According to Julia, "You don't know the price you have paid until the price is so high that you cannot buy things back." A shiver raced down Richard's spine as he considered his relationship with Janice and his children. Suddenly he hated this young woman for what she said. How dare she pass judgment on his life? But part of Richard also understood that his anger could just as easily be turned inward. The call for new attendees to share went out and Richard hoped against hope that other AA virgins were present. They either were not present or refused to step forward. Richard walked slowly to the podium, looked out among the crowd and proclaimed, "Hello, my name is Richard and. . . ."

When the next words would not come, Richard bolted from the room, vowing never to return. But the power of the AA environment was almost as powerful as Richard's desire to drink. He found himself back at the same meeting 2 weeks later. Still not convinced that he had any problem himself, Richard found himself wanting to be convinced. As the weeks progressed, Richard found himself intermittently drawn to the meetings and, at still other times, ambivalent about attending them. His attendance was sporadic, but usually no more than 2 weeks would go by between his attendance at a meeting.

At each meeting that he did attend Richard would hear more stories that reminded him of his own life. He found himself at one moment hating each speaker for reminding him of himself and also being thankful that they shared what they had experienced. After 3 months of this see-saw attendance, Richard decided to ask Julia to be his sponsor. She agreed and the two of them began to develop a relationship that would move Richard through the step-by-step procedure that AA employs.

Richard has made amends for many of the events in his past, and has initiated new contacts with his grown children. Although neither of his children are yet at the healing point of granting Richard the forgiveness he seeks, they are at least willing to communicate with him. Janice has analyzed her own behaviors and has vowed to eliminate her tendency to reinforce Richard's patterns of drinking. For the moment, anyway, it seems that Richard is on his way to successfully achieving sobriety.

13

THE CASE OF PAULA H

Posttraumatic Stress Disorder

Introduction

Paula is a 30-year-old teacher. A single parent, she lived alone with her 6-year-old daughter, Carly. She made an appointment with her physician, Dr. Khatib, because of difficulty in getting to sleep at night plus a few other problems. Paula was rather subdued in the doctor's waiting room, sitting by herself in a far corner and avoiding her usual small talk with the office staff.

Dr. Khatib: How are you doing these days?

Paula: I guess I'm having a lot of trouble sleeping. I often wake up at night and can't get back to sleep. . . . Also, noises really bother me, and it seems I have bad dreams. Last week I woke my daughter up one night when I cried out in my sleep.

Dr. Khatib: Is anything going on in your life that might explain this problem?

Paula [largely avoiding the question]: Maybe it's a lack of sleep, or not eating much these days, but at times, I have difficulty concentrating, and once in a while I feel dizzy all of a sudden.

After a long pause, Paula went on to mention some soreness in her left shoulder and pain in her lower back. She hoped Dr. Khatib could prescribe something stronger than the over-the-counter analgesics and sleep aids she has tried.

Dr. Khatib was warm and supportive. Paula relaxed a little, and after hesitating as he made several notes in her chart, she decided to bring up the event that convinced her she had to come see him. She described how the previous week she drove through a stop sign, almost causing a serious accident that might have injured or even killed Carly. The intersection was a familiar one and Paula could not understand how she failed to stop.

Dr. Khatib paused to reflect on everything Paula had told him. As a group, her symptoms were rather diffuse and do not seem to center on any particular body system. With many illnesses, the symptoms center around a certain organ or certain body system (such as the respiratory tract). In Paula's case, however, multiple body systems appear to be involved (e.g., pain in her lower back, dizziness, trouble sleeping). Questioning Paula further, Dr. Khatib learned that none of these problems was present until a few months ago, which caused him to wonder about depression.

Dr. Khatib: Have you been feeling sad lately? Have you felt like crying?
Paula: "Yes . . . um, I've cried a few times . . ."
Dr. Khatib: Have you ever felt bad enough to consider hurting yourself?
Paula: [nervously] No!

Still thinking about depression, Dr. Khatib asked about social contact with her significant others.

Paula: I don't see people or go out much. . . .
Dr. Khatib: The last time you were in here I believe there was someone you were dating?

Paula tensed noticeably in response to the question. She felt the butterflies fluttering in her stomach but did not know what to do. "This man is a total stranger," she thought. "What business does he have asking such personal questions? All I want is a painkiller for my sore shoulder and maybe something to help me sleep better." These thoughts flew through Paula's mind in response to Dr. Khatib's question. She knew she should be honest, but did not know if she could trust this man. She also hated to think about "the events," as she had come to categorize them in her mind. Sometimes, she almost convinced herself that if she did not think or talk about the events, she could forget they ever happened.

Dr. Khatib paused, giving Paula a chance to answer if she wanted to. He noticed that she seemed to be mulling things over in her mind, and he wanted her to have a chance to answer without further prodding from him. After several minutes, he rephrased the question and asked it again.

Dr. Khatib: Are you still dating that young man you were dating the last time you came in for a visit?
Paula: N–no.
Dr. Khatib: I see.
Paula: You see what? What could you possibly know about it?
Dr. Khatib: Nothing. I simply meant, I see that you are not dating him anymore because that is what you just told me.
Paula: Oh.

Dr. Khatib: Is there anything you would like to tell me about that relationship?

Paula: I don't know.

Dr. Khatib: You don't know if there is anything about that relationship you want to tell me or you don't know if you want to talk about it?

Paula: Both.

Dr. Khatib: I promise you, Paula, that anything you tell me stays in this room. Why don't you just think of a good place to start and just start talking? If you decide that you want to stop talking, I won't pressure you to keep going. Okay?

Paula: I don't know.

Dr. Khatib: Talking about things is always better than holding them inside, don't you think?

Paula: I guess so. Things hurt to talk about too, though.

Dr. Khatib: Remember what I said? If you start telling me anything about that relationship that you think I should know but decide you want to stop, I won't pressure you. Okay?

Paula: I . . . I . . . I guess.

Paula teared up, looked away, and seemed to struggle with her emotions. To Dr. Khatib, she appeared to be struggling between keeping her private life private and wanting desperately to share something. He knew to give her time to make the decision for herself. By not pushing and letting her be in control of the conversation, he gave her more of a sense that she can trust him. When Paula looked back, tears were running down her face but she looked determined to tell him what she had, just moments ago, been uncertain she could reveal.

In a rush of emotion, Paula blurted out that Mark, the man she had been dating, beat her severely on two occasions. The second time was 4 months ago. He left her house in a rage, and she hasn't seen or heard from him since.

Dr. Khatib: Why haven't you taken legal action against him?

Paula: I'm afraid of what Mark might do, and I don't want to talk about what happened in front of anyone. I haven't even told my parents, because I am afraid of what they might do. It's possible they will blame me, since they did not like Mark and didn't like how we used to go out drinking a lot. If I tell them, I'm afraid Mark might do something to hurt them, or even worse, that he will hurt Carly somehow.

Dr. Khatib asked if Paula had experienced any other medical and psychological problems recently, including alcohol and drug use (more than likely Dr. Khatib used the CAGE questionnaire already discussed in several other cases—such as the cases of Barbara M and Richard B—in this casebook). He referred Paula to a neurologist for a thorough examination.

Dr. Khatib was concerned that the dizziness and difficulty concentrating, while they might be due to anxiety over the severe traumas Paula experienced, could also have been caused by blows to her head. The neurologist did a mental status exam and performed other neurological tests. He found no physical abnormalities that would explain Paula's symptoms, and after discussing the idea of psychotherapy at some length with Paula, referred her to Dr. Frank, a female psychologist who specializes in treating trauma.

The Diagnostic Interview

Dr. Frank was warm and cordial, but immediately got down to business. Because she knew why Paula was referred to her, she began by emphasizing how important it was for Paula to tell her everything that happened, and everything she thought and felt about it. (This is always useful in therapy, but it is especially difficult for people who have been through humiliating traumas like those Paula suffered.) Although Dr. Frank was ready to hear about everything, it took several sessions for Paula to give many details. (Noting this later, Paula explained that she did not really trust Dr. Frank to listen to all of it without becoming "turned off.")

Because it was the easiest way to start, Paula told Dr. Frank about her relationship with Mark. They met during a period of loneliness following her divorce. At first, Paula felt flattered by Mark's attentiveness and his intense interest in her. Later she became disenchanted by what later seemed like warning signs. For example, Mark was a heavy drinker and also regularly used marijuana. He showed a streak of cruelty toward a neighbor's dog, and he sometimes drove dangerously, especially after drinking. He could be very self-centered, and he seemed to have rigid expectations about how Paula should behave.

Mark became jealous when Paula spent time working with a male fellow teacher on an after-school project. He could be sweet and romantic at times, but could also be hypercritical, belittling Paula to the point of embarrassing her in front of others. Mark also imposed rather petty conditions on their relationship. He discouraged Paula from socializing with her fellow teachers after work, and sometimes listened in on her phone conversations. He insisted that she destroy all correspondence from her former husband, and consistently preferred that the two of them do things alone together. Eventually he objected even to Paula having more than brief phone conversations with her girlfriends.

Paula tried to end their relationship two or three times, but was not assertive about this: Her discomfort at making Mark unhappy and worries about loneliness made it hard to stick with this decision. Currently she was filled with doubt about her own role in bringing about Mark's violent behavior towards her. She wondered if there was any truth to his claim that she bore some responsibility for instigating his loss of control.

Once Mark had finally left for good, Paula was overwhelmed with fear and anxiety. The unexpectedness of the two assaults, and the fact that each went on for so long, were especially devastating. It was clear to Paula that she could never be as trusting of anyone as she used to be. She was frightened that since she had told the doctors about the beatings, Mark will find out and follow through with a threat he made that if Paula ever told anyone he would come back and hurt Carly. While Paula previously had been an enthusiastic fifth-grade teacher, she now felt like she was just "going through the motions." She stayed home nearly every evening. Her only social experiences were occasional weekend outings with Carly.

Eventually, Dr. Frank pressed Paula for an account of the beatings. She reluctantly provided this, indicating that as the assaults continued over a half-hour or longer, she felt as though she was watching from outside herself, with everything taking place in slow motion: "I was shocked and stunned . . . I couldn't say anything. I was on the floor and the room was spinning above me . . . I became numb."

Paula's Nightmare Following the First Beating

Paula told Dr. Frank that the nightmares started after the first beating and have since become almost a nightly ritual. It was following this dream on several occasions that she woke Carly with her screams. Dr. Frank knew that it would be difficult, but Paula must share those nightmares with her. Paula took a long time preparing herself to launch into a description of the nightmare. When she started, however, she barely stopped to take a breath. Dr. Frank suspected that Paula was afraid that if she were to stop in the middle of discussing the dream, she might never begin telling that story again.

> The dream started with me sitting in a rocking chair on a porch. I don't know where I am but it seems pretty calm and I remember thinking how happy I looked just sitting there rocking and soaking up the sun. But the scenery changes quickly and a storm starts rolling in. The clouds blacken and bolts of yellow and pink lightning start tearing through the clouds. I continued to rock in the rocking chair staring at the storm. Funnel clouds darted down toward the ground and tore trees out of the ground, roots and all. Then the clouds began to take on a new shape. At first, I could not make out the image. Then a sneering smile split the clouds and I could see teeth. It was Mark.
>
> The clouds had formed a horrible storm-like specter of Mark. I jumped up from the rocking chair and started to run. I don't know why I didn't run into the house. Something just told me that I needed to run away from the house. I had to keep Mark from going into that house. As I ran, tears started to run down my cheeks. I wiped a tear away and was only vaguely bothered when I looked at my fingers and they were streaked with blood. In comparison to the storm version of Mark, my own crying blood didn't seem all that surprising.

I was out in the middle of a field and running as fast as I could. The funnel clouds had retracted back into the Mark storm. Then, instead of funnel clouds, cloud versions of his arms bolted out of the cloud body and tried to grab me. I screamed and ran faster. But I could not outrun this monster version of Mark. One of his cloud fists closed around my body and tried to squeeze the life out of me. I tried to scream but I could not get enough air to make my lungs work. The only thing I could think of was Carly. Who would protect her when the cloud monster version of Mark killed me?

Then within the dream, I woke up in my own bed. I could hear Carly screaming and I knew Mark was after her. I tried to pull myself out of bed but I was tangled in the sheets. I tried to disentangle myself but I was wound up pretty tight. Then Carly screamed again and I ripped the sheets from around me. I jumped out of bed and ran toward the door. Then I felt something wrap itself around my ankle. I glanced back and it was one of the shreds of sheet. Suddenly, all of the shreds were slithering across the room toward me. They began to wrap around my other leg, both of my arms, my neck and my head. One wrapped itself around my mouth and I could not scream. One wrapped tightly around my nose and I could not breathe.

I heard Carly scream again and that energized me into action. I clawed my way toward the door and several of the sheet shreds tore and I broke free. Just as I reached the door, it slammed shut in front of me and Mark stepped out of the shadows. He was no longer a monster storm but he did not look any less evil. I swear I saw the fires of hell burning in his eyes. He had Carly's baby doll in his hands and he was holding it by the hair. While I stared at it in horror, the face changed and it was suddenly a tiny doll version of Carly.

That was all I could handle. I lunged for Mark and he disappeared. I yanked the door open and started to run down the hall. It was like all the dream sequences I have ever seen in movies. The faster I ran, the longer the hall became. But unlike the movie scenes, this was terrifying to me. I knew I had to reach Carly. God only knows what unspeakable things Mark would do to her. I ran as fast as I could but continued to lose ground. I saw Mark up ahead of me. He had a butcher knife in his hand and was just about to enter Carly's room. I tried to run faster. Then I heard it. Blood-curdling screams issued forth from Carly's room. That bastard was hurting my baby. I crumpled to the floor and started to scream. I wanted to scream so loudly that Mark would leave Carly alone.

It was those screams that came out of my mouth and woke up Carly. It was her touch on my arm that brought me out of that nightmarish hell. We held each other for the rest of the night and I kept vigilant watch while Carly slept in my arms. I will not let that bastard hurt my little girl. Do you hear me? I can't let him hurt Carly.

Dr. Frank handed the tissue box to Paula and gave her time to calm down from the emotions brought back from the memories of that nightmare. It was a horrible dream and Dr. Frank knew that such images did not fade very quickly with time. Nevertheless, the dream did reconfirm the stress and fear Paula was experiencing because of Mark's cruel treatment.

After the first attack, Paula convinced herself that the assault was an aberration, and she believed Mark when he said it would never happen again. After the second beating, Paula decided she could never trust Mark again, and she became especially worried about Carly's safety.

Paula continued to worry about her own safety as well, since Mark could easily determine her whereabouts at almost any time of day. As a consequence, Paula was sometimes seized with the thought of radically changing her appearance, such as getting her hair cut extremely short. She fantasizes that if Mark ever tried to surprise her, he might be startled enough by the change in her appearance that she could escape.

In the months since the second attack, Paula has kept to herself at work and avoided most informal social gatherings. She often skipped lunch, saying she is not hungry. Her fellow teachers have noticed some irritability in recent months that was not previously characteristic of Paula. The teachers closest to her have suggested that she has become distant and preoccupied, and much more sensitive to criticism (e.g., displaying a grimly silent response to their kidding about keeping to herself so much).

One morning, Paula was busy talking with a student when another student came up and touched her on the arm to get her attention. The sudden and unanticipated touch caused Paula to flinch and she jerked herself away. She stared in terror at the boy. Her reaction startled him so badly that he went running out of the room. The rest of the students in her class stopped and stared at her. On another occasion, the sudden slamming of a classroom door caused a similar overreaction that startled others.

Staying home most evenings has interfered with some of her job responsibilities (like school "open house" events) and has not helped Paula deal with her intrusive thoughts and physical symptoms any more effectively. Increasingly strained relations have developed with two male colleagues at school, who previously were among her close friends. She had few supports and felt trapped. She needed support (and possibly more) from her friends, but wasn't sure she could really count on them to give it once they found out what happened. All she could imagine was having to answer ceaseless questions, such as "How could you have let him do that to you?" She was discouraged enough about work that she was thinking of asking for an immediate medical leave of absence.

Dr. Frank's intake interviews also dealt with other issues. She concluded that Paula did not have immediate need of protective shelter, financial assistance, or medical treatment, and that she was demonstrating reliable care of herself and her child. Dr. Frank obtained sufficient information from Paula to indicate that she was not at special risk based on a previous history of abuse (e.g., as a child) or other mental disorders, and was not endangering herself (e.g., by excessive use of alcohol).

Dr. Frank asked Paula to do a careful enumeration of people she could still trust and use for support. There weren't many. Paula explained that because she had been able to deal with other negative experiences, like her divorce, by forcing her mind off them, she wanted to believe she could do the same thing this time. It turned out to be difficult, however, since the beatings came as such a shock and there were so many reminders of them around. She asked Dr. Frank if therapy can be used to make her forget, but Dr. Frank carefully explained that it is more effective to confront trauma directly and develop ways to manage it consciously.

Dr. Frank assured Paula that her symptoms of poor sleeping, distracting thoughts, being easily startled, and feeling socially ill at ease were normal for someone who had been through events like those she experienced. She explained that there is a name for the problems Paula had, that others have been through such experiences, that talking about it to a therapist will be helpful, and that recovery from the worst aspects of the experience is possible.

Nevertheless, Paula was ambivalent about entering therapy. Dr. Frank pointed out that seeking help indicates strength and motivation to overcome the setback created by her traumatic experience, and that entering therapy within a few months of being assaulted carries a more positive prognosis, with fewer complications, than waiting until much later.

The Assessment Model

Dr. Frank's intake interviews have developed these facts: Paula was reexperiencing aspects of two severe beatings through repeated, intrusive recollections and nightmarish dreams. She also showed physiological reactivity (irritability and difficulty sleeping) to stimuli associated with her traumatic experiences. Among other difficulties were the somatic complaints that brought her to Dr. Khatib, and also feelings of ineffectiveness and lack of interest in socializing. As a result, she was withdrawn and distant from others.

These facts made a diagnosis of PTSD seem quite obvious. However, Dr. Frank did not jump to that conclusion. Instead, she gathered systematic information from Paula to ensure that there were no other causal explanations for her symptoms. For example, the episode of running the stop sign, although not exactly a memory "blackout," triggered questions about substance use and the occurrence of any other "dissociative" episodes.

Only after a thorough evaluation did Dr. Frank conclude that the most appropriate diagnosis for Paula is PTSD. She displayed most of the classic symptoms of this disorder, including: (a) "reliving" the events of her abuse in her dreams, (b) increased arousal (and the subsequent problems associated with this such as insomnia), difficulty concentrating and hypervigilance (always being on the alert for danger), and (c) avoidance of stimuli and/or situations that remind her of the traumatic event (such as avoiding places she and Mark used to go, and even friends if they're the sort who might ask too many questions).

For a diagnosis of PTSD, the DSM-5 requires the direct experience of a very traumatic event, involving serious injury and possibly death, that continues to elicit intense emotional reactions, including fear, terror, helplessness, or a combination of these reactions. The violent physical abuse Paula suffered certainly qualifies, and the fact it was not a "natural" calamity but instead was perpetrated by a significant other makes the ordeal even more disturbing. Also significant in the diagnosis is the continuing impact of the event through intrusive thoughts and dreams about it, persistent avoidance of trauma reminders (people, places), diminished participation in significant activities, emotional numbing, increased arousal, and intense distress. The beatings Paula suffered were extremely serious in their consequences, and her symptoms were direct outcomes of those events (i.e., were not present previously), and has continued for more than 1 month. Dr. Frank decided against adding the specifier "with dissociative symptoms," since the inattention and memory problems Paula reported were not persistent or recurrent.

Treatment Considerations

Dr. Frank was sympathetic, sensitive, interested, and encouraging. She worked to establish a "therapeutic alliance" relatively quickly. She negotiated a contract with Paula that entailed a few very specific goals and specified what she and Paula would do throughout treatment. Paula's active involvement in the therapy process was intended to help her recover some sense of strength and control.

The challenge facing Paula and Dr. Frank was that Mark's beatings damaged Paula's psychological mastery of everyday life (her mental equilibrium) even more than her body. Paula needed to acknowledge, to Dr. Frank and to herself, the terrible things that happened, and she had to reestablish a sense of safety and control. She needed to rebuild her self-respect and her confidence in her ability to manage difficult situations, and to restore her connections to others. She had to come to understand that nothing she did or didn't do, no matter how careless or impulsive in hindsight, absolves Mark of being responsible for the criminal acts of assaulting her.

Treatment for PTSD differs from most other disorders, since in PTSD a return to the individual's pre-event level of functioning is a reasonable goal (i.e., there is no pressing need for substantive personality reorganization). In addition, the emphasis was on here-and-now issues and on what Paula could do or was doing rather than on possible "deficits" in her personality. To accomplish this, Dr. Frank maintained a present, problem-centered focus rather than looking at past difficulties, such as Paula's divorce. Also, she did not treat Paula as a "psychological cripple," but rather as a competent, responsible adult who had been through terrible experiences. This was important in counteracting a natural self-blame tendency shown by many trauma survivors.

Dr. Frank's treatment plan followed Herman's (1992) approach, where recovery is based on empowerment and reconnection that takes place in three stages. The first of these stages emphasized safety and stabilization. Thus, although Dr. Frank understood that it would be important for Paula to confront the trauma she experienced, initially it was even more important for her to experience a safe environment where she could recover some degree of trust in people.

Dr. Frank facilitated increased trust and competence in Paula by taking a collaborative stance that affirmed Paula's ability to manage her situation. Although she was available by telephone between sessions, she insisted that Paula had all the competence needed to carry out her recovery efforts between their meetings. Dr. Frank understood that Paula needed supportive, realistic input from her. She did not directly criticize Paula's actions, but also did not "sugar-coat" the damage that has occurred or the amount and difficulty of the work to be done.

In addition to helping Paula verbalize her feelings, Dr. Frank restated Paula's descriptions of what happened in ways that were more blunt and concrete; for example, when Paula said, "the time we had the bad fight," Dr. Frank corrected her with "when Mark assaulted you." She also helped to mobilize Paula's energy by helping her relabel her anxiety as "anger," understanding that the release of anger was crucial. However, Dr. Frank avoided letting Paula's anger take the form of fantasies about physical retaliation against Mark (which Paula may well have entertained but which were unlikely to assist her recovery) but instead encouraged a motivating kind of anger that helped Paula assign responsibility to Mark for what he did, and to herself for recovering from it.

For a person like Paula, the optimal solution to a given problem is rarely obvious, to her or to anyone else, and so it was best for Dr. Frank to support Paula in making her own decisions. For example, to an outsider, pressing charges against Mark may seem an almost mandatory response, but there are downsides to such an action (increased stress and perhaps danger) that may be very apparent to Paula.

Regarding Paula's ideas about radically changing her appearance, or taking a medical leave from work, Dr. Frank did not question these ideas directly, but instead encouraged Paula to think through the purposes of such actions and to consider a range of options first, from changing the locks on her house to getting a protective order against Mark. A key principle here is for Paula to make decisions that are consistent with her recovery and with which she can successfully follow through.

This "survivor-centered" focus was also shown in how Dr. Frank approached the issue of medication. There are medications that Dr. Khatib could have prescribed to help Paula get to sleep sooner at night, not to mention alleviate her depressive symptoms, but it was important that decisions such as the use of prescription medications be made by Paula. In the end, she decided not to use the antidepressant medication phenelzine (Nardil), concluding that it could restrict her lifestyle (e.g., she could not take medication and continue to ingest alcohol) and might also interfere with the psychological treatments Dr. Frank was proposing.

In stage one, Dr. Frank's treatment was primarily cognitive and behavioral. She helped Paula identify and address her maladaptive cognitions through self-monitoring of thoughts, and recognizing maladaptive connections between these thoughts and feelings of guilt and self-blame. Dr. Frank also applied the technique of prolonged "exposure," both during therapy sessions and as part of "homework" done outside of therapy. Although it may seem very counterintuitive, direct and sustained exposure to (or engagement with) trauma stimuli, even when the client is reluctant, is usually, much more beneficial than avoidance.

Dr. Frank was reasonably confident that Paula's other symptoms were not severe enough to diagnose her as having alcohol abuse, generalized anxiety, or depression, and also confident that exposure treatment would not exacerbate any of these other symptoms. Dr. Frank explained the rationale for using exposure to Paula, including the critical importance of full emotional engagement with no avoidance, since many clients are reluctant to try exposure. Dr. Frank was very understanding, and noted that "It may sometimes seem like we're doing surgery with no anesthesia." In the end, Paula was helped to overcome the worst of her anxiety and turmoil by the thought that she had to recover if she was to do the best job of which she is capable in raising Carly.

Sessions were held twice a week for 8 weeks. The exposure treatments included Dr. Frank guiding Paula to relive traumatic memories in her imagination (e.g., "close your eyes and describe the details of the assault as if it were happening now, focusing on details of the event and also your feelings and thoughts as the event occurs"). Paula described the beatings in the present tense (as though they were happening at that moment), and in great detail. She wrote out a script that she read during the exposure sessions.

As Paula read her script, Dr. Frank prompted her with "What sounds do you hear? What other sensations do you have?" and added anxiety-arousing details (pain, crying out for help). She plays back audiotapes of Paula's previous graphic descriptions of the beatings. Each dose of exposure lasts 45–60 minutes, until Paula's anxiety subsides. On occasions when Paula finished sooner, Dr. Frank had her start over at the beginning. Dr. Frank ended the exposure phase of each session with enough time remaining to allow Paula to regain her composure completely before she left.

Prolonged exposure to trauma stimuli in a safe situation drained Paula's arousal and shifted her thoughts from helplessness to the increasing manageability of her problems. A decline in distress over time (or "habituation") is associated with long-term successful recovery from trauma, and many authorities believe that exposure serves to undercut the way in which trauma stimuli and PTSD symptoms seem to remind clients like Paula that the world is dangerous and she is incompetent and helpless.

Though difficult to undertake, exposure eventually helps to render trauma stimuli much less potent as triggers for anxiety, distraction, and other symptomatic disturbances. Outside of therapy, Paula continued the exposure procedure by listening to at least one of her tapes every day, and also by spending time in some of the places she and Mark used to go together. Dr. Frank helped Paula attribute her success in these procedures to herself and the reservoirs of strength and courage she turned out to possess.

PTSD has multiple dimensions that entail cognitive (intrusive thoughts), behavioral (avoidance), emotional (numbing), and vegetative disturbances. Exposure may help reduce cognitive symptoms more than the others. The second stage of Herman's (1992) approach concerns remembrance and mourning, and involves reconstructing the trauma story. Here Paula came to realize that she could not get her innocence back and be the way she once was, and that she wouldn't get restitution from (or revenge against) Mark, but that what was available to her was the opportunity to resolve the loss of some of her prior carefree ways under terms that she controlled.

The third stage of Herman's approach shifts the emphasis to reconnecting Paula to her community, and here she worked to build and rebuild her social support resources. With Dr. Frank's help, Paula had come to see the strengths she possesses to have survived, come to therapy on her own, and to have resolved many of her trauma-related problems. She was increasingly confident that she would be able to integrate the facts of her abuse with the rest of her life, and understood that just as she held Mark accountable for what he did, she too is accountable for where she goes from here. Paula decided that it would be very meaningful for her to use her strengths to help others, and in so doing to make her trauma experiences part of her life in a positive sense. She decided to do this in two steps. First, she had gained sufficient control over the entire ordeal to sit down with Carly and talk about everything in detail. Second, as her own blamelessness (and Mark's culpability) finally sank in, Paula decided to work as a volunteer at a shelter for women who have experienced domestic violence. She also enrolled in a fitness club to improve and rebuild her physical condition as she has rebuilt her psychological condition.

A Biologist's View of PTSD

PTSD is the one disorder discussed in this casebook that is necessarily associated with trauma. The traumatic event must involve actual or threatened death or serious physical injury to the patient or others and must elicit a response of intense fear, horror, or helplessness on the part of the patient. It is often associated with the experiences of war (Thomas et al., 2010). However, there are other kinds of trauma that can also lead to the reexperiencing of the trauma through unexpected, recurring flashbacks or nightmares. Persons who have experienced rape; abduction; floods; airplane crashes; or physical, sexual, or other abuse during childhood may suffer PTSD.

Questions that the biologist asks in looking at this disorder revolve around the damage that is done to the neuroendocrine system under such traumatic conditions that changes are made that come back to "haunt" the one traumatized. In this section, we will look at one such change that might account for the symptoms of PTSD.

When there is acute physical stress, the body releases several hormones and neurotransmitters into the blood. The source of these molecules is the adrenal gland. The outer layer, the cortex, secretes glucocorticoid (GC), and the inner adrenal, the medulla, secretes epinephrine (adrenaline) and norepinephrine. There is evidence that several days of stress are damaging to the hippocampal neurons and that long-term stress can actually result in loss of the hippocampal neurons. The hippocampus is a part of the brain that is of critical importance in processes involving learning and memory (Wang et al., 2010).

Some genes make proteins that provide protection from creating fear memories. An example is stathmin, a protein that, when lacking in mice, results in a loss of the "freeze" response that protects them from danger and gastrin-releasing-protein (GRP). These and many other genes may provide some effects at work in PTSD. Brain structures, other than the hippocampus mentioned earlier, that are of research interest are the amygdala and certain areas of the pre-frontal cortex (PFC).

The other matter of extreme interest to a biologist that becomes especially relevant in Paula's case relates to sex (gender) differences and PTSD. The patient here is female. There are studies conducted by Kathleen T. Brady and her colleagues related to PTSD and cocaine and alcohol abuse (Brady, Dansky, Saladin, & Sonne, 1996) and gender differences (Brady, Grice, Dustan, & Randall, 1993).

One such study was of 100 cocaine and alcohol abusers (50 men and 50 women). One of the items studied was the percentage of these persons that were ever diagnosed with comorbid psychiatric disorders. Of the men, 24 percent had at some time been diagnosed with PTSD, compared to 46 percent of the women. The further question studied was who had psychiatric disorders before the onset of the substance dependence. Eight of the 11 men had the disorder first, whereas 18 of the 23 women had the disorder first. Perhaps the most interesting aspect of the study was that of the 50 men and 50 women whom Brady studied, 46 percent of the women were diagnosed with lifetime PTSD compared with only 24 percent of the men.

There have been a number of articles more recent than Brady's work that have added to the complexity of our understanding of gender differences in PTSD. These studies have all been conducted on US military veterans. One such study was conducted noting mental health diagnoses of US military personnel serving principally in Afghanistan and Iraq. This article states that the studies that exist for these service members are limited and show mixed results. However, reading the details of these studies leads to an understanding of the complexity of the topic of gender differences in PTSD (e.g., Smith et al., 2008).

The reason that biologists would take an interest in Brady's work is because it approaches the complexity of these disorders and the intertwining of a variety of parameters, of which gender difference is one to consider. Biologists rarely view questions proposed or answers sought as anything but complex—and when answers come, they use the answers to form new questions.

A Final Look at Paula's Case

As the end of therapy approached, Dr. Frank helped Paula anticipate possible future problems. PTSD reactions do not dissipate easily, and Paula could benefit from further counseling later. She gave Dr. Frank a verbal commitment that if necessary she would seek help again. In their final session, Dr. Frank used Herman's (1992) metaphor that recovering from trauma is like running a marathon: Recovery requires great preparation and commitment, and in the end is completed by Paula, not her therapist/coach.

In the months that followed, Paula learned to adjust better to difficult interactions with others, but remained uncomfortable about her safety and was more guarded about intimate relationships than she was before she met Mark. Paula may never fully resolve her trauma experience. Certainly there will be reminders, occasional bad dreams, and further life stresses. Paula was prepared for the possibility that Mark will contact her, and for "anniversary" reactions. On a more positive note, Paula also realized that, while it wouldn't be easy, she was ready to get on with the rest of her life.

14

THE CASE OF BRIGHID C

Dissociative Identity Disorder

Introduction

The McClintocks sat down at the dinner table precisely at 6 p.m. as had been their tradition every night since the children were born. The McClintocks had decided that a regular and consistent routine was important in the lives of their young children. Given that both of them had full-time careers, however, such a routine was impossible to accomplish alone. So the hiring of Brighid as a nanny and her subsequent stellar performance had been a blessing. Brighid had quickly settled into the dynamics of the family. The children adored her, and the McClintocks had nothing but high praise for her performance.

Katie led them through the usual pre-meal prayer, and Mrs. McClintock filled the children's plates. Within moments the bowls were being passed, but each time a bowl was offered to Brighid, she simply looked at it in numb silence. Several attempts were made to communicate with her but she seemed unresponsive.

"Brighid . . . Brighid . . . say something, please." Mrs. McClintock tried to break through to Brighid but she seemed utterly unaware of the attempt. Fearing that the situation would startle the children, Mrs. McClintock walked around the table and placed a hand on Brighid's shoulder. That seemed to make a connection because Brighid responded with a startled shriek and then began to shake uncontrollably.

"I can't eat . . . I can't eat . . . I . . . I . . ."

That feeble attempt to explain what she was so tense about appeared to be all that Brighid could muster. Her voice trailed off and she slumped face first to the table. The last movement energized the McClintocks into action. Within moments, they were able to help Brighid into her coat, and Mrs. McClintock was pulling out of the driveway and heading toward the hospital. Mrs. McClintock had noticed Brighid's odd comments about eating and her somewhat unusual eating habits before. This was by far, however, the most troublesome experience.

The Diagnostic Interview

"Hello, Brighid, I'm Dr. Scott, a staff psychiatrist here at St. Lawrence."

Brighid responded only with a slight nod. In fact, she seemed somewhat confused and unaware of where she was. Her employer, Mrs. McClintock, had brought her to the hospital access center for evaluation after Brighid became dizzy and confused following an inability to eat. Actually, Brighid was to share later that she did not remember keeping her responsibilities as a nanny to Mrs. McClintock's children. Though she appeared to ensure they were bathed, clothed, and ready to enjoy the full meal she had prepared, she did not remember doing these things.

Because Brighid seemed currently unable to be interviewed, Dr. Scott decided to interview Mrs. McClintock. Obviously, Mrs. McClintock was truly worried about Brighid. She was also very much concerned about the possibility of losing Brighid's services. Katie, four and a half years old, and Johnny, three, not only love Brighid, but her care of them was faultless. Over the next hour, Mrs. McClintock described Brighid and her behavior as best she could, and a number of interesting details emerged.

As a nanny, Brighid was somewhat of a perfectionist, and she worked very hard to please Mrs. McClintock. She was sometimes forgetful, and several misunderstandings had occurred recently. Brighid was always very apologetic when this happened, but on occasion her explanations have not entirely "added up." For example, once someone who sounded like Brighid left a brief message on Mrs. McClintock's answering machine the first thing in the morning asking her to give Brighid the day off, and Mrs. McClintock was unable to make other arrangements on such short notice.

Brighid arrived only slightly later than usual and claimed to know nothing about the earlier phone call. Another time, Brighid did not show up on time for work, which was very unusual for her, and when Mrs. McClintock called Brighid's apartment, a woman named Ginger answered the phone and claimed she had never heard of Brighid. Adding to the confusion, Ginger's voice sounded very much like Brighid's. Brighid showed up later that day and explained that she was late because of a very bad migraine headache. More baffling to Mrs. McClintock was that Brighid had no awareness of Mrs. McClintock's phone call and did not know who Ginger was. Mrs. McClintock was sure she had dialed the correct phone number, but Brighid's assertions were very convincing, and she was very apologetic, so Mrs. McClintock decided to forget the incident.

Brighid told Mrs. McClintock that she never drank alcohol or used drugs of any kind, and Mrs. McClintock has never seen her do so. However, once when Mrs. McClintock walked Brighid to her car, she noticed a rather large box of empty liquor bottles among several boxes of pop cans and glass jars that Brighid was taking to be recycled. Out of curiosity, Mrs. McClintock asked, "Where did all those liquor bottles come from?" and she found Brighid's answer odd: Brighid said she had no idea where they came from and had never even noticed them before. The origin of two dozen empty liquor bottles in her car was as much a mystery to Brighid as to Mrs. McClintock! Mrs. McClintock decided that if Brighid really was a drinker and had wanted to hide that fact, she would have made the excuse that someone else gave the bottles to her to recycle, or she would have avoided keeping them in her car at all.

The hour-long interview with Mrs. McClintock turned out to have been time well spent. Brighid was a very different person when Dr. Scott returned. She was relaxed and composed, answered to the name "Brighid," and now remembered who Mrs. McClintock was—though in an earlier interview she did not remember Mrs. McClintock, despite having worked for her. Dr. Scott performed a brief mental status exam. Brighid was oriented and understood that she was in a hospital emergency room. However, she had no recollection of the headache and dizziness that had incapacitated her only 2 hours earlier.

A CRITICAL THINKING AND QUESTIONING PAUSE

Think about the unusual mixture of symptoms that Brighid exhibits. Before moving toward any form of diagnosis, think about what other questions Dr. Scott should ask Brighid. There is a pattern that has emerged throughout many of the cases in this casebook. That pattern centers around attempting to rule out as many potential physical causes for the symptoms before turning to other forms of diagnosis.

Dr. Scott asked Brighid about her use of alcohol and other drugs, explaining that using substances like these sometimes causes memory blackouts. She told him she was a teetotaler (abstainer), and always had been. In terms of her general medical condition, the only significant problem she reported is occasional, but severe, migraine headaches. At times, these headaches were disabling enough that Brighid was unable to go to work. Curiously, however, once a headache had passed she often forgot that it occurred, and usually has no recollection of what happened during the time she was having it.

Further questions from Dr. Scott about her migraine headaches uncovered evidence of other memory gaps, some lasting several hours or longer. For example, twice in the month since her roommate moved out, Brighid has gone out in the morning and found her car parked in a different place than she remembered leaving it. She was worried that someone else had been using her car. She was also puzzled that money was occasionally withdrawn from her bank account without her knowledge. This once caused a problem with Marcie, her former roommate, when Brighid was unable to pay her share of the rent that month.

Brighid also had a surprisingly poor memory for certain earlier periods of her life, some of which lasted more than a year. For example, from before the age of 5, she vividly remembers traveling overseas with her family, as her father's army career took them all over the world. Yet she has almost no recollection of her life from ages 5 to 10, after her family settled in the Midwest following her father's retirement.

Dr. Scott questioned Brighid closely about the possibility she might have been having seizures. She offered no evidence to support this idea, and he noted to himself that her memory lapses lasted much longer than seizures normally would (i.e., hours or longer, versus seconds or minutes as with most seizures). Brighid also denied any history of delusional beliefs, hallucinations, or extreme mood fluctuations. She also was unable to come up with any life events or other experiences that would have led Dr. Scott to consider PTSD as a possible basis for her symptoms.

Dr. Scott shared with Brighid that he believed her problems could be very serious. Mrs. McClintock might be correct about a possible eating disorder, but Brighid's memory problems were a more immediate concern to him. He did not think she was stable enough to return home.

Brighid was now genuinely worried about her condition and the possibility she would lose her job. She was cooperative and agreed to sign all of the necessary forms to release her medical records to St. Lawrence. Dr. Scott explained that he wanted to wait to prescribe any medication, unless she needed something to help her sleep, so that he could evaluate her symptoms more accurately, and to give him time to receive and review her records. Dr. Scott wrote the prescription for a medication to help her sleep, if necessary, and left Brighid to be cared for by inpatient staff. He ordered complete physical and neurological exams for her, and asked that requests be sent for records of her previous medical care.

Dr. Scott obtained Brighid's permission to talk to Marcie, Brighid's former roommate. He was not surprised to learn from her that while Brighid was usually the earnest, shy person he had come to know, at times her behavior could be erratic and unpredictable. For example, Brighid and Marcie would sometimes agree to meet somewhere after work, but on several occasions Brighid never showed up and later claimed she had never agreed to meet Marcie. Brighid claimed not to drink, but over 7 months several bottles of Marcie's liquor disappeared from their apartment. Brighid convincingly denied any knowledge of what happened to the liquor, leaving Marcie baffled.

On weekends and other days when she was not busy at work, Brighid's moods, attention span, and even how she spent her time could vary widely. In contrast to her demeanor during the week, on these days she could be very cheerful, depressed (once in a while to the point of talking about suicide), or explosively angry. Marcie found that angry outbursts were especially likely on days when Brighid had migraines, or when they had argued over some misunderstanding (as when Brighid had promised to meet her but did not show up). For most of the week following one such conflict, Marcie was puzzled and then very irritated about a barrage of telephone calls to their apartment for someone named Ginger. Neither she nor Brighid knew anyone by that name.

Marcie concluded that Brighid quits difficult situations (jobs, relationships) much too quickly, and was amazed by how often Brighid has simply picked up and moved to another city in order to "get a fresh start on life." The final straw for the two of them came when Brighid did not have money for her share of the rent and made the rather lame excuse that someone had been withdrawing money from her account. Given Brighid's penchant for leaving problem situations abruptly, Marcie did not want to be left responsible for the apartment by herself. She liked Brighid, but grew tired of the misunderstandings and unpredictability so she decided to live elsewhere.

A week had passed since Dr. Scott first interviewed Brighid, and he ponders what he knows about her. The neurologist's exam turned up no indications of disorder beyond the headaches and memory lapses reported earlier. The doctor who performed Brighid's physical exam reported that she is in good health, but also added that Brighid has several old scars on her back and thighs for which she cannot account. Many pages of records have begun arriving from numerous facilities that previously provided care for Brighid. Dr. Scott was amazed at the number of diagnoses and treatments that his 20-year-old patient has received. The diagnoses include PTSD, OCD, Schizo-Affective Disorder, Bipolar (Manic-Depressive) Disorder, Paranoid Schizophrenia, ADHD, Antisocial Personality Disorder, BPD, and Bulimia Nervosa.

A CRITICAL THINKING AND QUESTIONING PAUSE

Even without the chapter title, you should begin to see a pattern in Brighid's case history that strongly suggests the disorder from which she suffers. Although much of the information in Brighid's records was surprising and hard to decipher, what did not surprise Dr. Scott about Brighid's records were those that indicated severe abuse. Already he had realized that Brighid was able to dissociate from painful memories. He had even begun to realize that she probably had alter egos. Receiving the records served to confirm the diagnosis that he was favoring: dissociative identity disorder (DID). This disorder, formerly referred to as "multiple personality disorder," is probably one of the most misrepresented disorders in the media. Most individuals suffering from this disorder do not have an "evil" personality that becomes a murderer unknown to the "other" personalities. Individuals suffering from this disorder experience a separation between various aspects of their personality. Severe abuse is a common background characteristic in most cases of DID.

Imagine the mental chaos brought on by psychological, sexual, and emotional abuse. Magnify the impact of this abuse when the victim is a child. However, abuse seldom leads to dissociation of the magnitude of DID. What appears to be unique in such cases is the level of chaos. Many parents use harsh punishments, even what borders on beatings, to discipline their children. Typically, this punishment is expected; at least the child is told, "If you do that . . . you will be punished." But chaotic abuse is unpredictable: It may not even involve punishment for specific actions on the part of the child. The same behavior that one moment may be praised by the parent or caregiver may the next moment be condemned and severely reprimanded. The child, therefore, is trying to make sense of situations that are inconsistent, contradictory, and confusing. This makes understanding his or her environment difficult at best. The child may be praised for being such a "good girl" and just a moment later, be branded as "evil." It is extremely difficult for the child to process this information and make sense of who she is. In effect, then, the various aspects of who he or she is become disconnected from each other.

Most of us have multiple sides to our personality but maintain an integration between those aspects. Brighid and others who have DID do not maintain such an integration. This difference results in a dissociation between those aspects that define the person. The most common characteristics of persons suffering from DID involve traumatic experiences in childhood. Such was the case with Brighid as well. She was labeled by her own mother as "an unplanned mistake." This, coupled with the chaotic and abusive environment created by her parents, was the root of Brighid's disorder.

Many children suffer from neglect in childhood. Many also suffer abuse. What appears to be different in the childhoods of many persons suffering from DID, as already mentioned, is the sheer unpredictability of the neglect and the abuse.

Brighid's mother, for example, would occasionally burn her with cigarettes for no apparent reason. Because Brighid could never predict when such abuse would occur, she could do little to avoid it. Although she attempted to find ways to predict when her behaviors would or would not initiate such an attack, they appeared to be entirely random. The chaos and confusion was magnified by the fact that Brighid's mother would often follow these abusive acts with equally random acts of love and kindness. One of her mother's "favorite" actions, for example, was to call Brighid downstairs with an angry voice, make her stand in the corner, telling her that she "had something for her." Sometimes her mother would bring her cookies and tell her what a good girl she had been. Other times, however, the same scenario would culminate with her mother thrashing the backs of her legs with a leather belt. Brighid had absolutely no way of knowing which times the scenario would play out pleasantly or unpleasantly.

The Assessment Model

Assessing DID is difficult because it can be masked by many other problems. It is common, for example, for individuals suffering from DID to also suffer from such problems as phobias or substance abuse disorder. Dr. Scott had found that many of the patients whom he treated whom he finally diagnosed with DID first came into treatment due to an eating disorder. Clearly, these problems can confuse the diagnostic picture.

In order to be diagnosed with DID, the individual must have at least two separate and distinct egos showing consistent differences in behavior, feelings, thinking, and/or identity (or sense of self). These different states of being resemble "personalities," known as *alters*, hence the original label of multiple personality for DID. These alter states can be and often are quite different from each other. Whereas one might be shy and reserved, the other may be outgoing and daring. Again, think of the many sides we all have to our own personalities. In some situations and around some people, we may be outgoing and entertaining yet, in other situations, we may be quite reserved and even shy.

One of the coauthors of this casebook frequently explains such a situation to students. Although he is described by students from his classes as entertaining, outgoing, and as having a great sense of humor, the same students, seeing him outside of the classroom around a group of people, such as at a party, would find him to be shy, quiet, and somewhat withdrawn. Most of us do not have a hard time reconciling the fact that we are somewhat contradictory beings. In fact, most people who know us help us to deal with our contradictions.

Several points are critical to this diagnosis:

1. Brighid displayed a striking inability to remember significant information about herself—although, at times, these memory gaps were "reversible." This means "Ginger," Brighid's alter, knew things that Brighid did not, such as where the liquor bottles came from. Ginger knew because she bought and consumed that liquor. Brighid was unaware of where the liquor bottles came from or where her money went because, in effect, *Ginger* bought them, Brighid did not. Such notable gaps in memory are completely inconsistent with ordinary forgetting.
2. Others (Mrs. McClintock, Marcie) had accounts of certain events that were at variance with Brighid's recollections.
3. There were objects in her possession (e.g., the liquor bottles) that Brighid could not account for.

4. The memory lapses were not directly caused by active use of alcohol or drugs, or by another medical illness.

It is also significant that Brighid's personality dissociations were upsetting to her and were causing genuine difficulties in her life and her employment situation. She received no significant "gains" from having this problem, and had no history of excessive attention seeking. In short, she is not "malingering."

Stress often precipitates these personality dissociations, and new personalities tend to complement those already in existence. The fact that these distinct ego states coexist within the person but will not be dominant at the same time helps to explain the "blackout" periods Brighid has experienced. While one of the identities is at the forefront, the others are, in effect, not present. When one ego state is dominant, there will be a perceived loss of time for the others. As one can imagine, these unexplained periods of lost time and memories are quite disturbing to the individual. This disorder can severely disrupt the person's life, depending on the severity and number of times the individual switches back and forth between identities.

An individual who has suffered severe and chaotic abuse is already confused about who he or she is. Dissociation, in fact, may become a coping mechanism. If the individual can "separate" and let the stronger side take over, the abuse may be more tolerable. Consider the individual trying to convince herself that the person being abused is *not her* because her mommy would never do that to *her*. It is a powerful way for the individual to maintain a sense of worth in the face of remarkably defeating circumstances. The real problem, however, is that this separation can become "fuzzy" and the person may lose sight of what is real and what is fantasy. When the line between fantasy and reality gets lost, the person loses the ability to understand that these multiple sides of his- or herself are just sides of the same person.

The Alternate Sides of Brighid

In order to begin to assess what needed to be done for Brighid, Dr. Scott asked to interview family members and friends. The picture that was built from these interviews was disturbing. Several of Brighid's friends reported instances in which Brighid would report losing track of time and be unable to recall what she had done for long stretches. Other friends mentioned that Brighid could be "unpredictable" and sometimes would go from being pleasant and even-tempered one moment to negative and cruel the next. One friend looked at Brighid's photograph and said, "I don't know who she told you she was, but she told me her name is Ginger." This friend described Ginger as "a girl who exchanges favors for money."

Unfortunately, none of this surprised Dr. Scott. He could not deny the evidence: the pattern of chaotic abuse, the inconsistent yet formidable history of diagnoses and treatment regimens, and the severe self-uncertainty that Brighid displayed when discussing herself. Although hypnosis has some documented usefulness to verify the existence of and treatment for the disorder (see Boyd, 1997), Dr. Scott did not consider using hypnosis to diagnose Brighid. Even before all of her records arrived, he was certain that Brighid had at least one alter that was completely separate from her identity as Brighid. When discussing such a possibility with Brighid, he discovered she was totally unaware of the activities of the alter, Ginger, the prostitute.

Beginning the Treatment

Dr. Scott did prescribe an antidepressant, one of the tricyclic choices, and intensive psychotherapy. The tricyclic would help bring Brighid's anxiety under control so that she could become an active part of her own therapy. Dr. Scott would enlist the aid of a therapist to deal with Brighid's dissociation. The goal of her therapist, Ms. Reese-Smythe, was to aid Brighid in reintegration of those aspects of who she was that had become dissociated or separated from each other. In fact, such total reintegration is the goal of most therapists who treat DID.

Brighid met with Ms. Reese-Smythe daily for 2 to 3 hours. Therapy for Brighid needed to be intensive so her dissociation could be confronted and resolved. Brighid needed to recognize the dissociative pattern and work to resolve the reasons that caused her to adopt such a pattern. Such a treatment schedule, however, is not very plausible, financially. Brighid's case was so intriguing to Ms. Reese-Smythe that she took it pro bono in light of Brighid's limited financial means. This is, by no means, the norm in treatment. Ms. Reese-Smythe, however, was committed to helping Brighid and learning all she could about this intriguing disorder. She believed that such intensive treatment was necessary in Brighid's case. As such, she committed to it despite the fact Brighid could not afford it.

Slowly, Brighid worked to confront the realities of her childhood and the difficulties that had caused her to dissociate. One of the most difficult aspects of treatment involves Brighid confronting her relationship with her abusers (who, in this case, happened to be both the mother and the father) and attempting to understand how and why she responded to the abuse the way she did.

For Brighid to consciously integrate her alternate personalities, she needed to first recognize their existence. Ms. Reese-Smythe made limited use of hypnosis to identify alternate personalities and their peculiar memories and characteristics, but not to the point of encouraging Brighid to fragment further. This treatment confirmed the existence of Ginger, a prostitute, plus other alternate identities. Ginger was presumably the one withdrawing money, drinking liquor, and so on.

From Ginger, Ms. Reese-Smythe learned that Brighid was labeled by her own mother as "an unplanned mistake." Ms. Reese-Smythe also uncovered the existence of Jana. Jana, personality-wise, is somewhere in between the typically reserved behavior of Brighid and the outgoing, over-the-top behavior of Ginger.

Jana is sociable and outgoing but is self-effacing and sensitive to others. Jana volunteered some of her time at a local community center working with at-risk youth. Brighid was better able to recognize Jana's behaviors as part of her own personality than those of Ginger—but such recognition is necessary if Brighid was to integrate and come to terms with these different aspects of who she was.

With Brighid's permission, Ms. Reese-Smythe videotaped sessions to capture Brighid's alternate personalities. Brighid viewed these tapes of her alternate selves in disbelief. Ms. Reese-Smythe developed a therapy contract with each alternate personality. The contract with Brighid was easiest to negotiate; Ginger is hostile and wants nothing to do with therapy. The alternate personalities learned to interact with each other, sharing information and emotions. Ms. Reese-Smythe insisted that Brighid minimize her use of avoidance in the face of reminders or other stresses. Integration progressed slowly as she learned that her transformations into alternate others reflected extreme dissatisfaction with key aspects of her life and her understandable desires, at times, to be someone else.

Brighid came to accept that her ability to maintain other identities was a coping skill that, while partially successful in the short term, would be better applied in a more conscious, flexible way. Brighid felt very guilty about not having done more to protect "the others" and was now able to understand how this led to the emergence of Ginger, a side of her who is angry and assertive.

Brighid met with Ms. Reese-Smythe for 2 months. After that time, Brighid was considered well enough to leave St. Lawrence—but treatment for Brighid is not over. In the several years that have passed, Brighid has been in and out of therapy. Treatment for DID is often intensive and long-term. This should come as no surprise. It takes many years of chaotic abuse to develop such a dissociative pattern. It only stands to reason, then, that it would require multiple years of therapy and treatment to resolve it.

Brighid has continued to take antidepressants to "take the edge off." As we mentioned before, she began with tricyclic antidepressants. The psychiatrists moved from one to another and then tried several SSRIs. At one point, they tried an MAO inhibitor, but Brighid could not tolerate that because it caused her to be nauseated and to vomit. She has been fortunate to have several very positive experiences and today is doing much better. In a few moments, you will hear Brighid's story in her own words. Until then, however, let us consider the biological aspects of DID.

Dissociative Identity Disorder From a Biologist's Vantage Point

Of all the people whose stories are told in this book, Brighid's is the most difficult for the biologist to evaluate. It has only been in recent years that biology has emerged as an important component of psychiatric disorders. One of the first to gain attention as having a significant biological component was schizophrenia. Because of the unfortunate confusion raised by the etiology of the illness's name—*schizo* (split) and *phrenia* (reality)—there was confusion by the public that schizophrenia was a split personality. DID was formerly called *multiple personality disorder.*

Public education about schizophrenia and its biological basis as an explanation of etiology tended to result in a discounting of DID as an actual disorder. Instead, it was often perceived as something simply explored in movies and not something present in real life. In fact, DID is less common than other mental illnesses and less able to be tied to specific anatomical and physiological processes. Its only clearly defined criteria are the existence of more than one personality in one human body. Most who suffer from DID report sexual, verbal, or other forms of abuse in childhood that were unpredictable in nature. Perhaps it is a strength of some persons to have been able to provide a "safe place" to have gone in the face of such trauma. However, the ability to "retreat" from the cruelty of reality ultimately seeks its price. When there are two or more separate identities sharing a single body, there are holes in time. For the patient, those translate as memory loss.

Often persons who have DID also suffer the symptoms of PTSD as a result of the exposure to extreme and intense stress. People who have DID also frequently have symptoms that overlap with those of psychosis or BPD. The advent of using imaging to open the cranial vault to attempt to learn more about its well-protected contents emerged at the end of the 20th century and the beginning of the current one. Although imaging has improved and expanded in its use for researching both animal and human brains, it is still far from being precise and accurate enough to distinguish differences that would both enhance our understanding and assist physicians with diagnoses.

A brief synopsis of several studies indicates how imaging has helped us move forward in understanding the biology of DID and provides hope for further understanding through ongoing research studies. Two of the studies were reported in 2006 and the third in 2008. We present these in part to show how answering some questions leads scientists to either ask new questions or narrow the focus of the search.

The first study (Sar, Unal, & Ozturk, 2008) used imaging technology to measure regional blood flow in patients who were carefully screened and determined to have DID. These authors carefully eliminated patients who had co-occurring BPD; however they made no mention of excluding persons who may have had co-occurring PTSD. Persons who served as controls were healthy, nontraumatized adults who had no history of childhood abuse. All persons in the study were right-handed to avoid lateralization issues. The authors reported decreased blood flow in the orbitofrontal regions and increased perfusion in the medial and superior frontal and occipital regions.

The second study that was also reported in 2006 (Vermetten, Schmahl, Lindner, Loewenstein, & Bremner) used MRI technology to study the volume of the hippocampus and amygdala in adult female patients who were carefully screened to determine that they met the diagnostic criteria for DID; however, the authors acknowledged that they did not screen to exclude those with co-occurring PTSD. The results of this study indicated decreased volumes of both the hippocampus and the amygdala in the patients with DID but not in those serving as healthy controls.

The study reported in 2008 (Weniger, Lange, Sachsse, & Irle, 2008) stated as its purpose to determine volume differences. The results of this study indicated volume differences in the hippocampus and the amygdala determined through 3D MRI, between female patients with dissociative amnesia (DA) or DID and those of patients with PTSD. The authors acknowledged small sample sizes as a limitation of the study. Both test groups were compared with results from persons who served as healthy, normal controls. The results indicated that there were reduced sizes in both of those structures in the patients with PTSD but not in those with DA/DID. Among other implications of these outcomes, the authors suggested that it is possible that normal amygdala and hippocampal size is protective against PTSD and cognitive disorders in traumatized individuals.

Research into the biology of DID remains limited, and the low prevalence of this diagnosis compared with the others described in this book suggests that future progress will be relatively slow.

Brighid Tells Her Story

Yes, I remember Dr. Scott very well. I don't remember much about the meetings with him though. The one that is clear in my mind is the one when he told me my diagnosis. When he told me that I have dissociative identity disorder, I yelled at him. I informed him of three things: One, that he was crazy; two, that he had no business being a doctor; and three, that I was not nuts.

Now I realize how correct his diagnosis is. Everything "fits." I knew when I was little that things just were not right. Life seemed to be all mixed up from my earliest memories. My father was an E-8 in the United States Army. I don't know what E-8 means to this day, but he was one. We lived in countries all over the world. It seems that we were always moving until I was 5. I remember that year because we came home to the Midwestern United States when my father was discharged from the army.

He worked as a counselor after that. And that was the year that my father spoke directly to me for the first time. My mother said that she wanted to have me, but my father didn't. And even though he didn't speak to me directly until I was 5 years old, he came in to my room at night to mess with me and my older sister, Belinda, from as far back as I can remember. His treatment wasn't as hard to deal with in some ways as my mother's. I could count on him to treat me bad.

But with mother, I could never figure her out. She told me how much she loved me and wanted me, but then just "out of the blue," she would burn me and Belinda with her cigarette. Or sometimes, even worse, she would burn us on our tongues with the matches that she lit her cigarettes with. No matter what she used to burn us with, she always did it where it wouldn't show.

She wasn't always as careful with the beatings. The bruises weren't in obvious places, but sometimes, when I wore a skirt, they showed. She would tie us up and secure us to the furniture. Then she beat us with the belt and then would tell us how much she loved us and would beg our forgiveness and say that she had been a bad mom. When I was 10, Belinda left home, and I never saw her again. It was several years after Belinda left that I finally had it out with my father. One night when he was about to beat me, I grabbed the belt and said in a very clear and firm voice, "You are never going to lay another hand on me again. Do you understand?" I was right. He did not touch me again, but it still was not a healthy environment.

When I was 15, I was having obvious problems with bulimia. The school counselor worked with the school nurse to see that I was admitted to the psychiatric ward in a pediatric hospital. They determined that I was too enmeshed with my mother and the stress of school made the problem worse. They placed me in an alternative home for 3 weeks, and the family started family therapy on Friday afternoons. I don't remember much about the therapy because we kept switching therapists.

Finally the workers at the Welfare Department were able to get me out of my home. I was placed in six consecutive foster homes that did not work well. In a few instances, the foster home was almost as chaotic as with my mother and father. Most didn't work because the foster parents just weren't prepared for a child with as many problems as I had. Finally, I was placed in the Hillcrest Home. It was a group home for adolescent girls who were wards of the state. It was when I was there that I began to receive intensive psychiatric care. Much of it was as an outpatient. They had a very hard time knowing what was the matter with me, and it seems that I was always taking some new medication.

I signed a release for you to talk with Dr. Scott, so I realize that you are aware of the fact that I took special training to become a nanny and was able to work for Mr. and Mrs. McClintock. They were really nice to me, and always told me how lucky they were to have me as the kids' nanny. Mrs. McClintock tried hard to help me. She realized that I had an eating disorder, but she just couldn't get me over the hump toward healthy eating. She talked me into letting her take me to St. Lawrence Hospital where they admitted me. You know about my stay there.

The best part of my journey came after I left St. Lawrence. I continued to have problems after I moved here to the state capital. I was being treated by therapists in a community mental health center. I saw the psychiatrist only occasionally. The psychiatric nurse followed-up by monitoring my antidepressant medication and its effectiveness.

My two big opportunities came later. I had been admitted to the acute care psychiatric unit of the hospital after one of my "blackouts" when I was gone all night. When I was "stepped-down" to the subacute unit, I met Dan Hollens,

MSW. He has made all the difference. For the first time in my illness, I had a therapist who empowered me with my own health management. He told me that my goals were the ones that counted, not his as a therapist.

"This is your life that we are talking about," Dan told me. "I am your personal consultant. We don't have to make reintegration our goal. I'd suggest that we get the team working together! What is good for one is in the best interest of all." How often I heard him say over again, "All for one and one for all!" Dan taught me that it is the same body that we are talking about, so if one hurts the body, all suffer. This patient man listened to everything I told him without judging. His interest was truly in guiding me so that I could manage my own recovery process.

The second opportunity that came my way was full-time employment with an agency that works with persons who are mentally ill. I am now an administrator and enjoy working with others and empowering them in their recovery process. Not only is the work important to me, but also I have made several close friends. One of them is a coworker who serves as my support person and mentor. She has helped me through tough times, sometimes gone to difficult sessions with Dan with me and invited me to share in her own family events. I have been successful in forming several close personal relationships, and for the first time in my life am in healthy dating situations. I am taking one day at a time and enjoying a much healthier life.

15
WRAPPING UP THE JOURNEY

Concluding Thoughts From Your Authors

By now, we have gone on quite a journey together. We truly believe we, as authors, have learned as much from this journey as have you, the reader. We have learned to work together and recognize the individual contributions each of us makes. In addition, we have learned to look at abnormal behavior from a myriad of angles. This "multiple perspectives" approach makes understanding abnormal psychology more complex but it also offers a more accurate representation of what mental illness is really all about. So many comments stand out in our minds about the cases in this book—but several points strike us as the most important. Let us share these with you and stress why we think they are important.

Biased first-impression research was one of the coauthors' first major forays into the field of psychological research (Gilbert & Osborne, 1989; Osborne & Gilbert, 1992). In the beginning of the research program, Dr. Osborne had no idea that he would come full circle and see so many connections between biased first-impression research and a casebook on abnormal psychology, but the connection is striking. It is easy to make quick judgments about others on the basis of a few seconds of behavior. Many times, such first impressions are harmless. On one hand, a man who stoops to pick up a young woman's books that have fallen is seen as a "gentleman." In reality, we have no real basis for making that assumption—but, in this case, no one is harmed by that impression.

Consider, on the other hand, a mentally ill person who is hearing voices telling him to do bad things (like Ricky G in this casebook). How "fair" will Ricky's first assessment be? If someone decides this person is "just weird," they will probably never take or make the opportunity to get to know Ricky. This saddens us. Remember in Chapter 7, that Carl V's girlfriend, Rachel, commented that she is a person first, and has a mental illness second? That is the major problem with basing first impressions on such limited information. How many wonderful people have we never gotten to know in our lives because we had an erroneous first impression? We will probably never know.

By using quotes and personal statements from individuals struggling with these disorders, and from their family and friends, we were trying to help you see each person as an individual rather than a "case" of some particular DSM disorder. While we wanted you to learn about the specific disorders illustrated with the help of these individuals, we also wanted you to understand that each individual's identity as a person is more important than his or her diagnosis.

A second point that stands out in our minds is the integration of biology and psychology. Surely by now, you have learned in other psychology courses that an understanding of biology is fundamental to your building a strong understanding of psychology. Thankfully, we had Dr. Esterline Lafuze on our team to reinforce this integration, this interplay. We believe remembering the biological bases of these illnesses will aid in our ability to avoid those negative first impressions we have already mentioned. Perhaps enhancing our understanding of the biological bases of these illnesses will also help to lessen the stigma that is such a pervasive aspect of the life of a person suffering from mental illness. Again, Dr. Esterline Lafuze has been an important player in that respect. She constantly reminded Drs. Osborne and Perkins to avoid using terms such as *admit* and to use a word such as *acknowledge* instead.

It is amazing how powerful such word choices can be. If a case included a comment such as "Barbara *admits* to regular drinking," it comes across as assigning blame. The same point can be made in a nonjudgmental way, however, by rewriting the sentence to read, "Barbara *acknowledges* she drinks regularly." We are not suggesting that persons that ingest substances are "guilt free"—but no one wants to become addicted. Biology is beginning to help us understand which persons are most likely to become addicted and what biological systems are involved in addiction.

We were also powerfully moved by the inclusion of interviews with family members. We were bolstered by the courage of family members. The accounts that we have presented result from extensive consultation with many families that live with the reality of mental illness, in some instances including those who have the illnesses themselves. Thus, you have been given a very real and close-to-the-heart description of family member involvement in many of these cases.

We promised ourselves as we began to formulate the outline for this book that we would do everything in our power to enhance the critical thinking and evaluation skills of our readers. Most of the time, this is done by modeling. Assessing and diagnosing illness of any kind is difficult. Many mental illnesses have overlapping symptoms, which complicates the process even more. Portrayal of the care providers in this casebook is the result of consultation and interaction with persons who provide services. We are appreciative of those whose lives are affected as consumers and family members, and also of the care providers who read and acknowledged the authenticity of final versions of the cases before the book was published. Each of those professional persons who shared in this process demonstrated the critical thinking and evaluation skills that mark an excellent care provider.

We purposely used many different kinds of formal and informal resources—psychiatrists, psychologists, social workers, nurses, family members, self-help groups—because the fact is that any and all of these sources of help are relevant today. We also described in several cases how a diverse group of individuals (medical, psychological, family) worked together collaboratively to help the individual manage the disorder and work towards recovery. This level of cooperation may or may not occur in all treatment settings today, but we depict it as happening this way because we want to support the idea of using this kind of cooperative network for coping and recovery.

We made extensive use of significant others because they are so important. It is in the individuals' interactions with their family, friends, teachers, family physicians, police officers, employers, and so on, that key decisions get made ("Should I seek or accept help? From whom?") and identities start to shift (e.g., from "drinker" to "alcoholic," or from "child who is oppositional and defiant" to "child who has autism"). The extent to which a person maintains adherence to a treatment regimen and "stays the course" toward recovery also depends a great deal on input and other support from his or her significant others. We also included significant others because it is important to illustrate the impact of these illnesses on those around the person who suffers from the illness. Many of the comments from family members illustrate the courage and burden these individuals share as they attempt to cope with the suffering of their loved ones.

While most of the people we describe in this book are "only too human," we have tremendous admiration for all of them—providers, families, friends, and significant others—but most of all, we admire the individuals who struggle with symptoms and mental disorders every day of their lives. For us, Linehan's (1993) constructive assumptions about patients who have BPD have broad relevance to all persons struggling with mental disorders. For example, we assume that people always do the best they can to manage their symptoms and cope with their lives.

It serves no constructive purpose to say that a person like Carl V (BPD), Jacob T (Autism Spectrum Disorder), or Richard B (Alcohol Use Disorder) is not trying hard enough to survive and adapt to the challenges he faces. In a sense, their symptoms (Carl cutting his forearms, Jacob taking off his clothes at school) can be understood as calls for help in what are difficult and sometimes almost unlivable situations, and it is important to see the survival value for these individuals in what to us seem like terribly self-defeating symptoms of mental disorder.

We made a point of describing assessment and treatment procedures that would be desirable to use, even if for practical or other reasons most of today's practitioners would not always be able to follow them. For example, many of the professionals who first make contact with the individuals we describe do careful mental status exams, ask the CAGE questions regarding substance abuse, and have the individuals receive medical checkups, including full physical exams in some cases. We wanted to illustrate thorough and methodical intake procedures that are desirable to use, even if not all of them would occur exactly as we describe here.

Many of the individuals whose disorders are described in this book turned out to have simpler, more "cut and dried" symptom patterns than might be found among persons with mental disorders such as those who are brought by the police to hospital emergency rooms. For example, as a rule, the individuals depicted here have only one primary diagnosis and do not qualify for second or third diagnoses of other disorders. Although "dually diagnosed" individuals of the latter sort are relatively common, our goal in this book was to show one particular diagnosis as clearly as we could.

Another benchmark we planned to use to assess the quality of our work was realism. We felt that a casebook should be realistic. To this end, not everything written in these pages has been pleasant—but illness makes no promise to be pleasing. We have tried to provide a broad picture of the illnesses, the trials, the tribulations, and the triumphs. Along with this broad picture has come a broader understanding of treatment options and the many hurdles that individuals suffering from these illnesses face. Consider some of the challenges confronted within these cases:

1. dual diagnosis
2. involuntary commitment
3. treatment options when there is no money
4. maintaining adherence to the treatment regimen
5. challenges confronted by the care providers ("splitting" in the Carl case, falling in love with a client in the Sally case, etc.)
6. dealing with the side effects of medications.

Although these are only a few of the challenges that we presented within the cases in this book, we hope they have broadened your understanding of all that is involved in the successful (and nonsuccessful) treatment of persons who suffer these illnesses. Although this approach presents diagnosis and treatment as complicated (and, indeed, it is), we also believe that such honesty in our portrayal will go a long way to reinforce the subtitle of this text. If we have helped a few of our readers to learn to look beyond the symptoms and see the person behind those symptoms, then every hour of labor that went into this book will be validated.

Our approach throughout is consumer-driven rather than cookbooklike. For example, other than using a battery of tests with Jacob T to evaluate his verbal and adaptive behavioral functioning, we made little use of psychological tests. The primary reason for this is that the professionals we describe were interested in providing immediate, direct help. The diagnoses were not uncertain, which meant further time and expense devoted to psychological testing was unnecessary.

The treatments we reviewed were usually those for which there is some empirical support. Otherwise, our approach always endorses the consideration of more than one option, and of some role played by consumer and/or family choice. Another important point is that even with our increasing understanding of the role played by biology, the options include more than medication, and the responsibilities touch more people than the individual or the provider (i.e., the family too).

Another assumption we make is that if the person is not able to use treatment or the other help that he or she receives to improve or recover, it is not the person who failed the treatment, but the treatments and other supports that failed the person. To those who argue that a person who is not sufficiently motivated to use therapy has failed simply for that reason, we respond that the person's suffering and desire for relief give them more than enough motivation to change, and the problem is more usefully understood as being that the treatment and the therapist have been unsuccessful in translating this distress into a serious effort to recover.

Furthermore, a failure of one treatment attempt, no matter how intensive and long-lasting it was, does not mean that there will not be a different outcome—perhaps even a very successful one—on the next attempt, or the one after that, or the one after that. Most disorders, including all of those described in this book, tend to carry a lifelong risk of relapse or deterioration, but the chances people have for improvement and recovery are also almost unlimited. Treatment cannot change past events, such as Barbara M's husband's death or Brighid C's dysfunctional childhood, nor can it eliminate current risks, such as the chances of Paula H's ex-boyfriend returning to threaten her, or future setbacks, like stresses that may provoke a major relapse in Ricky G. However, therapy can be very helpful in opening a person's eyes to new options, and in channeling his or her current coping efforts in more effective directions.

We used hospitalization as a response to very risky situations that some of the individuals in these cases were facing (Ricky G and Sally W, for example), but in general we believe that people should be able to live with as little restriction and as much independence as they can manage.

Before moving on to other closing thoughts, let us focus on heroism. In most instances, society does well in honoring our heroes. "You know that you are a hero," one of the authors said to one young man, who was fairly new at dealing with the challenge of schizophrenia as he left to struggle with the pressures of a job rehabilitation program for persons with a wide range of disabilities. It was obvious that he was dreading the constant pressure to keep the production pace and the continual verbal push to go faster, which only made his hallucinations worse. Few supervisors, at least at that time, had a clue as to what schizophrenia was or what helped or worked against the person who suffered its symptoms.

"I don't feel much like a hero," he replied. His head was bowed, and his shoulders sagged.

"No. It isn't while the battles rage and the bullets are to be dodged, that we know. It is after the battles are over and the dust and smoke clear, that the truth dawns. It is then we know who has fought hard and well."

In other arenas of heroism, we have "caught on" more quickly. Whether it has been on the battlefield, the playing field, the courtroom, the intensive care unit, or the hospice program, we have done much better. Even in the "decade of the brain," for those who suffer the neurobiological disorders that we call mental illness and their families, the acknowledgment of heroism has been slow. Persons with the disorders still face stigma and misunderstanding. Still, they fight the sting of cruel assumptions that they are self-centered, manipulative, lazy, or worse. At the same time, their families are blamed—if not for causing the illness, then they are blamed for not being helpful or for making matters worse.

We believe that someday there will be a wave of enlightenment that will sweep over us and cause us to look back in amazement on the cruelty that we have inflicted on these persons of true courage who dealt with life the best that they could in the face of often overwhelming odds.

For all who read this casebook, we feel that an important goal is to enroll you into honoring our heroes. We ask that you regard the behaviors that are difficult as symptoms of disorders that are rooted in biology. That thought leads to another about understanding the biological component of these disorders. There are many primary consumers and family members who avoid considering the biology because they believe that it must carry a component of "determinism" with it. Somehow, then, it seems that they face an unchanging and unchangeable condition with little hope of wellness.

For us, however, it is the discovery of biological implications that frees us to hope that there are endless possibilities for recovery and wellness. There is something to get ahold of to measure, to evaluate, to use to develop strategies for intervention, observation, and analysis of outcomes. Such discovery brings the opportunity for education of the kind in which you are currently involved by reading this book—and for those who walk daily with one of the disorders and for those who walk closely beside them, understanding reduces fear.

Another important statement to make here is about "team." One of the greatest joys of coauthoring this book was the opportunity for the three of us to work together as a team. High-trust relationships are based on mutual respect, mutual honesty, and a degree of mutual affection. Working as part of a team we, as coauthors, were made even more sensitive to the importance of "team" in meeting all of life's challenges. There was no effort when a problem surfaced or a special challenge arose to spend any time in trying to assign blame. We scrambled to find a solution to the problem, and whoever came up with the ball either carried it or passed it off to a teammate.

We take that analogy to meeting the challenge of living with mental illness. Much time can be spent trying to find someone at fault. There is sometimes a primitive feeling that if we can just find the right person to blame, the problem will disappear. In fact, our observation has been that exactly the opposite is true. Even if we could find the "correct" person to blame, it often would not be helpful. Sometimes it is couched subtly in a goal to make a person independent (whatever that means). It seems that homeostasis, or balance, reaches far beyond the biological understanding of the word. Through carefully developed signaling and feedback processes that involve eloquent communication, honesty, respect, and trust, we will achieve healthy interdependence. As an unbeatable team of consumers, family members, and professional providers from a multitude of disciplines, we can learn from one another how best to live.

This thought leads to the concept of "outcomes." When considering outcomes, it is very important to understand that for none of these individuals is the realistic goal one of complete "cure." Instead, we agree with a philosophy that emphasizes a process of managing one's disorder and of "recovery."

As a last point, let us turn your attention more fully to the concept of recovery. Typically, recovery is seen as the period of transition between being seriously ill and being able to function fully. This is, as you probably have guessed, very complicated. The reality for many persons suffering with mental illness will be lasting recovery. Few of these illnesses can currently be cured. Although many treatments can help persons return to relatively "normal" levels of functioning, recovery is ongoing. Consider Sally W, who may need to take medication for the rest of her life. Consider also Richard B, who must constantly be vigilant to maintain sobriety. These are both examples of the ongoing nature of recovery for persons with mental illness.

Recovery is not a bleak concept, however. It is a concept that can mean "hope" as well. A shining example of the hope of recovery is the National Empowerment Center. This nonprofit organization is run by consumers/survivors of psychiatric services. The Center focuses on a mission built upon the concept that recovery (empowerment, hope, and healing) is possible for each person diagnosed with mental illness. Certainly recovery will be more complete for some persons than for others, but the Center's mission is on aiding recovery for each person.

The Center is a clearinghouse for information about support groups, statewide organizations, video and audiotapes, and education and training to providers from a consumer/survivor perspective. Many of the Center's staff are considered experts on alternative approaches to treatment and are advocates for clients' rights. Video resources include tapes that aid consumers in designing their own recovery process, including the development of peer support networks. What impresses us most about this approach to recovery is the emphasis on getting the client involved actively in the recovery process. This approach will go a long way toward dispelling the misconception that individuals with mental illness cannot help themselves. This is not to say that alternative approaches to treatment can and should replace traditional ones. Instead, such approaches to recovery focus on supplementing and enhancing traditional approaches. These features fit in nicely with the open and realistic picture of mental illness and treatment we have endeavored to develop.

REFERENCES

ACOG. (2015). Tobacco, alcohol, drugs and pregnancy. Retrieved on January 21, 2016 from: http://www.acog.org/Patients/FAQs/Tobacco-Alcohol-Drugs-and-Pregnancy.

ACOG Committee on Practice Bulletins (2008). Use of psychiatric medications during pregnancy and lactation: Clinicial management guidelines for obstetrician-gynecologists. *Obstetrics & Gynecology, 111*(4), 1001–1020.

American Psychiatric Association (1994). *Diagnostic and statistical manual of mental disorders, 4th Edition.* Washington, DC: Author. (1st ed., 1952; 2nd ed., 1968; 3rd ed., 1980, rev., 1987).

American Psychiatric Association (2013a). *Highlights of changes from DSM-IV-TR to DSM-5.* Arlington, VA: American Psychiatric Publishing. Retrieved on October 4, 2014 from: http:www.uic.edu/docassist/changes-from-dsm-iv-tr-to-dsm-5-51.pdf.

American Psychiatric Association (2013b). *Diagnostic and statistical manual of mental disorders, 5th Edition.* Arlington, VA: American Psychiatric Publishing.

American Psychiatric Association (2013c). *DSM-5 fact sheet: Personality disorders.* American Psychiatric Publishing. Retrieved on October 5, 2014 from: http:www.dsm5.org/Documents/Personality Disorders Fact Sheet.pdf.

American Psychiatric Association (2013d). *DSM-5 fact sheet: Paraphilic disorders.* American Psychiatric Publishing. Retrieved on October 8, 2014 from: http:www.dsm5.org/Documents/Paraphilic Disorders Fact Sheet.pdf.

Arco, L. (2015). A case study in treating chronic comorbid obsessive–compulsive disorder and depression with behavioral activation and pharmacotherapy. *Psychotherapy, 52*(2), 278–286.

Barlow, D.H., & Durand, V.M. (1999). *Abnormal psychology: An integrative approach.* Pacific Grove, CA: Brooks/Cole.

Baron-Cohen, S., Auyeung, B., Nørgaard-Pedersen, B., Hougaard, D.M., Abdallah, N.W., Melgaard, L., Cohen, A.S., Chakrabarti, B., Ruta, L., & Lombardo, M.V. (2014). Elevated fetal steroidogenic activity in autism. *Molecular Psychiatry, 20*(3), 369–376.

Becker, A.E., Grinspoon, S.K., Klibanski, A., & Hertzog, D.B. (1999). Current concepts: Eating disorders. *New England Journal of Medicine, 340*(14), 1092–1098.

Blackwood, D.H.R., He, L., Morris, S.W., McLean, A., Whitton, C., Thomson, M., Walker, M.T., Woodburn, K., Sharp, C.M., Wright, A.F., Shibasaki, Y., St. Clair, D.M., Porteous, D.J., & Muir, W.J. (1996). A locus for bipolar affective disorder on chromosome. *Nature Genetics, 12*(4), 427–430.

Blatner, A. (2006). The art of case formulation. Retrieved on September 22, 2014 from: http:www.blatner.com/adam/psyntbk/formulation.html.

Bloom, F.E., & Lazerson, A. (1988). *Brain, mind and behavior.* New York: W. H. Freeman.

Bohon, C., & Stice, E. (2011). Reward abnormalities among women with full and subthreshold bulimia nervosa: A functional magnetic resonance imaging study. *International Journal of Eating Disorders, 44*(7), 585–595.

Boyd, J.D. (1997). Clinical hypnosis for rapid recovery from dissociative identity disorder. *American Journal of Clinical Hypnosis, 40*(2), 97–110.

Brady, K.T., Dansky, B., Saladin, M., & Sonne, S. (1996). *PTSD and cocaine dependence. The effects of order of onset.* Presentation at the annual meeting of the College on Problems of Drug Dependency, San Juan, Puerto Rico.

Brady, K.T., Grice, D.E., Dustan, L., & Randall, C. (1993). Gender differences in substance use disorders. *American Journal of Psychiatry, 150,* 1707–1711.

Campbell, C.M., & Edwards, R.R. (2012). Ethnic differences in pain and pain management. *Pain Management, 2*(3), 219–230.

Clark, D.M. (1996). Panic disorder: From theory to therapy. In P. Salkovskis (Ed.), *Frontiers of Cognitive Therapy* (pp. 318–344). New York: Guilford Press.

Crowe, R.R., Noyes, R., Pauls, D.L., & Slymen, D.J. (1983). A family study of panic disorder. *Archives of General Psychiatry, 40,* 1065–1069.

Dager, S.R., Friedman, S.D., Heide, A., Layton, M.L., Richards, T., Artru, A., Strauss, W., Hayes, C., & Posse, S. (1999). Two-dimensional proton echo-planar spectroscopic imaging of brain metabolic changes during lactate-induced panic. *Archives of General Psychiatry, 56*(1), 70–77.

Donegan, N., Sanislow, C.A., Blumberg, H.P., Fulbright, R.K., Lacadie, C., Skudlarski, P., Gore, J.C., Olson, I.R., McGlashan, T.H., & Wexler, B.F. (2003). Amygdala hyperreactivity in borderline personality disorder: Implications for emotional dysregulation. *Biological Psychiatry, 54*(11), 1284–1293.

Durand, V.M., & Barlow, D.H. (2013). *Essentials of abnormal psychology, 6th Edition.* Belmont, CA: Wadsworth, Cengage Learning.

Eells, T.D., Kendjelic, E.M., & Lucas, C.P. (1998). What is Case Formulation?: Development and use of a content coding manual. *The Journal of Psychotherapy Practice, 7,* 144–153.

Eisch, A.J., & Petrik, D. (2012). Depression and hippocampal neurogenesis: A road to remission? *Science, 338,* 72–75.

Elbogen, E., & Johnson, S. (2009). The intricate link between violence and mental disorder: Results from the national epidemiologic survey on alcohol and related conditions. *Archives of General Psychiatry, 66*(2), 152–161.

Escamilla, M.A., & Zavala, J.M. (2008, June). Genetics of bipolar disorder. *Dialogues in Clinical Neuroscience, 10*(2), 141–152.

Ewing, J.A. (1984). Detecting alcoholism: The CAGE questionnaire. *Journal of the American Medical Association, 252*(14), 1905–1907.

Faedda, G.L., Tondo, L., Baldessarini, R.J., Suppes, T., & Tohen, M. (1993). Outcome after rapid versus gradual discontinuation of lithium treatment in bipolar disorders. *Archives of General Psychiatry, 50,* 448–455.

Gilbert, D.T., & Osborne, R.E. (1989). Thinking backward: Some curable and incurable consequences of cognitive busyness. *Journal of Personality and Social Psychology, 57*(6), 940–949.

Gilbert, D.T., Pelham, B.W., & Krull, D.S. (1988). On cognitive busyness: When person perceivers meet persons perceived. *Journal of Personality and Social Psychology, 54*(5), 733–740.

Glantz, L.A., & Lewis, D.A. (2000). Decreased dendritic spine density on prefrontal cortical pyramidal neurons in schizophrenia. *Archives of General Psychiatry, 57*(1), 65–73.

Gonsalves, L., & Schuermeyer, I. (2006). Treating depression in pregnancy: Practical suggestions. *Cleveland Clinic Journal of Medicine, 73*, 1098–1104.

Gorman, J.M., Fyer, M.R., Goetz, R., Askanazi, J., Leibowitz, M.R., Fyer, A.J., Kinney, J., & Klein, D.F. (1988). Ventilation physiology of patients with panic disorder. *Archives of General Psychiatry, 45*, 53–60.

Gorwood, P., Bouvard, M., Mouren-Simeoni, M., Kopman, A., & Ades, J. (1998). Genetics and anorexia nervosa: A review of candidate genes. *Psychiatric Genetics, 8*, 1–13.

Gregory, A.M., Caspi, A., Moffitt, T.E., Koenen, K., Eley, T.C., & Poulton, R. (2007). Juvenile mental health histories of adults with anxiety disorders. *American Journal of Psychiatry, 164*, 1–8.

Guido, K.W.F., & Kaye, W.H. (2012). Current status of functional imaging in eating disorders. *The International Journal of Eating Disorders, 45*(6), 723–736.

Gunderson, J.G. (2011). Borderline personality disorder. *New England Journal of Medicine, 364*, 2037–2042.

Hall, J., Trent, S., Thomas, K.L., O'Donovan, M.C., & Owen, M.J. (2015). Genetic risk for schizophrenia: Convergence on synaptic pathways involved in plasticity. *Biological Psychiatry, 77*(1), 52–58.

Hedman, E., Ljótsson, B., & Lindefors, N. (2012). Cognitive Behavior Therapy via the Internet: A systematic review of applications, clinical efficacy and cost–effectiveness. *Expert Review of Pharmacoeconomics and Outcomes Research, 12*(6), 745–764.

Hedrick, M. (2015). Dating with schizophrenia. Retrieved on June 18, 2015 from: www. NewYorkTimes.com.

Herman, J.L. (1992). *Trauma and recovery.* New York: Basic Books.

Hilty, D.M., Brady, K.T., & Hales, R.E. (1999). A review of bipolar disorder among adults. *Psychiatric Services, 50*, 201–213.

Hyman, S.E. (2008). A glimmer of light for neuropsychiatric disorders. *Nature, 455*(16), 890–893.

Johnson, P.L., Truitt, W., Fitz, S.D., Kelley, P.E., Dietrich, A., Sanghani, S., Traskman-Bendz, L., Goddard, A.W., Brundin, L., & Shekhar, A. (2009). A key role for Orexin in panic anxiety. *Nature Medicine.* Retrieved on September 14, 2015 from: http:// www.nature.com/nm/journal/v16/n1/full/nm.2075.html.

Keel, P.K., Mitchell, J.E., Miller, K.B., Davis, T.L., & Crow, S.J. (1999). Long-term outcome of bulimia nervosa. *Archives of General Psychiatry, 56*, 63–69.

Kiehn, B., & Swales, M. (1995, November). An overview of dialectical Behavior Therapy in the treatment of borderline personality disorder. *Psychiatry On-Line.* Available: http://www.seabhs.org/poc/view_doc.php?type=doc&id=1020&cn=8

Kieseppä, T., Partenon, T., Haukka, J., Kaprio, J., & Lonnqvist, J. (2004). High concordance of bipolar I disorder in a nationwide sample of twins. *The American Journal of Psychiatry, 161*(10), 1814–1821.

Kliemann, D., Dziobek, I., Hatri, A., Baudewig, J., & Heekeren, H.R. (2012). The role of the amygdala in atypical gaze on emotional faces in autism spectrum disorders. *Journal of Neuroscience, 32*(28), 9469–9476.

Lieb, K., Zanarini, M., Schmahl, C., Linehan, M., & Bohus, M. (2004). Borderline personality disorder. *Lancet, 364*, 453–461.

Linehan, M. (1993). *Cognitive-behavioral treatment of borderline personality disorder.* New York: Guilford Press.

Manji, H.K., & Lenox, R.H. (2000). Signaling: Cellular insights into the pathophysiology of bipolar disorder. *Biological Psychiatry, 48*(6), 518–530.

Marlatt, G. A., & Gordon, J. (1985). *Relapse prevention.* New York: Guilford Press.

Miller, W.R., & Rollnick, S. (1991). *Motivational interviewing.* New York: Guilford.

National Institute on Drug Abuse (NIDA). (2015). Addiction science. Retrieved on September 12, 2015 from: http://www.drugabuse.gov/related-topics/addiction-science.

Nelson, K.B. (2001). Toward a biology of autism: Possible role of certain neuropeptides and neurotrophins. *Clinical Neuroscience Research, 1*(4), 300–306.

Neumeister, A., Bain, E., Nugent, A.C., Carson, R.E., Bonne, O., Leckenbaugh, D.A., Eckelman, W., Herscovitch, P., Charney, D.S., & Drevets, W. (2004). Reduced serotonin type 1A receptor binding in panic disorder NIMH mood and anxiety disorders program. *Journal of Neuroscience, 24*(3), 589–591.

Nietzel, M.T., Bernstein, D.A., & Milich, R. (1994). *Introduction to clinical psychology.* Englewood Cliffs, NJ: Prentice Hall.

Nowinski, J. (2014). *Hard to love: Understanding and overcoming male borderline personality.* Las Vegas, NV: Central Recovery Press.

Osborne, R.E., & Gilbert, D.T. (1992). The preoccupational hazards of social life. *Journal of Personality and Social Psychology, 62*, 219–228.

Ota, M., Sato, N., Sakai, K., Okazaki, M., Maikusa, N., Hattori, K., Hori, M., & Teraishi, T. (2014). Altered coupling of regional cerebral blood flow and brain temperature in schizophrenia compared with bipolar disorder and healthy subjects. *Journal of Cerebral Blood Flow & Metabolism, 34*, 1868–1872.

Papp, L.A., & Klein, D.F. (1993). Carbon dioxide, hypersensitivity, hyperventilation & panic disorder. *American Journal of Psychiatry, 150*, 1149–1157.

Post, R.M., Roy-Byrne, P.P., & Uhde, T.W. (1988). Graphic representation of the life course of illness in patients with affective disorder. *American Journal of Psychiatry, 145*, 844–848.

Rajkowska, G., Miguel-Hidalgo, J.J., Wei, J., Dilley, G., Pittman, S.D., Meltzer, H.Y., Overholser, J.C., Roth, B.L., & Stockmeier, C.A. (1999). Morphometric evidence for neuronal and glial prefrontal cell pathology in major depression. *Biological Psychiatry*, 1085–1098.

Rapee, R.M., & Barlow, D.H. (1988). Cognitive-behavioral treatment. *Psychiatric Annals, 18*, 473–477.

Raudzus, J., & Misri, S. (2008). Managing unipolar depression in pregnancy. *Current Opinion in Psychiatry, 22*, 13–18.

Reichenberg, A., Raz, G., Mark, W., Bresnahan, M., Silverman, J., Harlap, S., Rabinowitz, J., Shulman, C., Malaspina, D., Lubin, G., Haim, Y., Knobler, H.Y., Davidson, M., & Susser, E. (2006). Advancing paternal age and autism. *Archives of General Psychiatry, 63*(9), 1026–1032.

Reynolds, F.G., Shott, M., & O'Reilly, R. (2011). Altered temporal difference learning in bulimia nervosa. *Biological Psychiatry, 70*, 728–735.

Saijdyk, T.J., Katner, J.S., & Shekhar, A. (1997). Monoamines in the dorsomedial hypothalamus of rats following exposure to different tests of "anxiety." *Progress in Neuro-Psychopharmacology & Biological Psychiatry, 21*, 193–209.

Sansone, R.A., & Sansone, L.A. (2011). Gender patterns in borderline personality disorder, *Innovations in Clinical Neuroscience, 8*(5), 16–20.

Sar, V., Unal, S.N., & Ozturk, E. (2008). Frontal and occipital perfusion changes in dissociative identity disorder. *Psychiatry Research: Neuroimaging, 156*(3), 217–223.

Schultz, R.T. (2005, April–May). Developmental deficits in social perception in autism: the role of the amygdala and fusiform face area. *International Journal of Developmental Neuroscience, 23*(2–3), 125–141.

Schultz, S.K., & Andreasen, N.C. (1999). Schizophrenia. *Lancet, 353*, 1425–1430.

Self, D.W. (1997). *Neurobiological adaptations to drug use in hospital practice: A special report—new understandings of drug addiction.* Needham Heights, MA: McGraw-Hill.

Shekhar, A., & Keim, S.R. (1996). The effects of GAGAA receptor blockade in the dorsomedial hypothalamic nucleus on corticotrophin (ACTH) and corticos-terone secretion in male rats. *Brain Research, 739*, 46–51.

Shekhar, A., & Keim, S.R. (1997). The circumventricular organs form a potential neural pathway for lactate sensitivity: Implications for panic disorder. *The Journal of Neuroscience, 17*, 9726–9735.

Shekhar, A., Keim, S.R., Simon, J.R., & McBride, W.J. (1996). Dorsomedial hypothalamic GABA dysfunction produces physiological arousal following sodium lactate infusions. *Pharmacology, Biochemistry and Behavior, 55*, 249–256.

Shenton M.E., Kikinis, R., Jolesz, F.A., Pollak, S.D., LéMay, M., Wible, C.G., Hokama, H., Martin, J., Metcalf, D., & Coleman, M. (1992). Abnormalities of the left temporal lobe and thought disorder in schizophrenia. A quantitative magnetic resonance imaging study. *New England Journal of Medicine, 327*(9), 604–612.

Shepherd, G.M.G. (2013). Corticostriatal connectivity and its role in disease. *Nature Reviews Neuroscience, 14*(4), 278–291.

Siassi, I. (1984). Psychiatric interviews and mental status examinations. In G. Goldstein & M. Hersen (Eds.), *Handbook of psychological assessment* (pp. 259–275). New York: Pergamon Press.

Silk, K. (2000). Borderline personality disorder: Overview of biologic factors. *The Psychiatric Clinics of North America, 23*(1), 61–75.

Smith, K.A., Fairburn, C.G., & Cowen, P.J. (1999). Symptomatic relapse in bulimia nervosa following acute tryptophan depletion. *Archives of General Psychiatry, 56*, 171–176.

Smith, T.C., Ryan, M.A., Wingard, D.L., Slymen, D.J., Sallis, J.F. & Kritz-Silverstein, D. (2008). New onset and persistent symptoms of posttraumatic stress disorder self-reported after deployment and combat exposures: Prospective population based US military cohort study. *British Medical Journal, 336*(7640), 366–371.

Sperry, L. (2010). *Highly effective therapy: Developing essential clinical competencies in counseling and psychotherapy.* New York: Routledge.

Sperry, L., & Sperry, J. (2012). *Case conceptualization: Mastering this competency with ease and confidence.* New York: Routledge.

Steadman, H.J., Mulvey, E.P., Monahan, J., Robbins, P.C., Applebaum, P.S., Grisso, T., Roth, L.H., & Silver, E. (1998). Violence by people discharged from acute psychiatric inpatient facilities and by others in the same neighborhoods. *Archives of General Psychiatry, 55*, 393–401.

Stober, G., Ben-Shachar, D., Cardon, M., Falka, P., Fonteh, A.N., Gawlik, M., Glenthoj, B.Y., Runblatt, E., Jabljensky, A., Kim, Y., Kornhuber, J., Mcneil, T.F., Muller, N., Oranie, B., Saito, T., Saoud, M., Schmitt, A., Schwartz, M., Thome, J., Uzbekov, M., Durany, N., & Riederer, P. (2009). Schizophrenia: From the brain to peripheral markers. A consensus paper of the WFSBP task force on biological markers. *The World Journal of Biological Psychiatry, 10*(2), 127–155.

Stone, M.H., Hurt, S.W., & Stone, D.K. (1987). The PI 500: Long-term follow-up of borderline inpatients meeting DSM-III criteria. *Journal of Personality Disorders, 1*, 291–298.

Surtees, P.G., Wainwright, N.W.J., Willis-Owen, S.A.G, Luben, R., Day, N.E., & Flint, J. (2006). Social adversity, the serotonin transporter (5-HTTLPR) polymorphism and major depressive disorder. *Biological Psychiatry, 59*, 224–229.

Sweeten, T.L., Posey, D.J., Shekhar, A., & McDougle, C.J. (2002). The amygdala and related structures in the pathophysiology of autism. *Pharmacology Biochemistry and Behavior, 71*(3), 449–455.

Szeszko, P., MacMillan, S., McMeniman, M., Chen, S., Baribault, K., Lim, K.O., Ivey, M.R., Banerjee, S.P., Bhandari, R., Moore, G.J., & Rosenberg, D.R. (2004). Brain structural abnormalities in psychotropic drug-naive pediatric patients with obsessive-compulsive disorder. *American Journal of Psychiatry, 161*(6), 1049–1056.

Thomas, J.L., Wilk, J.E., Riviere, L.A., McGurk, D., Castro, C.A., & Hoge, C.W. (2010). Prevalence of mental health problems and functional impairment among active component and National Guard soldiers 3 and 12 months following combat in Iraq. *Archives of General Psychiatry, 67*, 614–623.

Torgerson, S. (1983). Genetic factors in anxiety disorders. *Archives of General Psychiatry, 40*, 1085–1089.

Vermetten, E., Schmahl, C., Lindner, S., Loewenstein, R.J., & Bremner, J.D. (2006). Hippocampal and amygdalar volumes in dissociative identity disorder. *The American Journal of Psychiatry, 163*(4), 630–636.

Wang, Z., Neylan, T.C., Mueller, S.G., Lenoci, M., Truran, D., Marmar, C.R., Weiner, M.W., & Schuff, N., (2010). Magnetic resonance imaging of hippocampal subfields in posttraumatic stress disorder. *Archives of General Psychiatry, 67*, 296–303.

WebMD (2015). Pregnancy and antidepressants. Retrieved on September 12, 2015 from: http://www.webmd.com/baby/pregnancy-and-antidepressants.

Wender, P.H., Kety, S.S., Rosenthal, D., Schulsinger, F., Ortmann, J., & Lunde, I. (1996). Psychiatric disorders in the biological and adoptive families of adopted individuals with affective disorders. *Archives of General Psychiatry, 43*, 923–1096.

Weniger, G., Lange, C., Sachsse, U., & Irle, E. (2008). Amygdala and hippocampal volumes and cognition in adult survivors of childhood abuse with dissociative disorders. *Acta Psychiatrica Scandinavica, 118*, 281–290.

Wickelgren, I. (1997). Getting the brain's attention. *Science, 278*, 35–37.

Wiedemann, G., Pauli, P., Dengler, W., Lutzenberger, W., Birbaumer, N., & Buchkremer, G. (1999). Frontal brain asymmetry as a biological substrate of emotions in patients with panic disorders. *Archives of General Psychiatry, 56*, 78–84.

Winchel, R.M., & Stanley, M. (1991). Self-injurious behavior: A review of the behavior and biology of self-mutilation. *The American Journal of Psychiatry, 148*(3), 306–317.

Woody, E.Z., Lewis, V., Snider, L., Grant, H., Mamath, M., & Szechtman, H. (2005). Induction of compulsive-like washing by blocking the feeling of knowing: An experimental test of the security-motivation hypothesis of obsessive-compulsive disorder. *Behavioral and Brain Functions, 1*, 1–11.

INDEX